ῼy ti

N 1980

The Science Fiction
of Isaac Asimov

The Science Fiction of Isaac Asimov

JOSEPH F. PATROUCH, JR.

London
DENNIS DOBSON

This edition first published in Great Britain in 1978
by Dobson Books Ltd,
80 Kensington Church Street, London W8 4BZ

ISBN 0 234 72008 5

Printed and made in Great Britain by
Billing & Sons Limited,
Guildford, London and Worcester

Dedicated to
EDMOND HAMILTON
whose *The Star Kings* started it all for me

Contents

Preface   vii

Introduction   xv

ONE: The Earliest Asimov   3

TWO: Asimov's Robots   35

THREE: Asimov's Foundations I   61

FOUR: Asimov's Foundations II   87

FIVE: Asimov's Novels I   111

SIX: Asimov's Novels II   151

SEVEN: Asimov's Collections I   183

EIGHT: Asimov's Collections II   221

Conclusions: The Most Recent Asimov   255

Bibliography   273

Index   277

Preface

This study has two primary goals: to describe Asimov's career as a science fiction writer and to analyze as much of that science fiction as possible. The first goal is relatively easy to achieve. Asimov's science fiction career is a matter of public record. In his *The Asimov Science Fiction Bibliography* M. B. Tepper made available a "meticulously accurate" (Asimov's words) listing of that public record. Marjorie Miller's *Isaac Asimov: A Checklist* should now be available in most libraries with any interest at all in science fiction. Those of us now working with Asimov will find that these two have done most of our preliminary work for us, and we owe Tepper and Miller a large vote of thanks.

The second goal is more difficult to achieve. The process of literary analysis involves different things for different people. Whatever specific critical approach one takes will seem sensible to some readers and entirely wrongheaded to others. People who are interested in a history of science fiction should consult such works as Brian Aldiss's *Billion Year Spree: The True History of Science Fiction* or Donald A. Wollheim's *The Universe Makers: Science Fiction Today*, because I propose to do a history of Asimov's science fiction rather than one of science fiction in general. I am interested only slantingly in the relationship of Asimov's science fiction to the general history of science fiction, in Asimov's biography, and in his nonfiction. My subject matter here is confined almost exclusively to that described by the study's title: *The Science Fiction of Isaac Asimov*.

I do not intend to develop high-sounding theories about aesthetics, philosophy, art, and science fiction, and I refuse to play the game of "my vocabulary is bigger than your vocabulary." This study is aimed at a popular rather than an academic audience. I think of what I do as "practical criticism." I am interested in Asimov's craftsmanship. How are his stories put together? What specific things in specific stories work and what things don't, and why? I am so much more interested in specifics than in generalizations that I sometimes think a good subtitle for this study would be "For Example," two words that I do not think can be overused.

In the actual sitting down and writing out of the criticism, I find that I have learned more from "how to" books than from books of literary theory. That is, theoretical books like Wellek and Warren's *Theory of Literature* have meant less to me in actual practice than "how to" books like Meredith and Fitzgerald's *The Professional Story Writer and His Art*. Admittedly because of my own desire to write, I am more interested in discovering what Asimov did than I am in whatever insights this or that story might give me into my relationship with God or Truth or Beauty or Keats.

This does not mean that I avoid the critical task of evaluation. But my evaluations tend to be comparative—this Asimov story is better than that one, or this technique is used better in this story than in that one—rather than absolute. I try to be very careful to distinguish among three terms as I think and write: assertion, demonstration, and evaluation. For example (there's those two words!), while reading *The Currents of Space*, I noticed that Asimov used the technique of the flashback so often that more than once it was difficult to tell when the "now" of the story was. But it is not enough simply to assert this: it must be—and I think it can be—demonstrated. When I have shown in what specific ways this flashback technique hurts the novel, and in what specific ways it helps it, I feel justified in making an evaluative remark like "*The Currents of Space* is seriously marred by the overuse of flashbacks." On the basis of other evidence so gathered and judgments so made, I might decide that the novel is not a very good one, that it is, in fact, one of Asimov's weakest. I observe, I assert, I demonstrate, I evaluate—all on the basis of craftsmanship.

Allow me one more paragraph on the subject of evaluation. Values are not in stories. They are in the people who evaluate. They are in the standards used to evaluate. I might be able to assert and then to demonstrate that a certain story is tightly plotted, and I might even get you to agree with me. But when I go on to say, "Therefore it is a good story," I am evaluating according to my own belief that tight plotting is a good property for stories to have. You might feel that plotted stories are lies, that real people don't live in neat little self-contained episodes, and that therefore the plotted story is a bad story. The point here is that evaluation is a matter of the evaluator and the standards used, not of the works themselves. Like beauty, value is in the eye of the beholder. Stories are better or worse than one another only if the people doing the comparing agree together beforehand what standards to use and how to use them. I hope that as I assert, demonstrate, and evaluate, I will always be able to make clear what my standards and procedures are.

Since I concentrate so much on Asimov's craftsmanship, and since I sometimes have negative things to say about it, I know that some staunch Asimovians are bound to rear up and bellow forth, "But how can a punk college teacher with only four published stories to his credit presume to tell the great and powerful Asimov how to write?" Well, the answer is that I'm not trying to tell Asimov how to write. I am examining what he has written as part of an attempt to tell myself how to write. This is flattery, not carping. My attitude toward the living Asimov exactly parallels that of Ben Jonson toward the dead Shakespeare: "I lov'd the man, and doe honour his memory (on this side Idolatry) as much as any."

In an effort to cut down on the number of footnotes, I have put the page references in parentheses after each quotation. The title is always clear from the context, and the edition used can be found in the Bibliography. I have not found it necessary to include a detailed chronological bibliography of Asimov's stories because Tepper and Miller, in the previously referred-to sources, have already made such materials available to us. Instead, I concentrate on the more accessible hard-cover editions published by Doubleday.

Many people have been of help to me in the preparation of

this study. Over a period of nearly three years now, I have corresponded with Dr. Asimov concerning this book's factual (but never its evaluative) content. He has always promptly and carefully answered my questions, and he has kindly given me permission to quote from those letters to me. (I must add here that in graduate school I was trained as a medievalist—specialty: Chaucer—and I wasn't really sure how to deal with a living writer. I couldn't ask questions of Chaucer or of the fifteenth-century English bishop I wrote my dissertation on. Dr. Asimov's free and easy co-operation made having the author around no trouble at all.) So my most immediate thanks must go to Isaac Asimov himself, most importantly for writing his science fiction in the first place, and secondarily for supplying me with data as I found I needed it and for reading the manuscript to help screen out errors of fact. Thank you, Isaac. Despite its not being all roses, I hope you like the book.

Two organizations have also been of immense help to me. Doubleday & Company and the University of Dayton. At Doubleday Lawrence Ashmead thought the first three chapters warranted encouraging me to finish the book (encouragement expressed in a contract and an advance), and David Krotz and Mike Ossias showed a warm humanity in their correspondence as the work continued. Here at the University of Dayton, my chairman, Dr. B. J. Bedard, and my assistant chairman, Dr. Michael H. Means, offered their encouragement both morally and in the form of favorable teaching schedules. The Graduate Research Council at the university awarded me two summer research grants, freeing me to do the second and third chapters. The University of Dayton Library staff (especially Mr. Raymond Nartker and Ms. Johannah Scherrer) was of great help in securing needed articles, stories, and theses. One does not produce a manuscript without typists, and Charan Niehaus and Debbie Anderson were very conscientious in the work they did for me.

Of course, a project that takes over three years to complete is not done without sacrifice and help from one's family. My special thanks go to my wife, Ruth, and to our kids, Joe, Kathy, Denise, and Jean. I would like also to express my appreciation to my parents, first for my life, then for encouraging and sharing my early enthusiasm for science fiction and for Asimov.

Whatever merits this study has are due in large measure to all these people, and I thank them sincerely. Whatever deficiencies it has are all my own.

The Science Fiction
of Isaac Asimov

Introduction

A Description of Science Fiction

Science fiction is differentiated from other kinds of fiction by its emphasis on setting. Since there is no commonly accepted definition of the term "science fiction," anyone interested in the field is forced to fall back on descriptions of it that best express his own individual attitudes. My own personal description of what I mean when I use the term is "Science fiction is that fiction which examines scientifically plausible alternate settings for human consciousness." Three key elements in this description deserve elaboration.

Scientifically plausible. Its emphasis on scientific plausibility distinguishes science fiction from fantasy. (Personally, I take "science fantasy" to be a contradiction in terms, like "circular square.") Granted that the understandings of science change with the passing of time. The sun was once conceived of as going around the Earth; combustion was accounted for by the consumption of phlogiston in inflammable materials; atoms were literally indivisible; Venus was a hot, swampy water-world; Mars had a relatively thin, cold, but breathable atmosphere. Science does not give us the truth. It gives us our best estimates and guesses about the truth. As a part of his voluntary self-discipline, the science fiction writer works within the limits of what science suggests in his own time. Science fiction represents one of man's most imaginative and enjoyable efforts to accommodate himself to the universe as it is understood in his own lifetime.

But if science is a relatively objective thing which a writer can make efforts at "keeping up with developments in," plausibility is an entirely different matter. Like beauty and values, plausibility is in the mind of the reader. What one reader may find plausible another may find implausible. It cannot be measured and objectified. It cannot be a subject for scientific study. As a result, a story or a gimmick that one person might classify as science fiction would be classified by another as fantasy. Very few scientific grounds exist for time travel, faster-than-light drives, or parallel worlds-other dimensions. None of these are scientific according to modern ideas about the universe. But a good writer can make any of them scientifically plausible. In fact, these three gimmicks have been so thoroughly established in the science fiction reader's mind by good writers that now anyone, good or bad, can use them and have them accepted as "scientifically plausible." By making the reading audience believe it, H. G. Wells gave time machines to all writers, and time-travel stories are a legitimate part of science fiction, even though time travel is not a legitimate part of science.

Alternate settings. Its emphasis on alternate settings distinguishes science fiction from historical novels and mainstream novels, both of whose settings either have been or are. Science fiction deals with what might have been, what may now be, and what may yet be, as that subjunctivity is controlled by the understandings of modern science. Stories of what might have been include Mark Twain's account of a nineteenth-century Yankee at King Arthur's court and those innumerable tales of interstellar ships seeding a geologically ancient Earth with Adams and Eves. Stories of what might now be include ones about the Earth being the property of aliens or about secret government research projects. And stories of what may yet be obviously include all stories laid in a (scientifically plausible) future.

One further thing: "Setting" does not mean simply a physical change in one's environment, the addition of spaceships, robots, or time machines. Setting could include an internal change like telepathy or prescience. A world in which someone could read other people's minds (as in Robert Silverberg's *Dying Inside*) is obviously just that much different from the one in which we think we live, and therefore such a story uses an alternate setting and is science fiction.

For human consciousness. This is the most difficult element to discuss. The only consciousness about which any of us have any direct knowledge is our own. On the basis of that one example, we infer consciousnesses similar to ours in other hunks of protoplasm shaped like our own. We then call that generalization-from-one-example "human consciousness." You can go in either of two directions from here (and this is a matter of terminology and classification rather than reality, if I may so express it): you can emphasize the "human" term and say that to have "human consciousness" a living creature must be conscious and shaped like me; or you can emphasize the "consciousness" term and say that regardless of a living creature's external shape it is human if it attains a human's level of consciousness. In general, science fiction negatively criticizes the first, that a creature must look like us to be like us, and assumes the second, that size, color, shape, metabolism, etc., are not indications of the intelligence, consciousness, *humanity,* of a creature.

Thus stories about aliens are really stories about ourselves, about what our physiques and psychologies would be if our environments happened to be different. Science fiction is a series of lab experiments, of demonstrations, on the subject of what I would have been like (would be like) under different environmental circumstances: the relationship of setting and psychology.

To put it slightly differently: Science fiction has at its thematic center a concern with the certainty of (primarily technological) change in man's contemporary environment. This concern is best expressed in its concentration on setting, on creative, imaginative, scientifically plausible settings. If we can adapt ourselves to the many worlds of science fiction, surely we can adapt to the one world of the day after tomorrow, whatever it really turns out to be like. This is what is meant when people say that science fiction prepares its readers to accept change. Science fiction is a consciousness-expanding activity.

All the above is implied for me in my description of science fiction as "that fiction which examines scientifically plausible alternate settings for human consciousness."

Narrative Techniques

A science fiction story is first and foremost a story, a work of fiction. The same expectations, the same assumptions, that one carries to the reading of any work of fiction can be brought to the reading of science fiction. Since I intend to criticize Asimov's craftsmanship, let me attempt to codify, to schematicize (and in the process, unfortunately, to rigidify and deaden), some of the things I know I try to be aware of when I read a work of fiction. If nothing else, this will notify the reader of my own sets and limitations so that he can keep them in mind as he reads through my commentaries on Asimov's fiction. Perhaps pompously, I call these things narrative techniques, and I concentrate on six of them: plot, action vs. summation, narrative point of view, character, setting, and theme.

Plot. For the sake of convenience and discussion, it is easy to divide a plot into five sections. The first is the initial situation. Here we learn the names of the major characters, their relationships, the town in which they live, etc. Into this situation is thrust a complication, a problem or a threat of some sort. The person who solves the problem or disposes of the threat would be the central character. His attempts to do so make up the third section of the story, the conflict. Finally, after a series of unsuccessful attempts, which serve to define the problem more sharply and to get the central character in deeper trouble, he does remove the threat/solve the problem in part four, the solution. And everything returns to normal or to a new status quo in the resolution. In summary, the five elements of a plot are (1) the initial situation, (2) the complication, (3) the conflict, (4) the solution, and (5) the resolution. Most stories will begin with the second element and filter the first out in the course of the conflict. Some stories will end with the solution, since once it is found, the resolution should be obvious.

While reading stories, perhaps the first two questions to ask are "What is the conflict in this story?" and "Who is trying to accomplish something in this story?" From the first question one can work backward to the initial situation and forward to the solution and resolution, and from the second question one can identify the central character of the story. Looking for these things during or immediately after the reading of a story provides (to me, at least) invaluable insights into how stories are put together, how they work as artificial creations.

Action vs. summation. What I have tried to schematicize so far is merely the skeleton of a story. One standard way of getting at its flesh is to look at the words used to tell it, but I don't find this entirely satisfactory. Stories don't exist in words on printed pages any more than music exists in printed notes. Music resides in the ears of listeners, and stories exist in the eyes of readers. The writer is creating a series of thoughts in the reader's mind. The mark of fiction is that those thoughts are—or ought to be—experiences. A reader should be participating in stories, not simply listening to them. If a writer is lecturing his readers, he is summarizing things for them. He is not letting them participate in the actions of the story. A writer helps the reader participate by giving him the events the same way life does, through the reader's senses.

So there are two more questions I try to ask myself as I read fiction: "Does the writer allow me to use my five senses to help me participate in the story?" and "Does he ask me to participate in the right actions?" No storyteller can tell a reader everything about his characters and their thoughts and actions over any given period of time. He must be highly selective in the details he chooses in a scene and in the scenes he chooses in a story. I like to ask questions of a writer as I read. Why has he bothered to make me present at this particular action? Is it really necessary —and how is it necessary—to the solving of the story's problem?

Narrative point of view. Instead of always thinking in terms of action vs. summation—of participating instead of being told— I like to remember that all language assumes a speaking voice. Whenever I read any sentence in a story, inside or outside of quotation marks, I have the right to ask, "On whose authority am I being told this?" and "How does he know?" The first question helps me to establish the narrative point of view of the story (the referent of the pronoun "whose"), and the second is a reminder that the speaker could be a limited human being just like you and me. One might decide that the authority is that of the author, in which case we usually call the narrator omniscient, since the author can know all, see all, tell all, in his own story. But when Isaac Asimov writes a story called "I'm in Marsport Without Hilda," we do not assume that the "I" is Asimov himself (who, so far as I know, has never been in Marsport, with or without Hilda). The speaking voice in this case is limited to one human being, the referent of the "I," and is therefore called a limited narrator. There are really two types of limited narrators, differentiated from one another by the pronoun used to refer to him.

When the pronoun is "I," as above, this is an I-narrator, or first-person limited narrative point of view. If the writer invents a character, allows us to participate in the story only through that character's thoughts and actions, and refers to him as "he," this is third-person limited narrative point of view. I try to notice who is speaking to me in the words of a story; an omniscient narrator, a first-person limited narrator, or a third-person limited narrator.

Character. Earlier, in the discussion of plot, I suggested that a reader might try to identify the central character involved in the conflict, the person trying to solve the story's main problem or stave off its major threat, the one trying to accomplish something. Most of us will make one of two mistakes here. Either we will assume that the speaking voice—the I-narrator, usually—is the central character, or we will assume that it is the character who is present most in the story. Remembering that the I-narrator of the Sherlock Holmes stories, Dr. Watson, is not their central character (Holmes is) should help correct the first mistake. Learning to distinguish between activity for its own sake and significant activity should help with the second. The central character in a story is the one who does significant things (quality), not simply many things (quantity). Sometimes it helps to look at a story from several different angles before deciding for sure who it is that is causing the story.

But this is all a continuation of the discussion of central character. What about characterization? Basically, characterization is the separation of an individual from the group to which it belongs. We usually apply the term to humans in a story. Humanity is the group, this person is the individual—and he is individual because of the ways he differs from his group. Proper names and physical features will do as a start in making one person distinct from another. We all have eyes, but our eyes are differently colored. We all have our little behavioral quirks. Perhaps when you are nervous, you crack your knuckles or chew your lower lip. Different speech patterns or vocabularies will help make people different from one another. Beyond the external characteristics, different thought patterns, different behavioral patterns, different responses to the same stimuli, all help distinguish an individual. One of the most important ways we all differ from one another is motivation. What moves one person to action and involvement may not necessarily move another. The question "Why does he do that?" should always have its answer primarily in psychology rather than in the necessities of the plot. "He did it because otherwise there would be no story" is not an adequate answer.

But a writer must also present his characters to his readers. Two general types of character presentation are discernible: editorial and dramatic. When the writer puts the character before the reader and explicitly tells that reader what to think about him, that is known as "editorial character presentation," because the writer editorializes. When he puts the character before the reader and implicitly shows that reader what to think, that is known as "dramatic character presentation," because the writer seems to be allowing the reader to make up his own mind on the basis of what the character himself says, thinks, and does and on the basis of what others say and think about him, without authorial intrusion. (I say "seems" because the writer, in controlling the data the reader has available, is at least to that extent controlling the reader's evaluation of that data.)

Setting. Science fiction, however, is not noted primarily for its characterization. In fact, rightly or wrongly, characterization is often mentioned as a weakness in the field. It is noted for its gimmicks and its settings, not its people. We remember H. G. Wells's time machine rather than his time traveler, the Martian war machines rather than the narrator or his brother. As I have already suggested, one major difference—and perhaps the only one—between most other fiction and science fiction is that, where other fiction assumes the setting (the suburbs, medieval Spain, an airport) and concentrates on the individual living in that setting, science fiction tends to assume the people and concentrates on the setting. Science fiction is more interested in the relationship between setting and people-in-general than it is in any particular person. A science fiction story is often a laboratory case. If we change his environment thus and so, how will mankind change in response? (Asimov's "Nightfall" is a classic example of this.)

Because science fiction creates its own settings, it tends not to date the way much other fiction does. Asimov's Foundation Series is more widely read today than it was when it first appeared in the forties and fifties. Of how many of its immensely more popular contemporaries can that be said? Their settings have rendered too many of them obsolete. Asimov's settings, never having been, are not out of date, and his work is still fresh and vigorous and contemporary. When isn't an analysis of the relationship between sentience and environment relevant?

In addition, in a very real sense setting is the lead character in a science fiction story. Science fiction is filled with very real, finely discriminated and individualized settings. Larry Niven's Beowulf Schaeffer and Louis Wu may not be the most memorable of characters, but who can forget the worlds and life forms of Known Space and the Ringworld. Frank Herbert's planet Dune lives in the memory long after Paul Muad-dib Atreides has faded. And who was the central character of Hal Clement's *Mission of Gravity?*

It seems to me that one quite legitimate way of looking at science fiction is that setting is the main character and plot is simply an expository device for exploring setting. Whether one agrees with this or not, the imaginary, carefully constructed setting is extremely important to a science fiction story, and science fiction readers reserve their highest praises for writers who can create Dunes and Ringworlds. The construction of scientifically plausible alternate settings for human consciousness is science fiction's game, and Asimov is one of its best players.

Theme. If one asks the question "What is the story about?" the immediate answer will be a plot summary. But if one then says, "Yes. Yes. I know that. But what is that about?" the answer will be the story's theme. The story may be about mining the rings of Saturn for water or trying to identify a menace that has killed off a human colony on a far-distant planet. But what that is about is ecology, the balance of nature, the relationship between man and his environment. When anyone finishes reading any story, it is perfectly legitimate for him to look up and ask, "So what?" An answer to that question will also be the story's theme.

On an entirely different level from the individual story, science fiction as a genre is permeated with certain themes and attitudes. I know there are things I believe, things that have become a part of me, which, traced back, almost surely had their origins in my reading of science fiction. Let me cite some of the themes of science fiction. 1. Science fiction readers have been taught that

Introduction xxiii

man's intelligence and reason are to be preferred over hysterical emotionalism. Science fiction is about problem-solving, not panicking in the face of problems. This is another way of saying that science fiction teaches a respect for the life of the mind. 2. Science fiction readers were among the first to be made aware that technological innovations had shrunk the world to a size where one man or one small group of men could realistically seek to take over the world, and this is the first time in human history when this has been so. It was a hard thing to see, but at core that's what all those stories about mad scientists inventing terrible weapons with which to take over were really about. 3. Science fiction readers have seen demonstrated time and again the insanity of racism. Having accompanied intelligent amoeba and giant brains and lizard men, they are not likely to object to mere differences in skin coloration. 4. Science fiction readers have also been taught the limitations of nationalism. They are not Brazilians or Russians or Americans or Germans. They are Earthmen, with all that implies. They know that the problems that face our world cannot be solved at the national level. 5. Science fiction readers feel in their very bones the inevitability and grandeur of man's expansion into the universe. They prefer that money be spent on space exploration rather than on violently preserving artificial and divisive national boundary lines. 6. Science fiction does not predict the future, and few of its readers and writers claim that it does. But what it does do is get us used to the idea that the future, in our own lifetimes, is going to be different from the present. And it constructs for us imaginary alternate worlds in which we can live while we read the story. With that practice, maybe we won't feel quite so alienated when the future gets here, whatever it turns out to be.

Science fiction readers get one other thing out of their reading, perhaps the most important thing of all. So far as any of us know, none of us chose the state of our own existence. We were not free to choose our century, our race, our sex, our parents, our economic and social status, the color of our hair, our height, or the number of our arms and legs. Nor did we freely choose to be born into a universe in which the boiling point of water at sea level on Earth is 212° F., the chemical composition of common table salt is NaCl, and light travels at a constant speed of 186,281 miles per second. Each of us is a conscious packet of sensations imprisoned in a specific body, place, and time not of his own choosing. Science fiction frees us from that prison. It lets us live other lives, not mere duplicates of our own, but as completely different as the human imagination can make them. Rightly or wrongly, I identify the feeling of exaltation this freedom brings with what many science fiction readers refer to as "the sense of wonder." The joy and wonder of sentience, of simply being, in a variety of forms and environments—that's what science fiction is all about. Science fiction quite literally is consciousness-expanding.

Let me round off this section of my Introduction with an anecdote intended to demonstrate that what we get from a work of fiction is a compromise between what the writer wants us to learn and what we want to learn. Asimov once listened to a college teacher explicate one of his stories. Afterward he went to the teacher and said, "Nothing of what you found in the story was in the author's mind when he wrote it." The teacher asked, "How do you know?" "Because," Asimov announced, "I am the author." "Well," replied the teacher, "just because you wrote the story, what makes you think you know anything about it?" Once a story is written, it exists only in being read. It's in the reader's mind, his experience. It's up to him to decide what to do with it. Using the tools outlined above has helped me to decide what to do with much of Asimov's fiction. Plot, action vs. summation, narrative point of view, character, setting, and theme—all these have given me material for thought and discussion on the subject of Asimov's skill at putting together his works of fiction. They have enabled me to study his craftsmanship as a writer.

Asimov's Career

For many people the name Isaac Asimov and the term "science fiction" are synonymous. Asimov is science fiction. His strengths and weaknesses are science fiction's strengths and weaknesses. He is the type of the science fiction writer. Although I don't think this is true anymore—anyone trying to gauge modern science fiction by reading the Foundation Series is simply wrong—I think it was nearly true between 1941, when he published "Nightfall," and about 1959, when he compiled *Nine Tomorrows*. (The

qualification in "nearly true" is my recognition that he shared
the mantle of leadership with Robert A. Heinlein.)

Born in Petrovichi, Russia, southwest of Moscow in the prov-
ince of Smolensk, on January 2, 1920, of Jewish parents, Asimov
was brought to the United States in 1923. He became a naturalized citizen five years later. At the age of nine he read his first
science fiction story, Harl Vincent's "Barton's Island," in the August 1929 issue of *Amazing Stories*. He immediately became an
avid fan of magazine science fiction. Although he started writing
stories for his own pleasure when he was eleven, it wasn't until
1937 that it occurred to him to try to write something for publication.

His subsequent writing career breaks easily into four main
periods. The first extends from "Marooned Off Vesta" in 1939
through "Nightfall" in 1941. In this period he wrote thirty-two
stories and published seventeen, with four more eventually seeing publication. His goal was to sell regularly to John W. Campbell, editor of *Astounding Science Fiction*, but Campbell bought
only five of these first seventeen: "Trends," "Homo Sol," "Reason,"
"Liar!" and "Nightfall." Actually, Frederick Pohl, by buying seven
of Asimov's stories at this time, gave Asimov more immediate
and practical encouragement than did the grail of Campbell's
hoped-for approval, and Pohl deserves more credit for getting
Asimov started than he usually receives. "Nightfall," which ends
this period, was the story that established Asimov's reputation as
a frontline writer of magazine science fiction.

His second period extends from immediately after "Nightfall"
through the last of the Foundation stories, ". . . And Now You
Don't," from 1941 through 1950. Throughout this period Asimov
was a valued member of Campbell's stable of writers. In this period he wrote for Campbell the two series of stories that form
the pillars of his science fiction reputation, the Robot Stories and
the Foundation Series. He had become what he had set out to be,
a respected writer of magazine science fiction. But such writing
did not pay very well. In eleven productive years, down through
1949, he had earned less than $8,000. So after receiving his Ph.D.
in chemistry from Columbia, he accepted a job teaching biochemistry at Boston University.

His third period runs from *Pebble in the Sky* in 1950 through

The Naked Sun in 1957. *Pebble in the Sky* was Asimov's first
hard-cover book. Originally written in shorter form for a *Startling
Stories* lead novel, it was rejected and set aside until Doubleday
decided to start publishing science fiction. From 1950 through
1957 Asimov published twenty-four books, seventeen of which
were either new science fiction (*Pebble in the Sky* and five of the
six Lucky Starr juveniles) or reprints from the magazines (*I,
Robot* and the Foundation Series from the forties, other novels
and collections from more recent magazine fiction). In the forties
Asimov was successful in the magazines when there were no
hard-cover outlets. In the fifties he was successful in both magazines and hard covers.

But a major change was coming in his writing career. For one
thing, the hard-cover market had increased his writing income
until by 1957 he was earning two and a half times as much writing
as he was teaching. Then again, an early biochemistry text had
been followed by a few other nonfiction science books, and he
found he enjoyed writing directly about science instead of doing
it encumbered with the need for plots and characterization and
dialogue. Finally, in late 1957 the Russians launched *Sputnik*,
and Asimov decided he would stop teaching in the classroom.
He would cut back on his science fiction production. He would
devote himself to helping close the science gap which *Sputnik*
had so dramatically revealed. *The Naked Sun* was the last original
full-length adult science fiction novel Asimov was to write until
The Gods Themselves appeared in the spring of 1972.

Period Four stretches, say, from *Earth Is Room Enough* in 1957
through *Nightfall and Other Stories* in 1969. In this period his
energies have gone into science writing. In science fiction he is
represented by a trickle of original stories, by collections of stories
largely drawn from the magazines of the fifties, by editing collections of science fiction stories, and by appearances at science
fiction conventions and on college campuses, at both of which
he is lionized. One collection of stories that he edited is of some
importance in his career, *The Hugo Winners*, Vol. I, 1962. Before
this collection Asimov had assembled and printed his own stories
without any commentary. (See *The Martian Way*, *Earth Is Room
Enough*, and *Nine Tomorrows*.) In *The Hugo Winners* Asimov
chatted amusingly about the stories, so amusingly and success-

fully that since 1962 he has provided similar informative commentary for his own collections. (See *Asimov's Mysteries*, where he plays it straight; *Nightfall and Other Stories*, where autobiographical banter is liberally inserted; *Opus 100*, which is a series of excerpts and stories surrounded by editorial material; *The Early Asimov*, an autobiography of his first eleven years as a science fiction writer, with twenty-seven stories added to illustrate the autobiography; and *Before the Golden Age*, an autobiographical account of the science fiction he read during his teens.)

The use of *Nightfall and Other Stories* to mark the end of this fourth period is somewhat misleading, as this period may or may not have ended yet. Still, the collection of previously printed magazine fiction marks this period as clearly as the publication of novels had marked his third and the magazine versions of the Robot Stories and the Foundation Series had marked his second. The publication of *The Gods Themselves* in 1972 may herald the return of Isaac Asimov to science fiction and the beginning of a fifth period. Whether this is so or not, and what the quality of that new fiction might be, we can only wait and see. For now, all we can say is that Asimov is our leading science writer and that he once produced a large body of science fiction that, with Heinlein's, dominated the field in the forties and fifties.

First Period

"Marooned Off Vesta" through "Nightfall"
(1939–41)

Order Written		Order Published
2	"The Callistan Menace"*	6
3	"Marooned Off Vesta"	1
5	"Ring Around the Sun"	5
9	"The Magnificent Possession"	7
10	"Trends"†	3
11	"The Weapon Too Dreadful to Use"	2
13	"Black Friar of the Flame"	22
14	"Robbie"*	9
15	"Half-Breed"*	4
16	"The Secret Sense"	12
19	"Homo Sol"†	8
20	"Half-Breeds on Venus"*	10
21	"The Imaginary"	28
23	"Heredity"*	13
24	"History"*	11
25	"Reason"†	14
26	"Christmas on Ganymede"	19
27	"The Little Man on the Subway"	49
28	"Liar!"†	15
30	"The Hazing"	27
31	"Super Neutron"*	17
32	"Nightfall"†	16

* Stories bought by Pohl
† Stories bought by Campbell

NOTE: Where a number is missing in the "Order Written" column, the story was written but never published and is now no longer extant. (See Asimov's own chart at the end of *The Early Asimov*.)

CHAPTER ONE

The Earliest Asimov

Isaac Asimov read his first science fiction story at the age of nine. He began writing for his own personal enjoyment at eleven. Then, in 1937, when he was seventeen, he decided to try to write a story for publication. As a result he wrote the first few pages of a story he called "The Cosmic Corkscrew." Writing for publication proved more difficult than writing for fun, however, and he set the story aside. A year later a visit to the editorial offices of *Astounding Science Fiction* (to inquire as to why his copy of the magazine had not arrived yet) moved him to return to the story. He finished it on June 19 and delivered it to editor John W. Campbell personally on June 21, 1938. Campbell rejected it two days later, Asimov put it aside permanently, and it was eventually lost.

We must rely on Asimov's own account of it:

> In it, I viewed time as a helix (that is, something like a bed-spring). Someone could cut across from one turn directly to the next, thus moving into the future by some exact interval but being incapable of travelling one day less into the future. My protagonist made the cut across time and found the Earth deserted. All animal life was gone yet there was every sign that life had existed until very shortly before—and no indication at all of what had brought about the disappear-ance. It was told in first person from a lunatic asylum because the narrator had, of course, been placed in a madhouse after he returned and tried to tell his tale. [*The Early Asimov,* p. 4.]

In *Before the Golden Age* Asimov remarks that the story began "with the scientist-hero lecturing a friend on cosmic rays and neutrinos" (p. 39). He also reports in *The Early Asimov* that Campbell rejected it because the beginning was too slow, it had a suicide at the end, it used first-person narration, the dialogue was stiff, and the nine-thousand-word length was inconvenient for piecing into a magazine made up of short stories and novelettes.

"The Cosmic Corkscrew" was written in June. In July he wrote two more stories, both of which were eventually published, so he sold two of the first three stories he wrote. His second written story, "Stowaway," was retitled "The Callistan Menace" by Frederick Pohl when he bought it for the new—and short-lived—*Astonishing Stories*. It became Asimov's sixth published story. His third written became his first published when Ray Palmer accepted "Marooned Off Vesta" for the March 1939 issue of *Amazing Stories*.

From the beginning, however, Asimov wanted to write for Campbell and be published in *Astounding*, and Campbell rejected all three of these fledgling efforts. In fact, though he submitted most of his stories to Campbell before sending them on to the other two major markets, *Amazing Stories* and *Thrilling Wonder Stories*, Asimov had to wait until his tenth written story before Campbell bought one. (The next story Campbell bought from him was to be his nineteenth, so Asimov did not start out selling regularly to Campbell by any means.) His first story in *Astounding* was "Trends," Asimov's original title having been "Ad Astra," from the Latin phrase for "through adversity to the stars." Remembering the reasons Campbell had rejected "The Cosmic Corkscrew," it is interesting to note that "Trends" has a first-person narrator and a lot of stiff dialogue. But it also has an idea, and ideas were always of transcendent importance for Campbell. Because of his early ambition to appear in *Astounding*, Asimov considers "Trends" his first important sale. It was his third published story.

In any study of "The Earliest Asimov," then, three stories must stand out initially: "The Callistan Menace," because it is his first extant story; "Marooned Off Vesta," because it was his first published story; and "Trends," because it was his first sale to Campbell and *Astounding*.

"The Callistan Menace" and "Marooned Off Vesta," produced

in the same month, are very similar to each other in one extremely important respect: they both show the effect of a great deal of preplanning. They are both well-made stories in which the parts are fitted together with great care. Asimov speaks of working in his father's candy store in Brooklyn at this time "without conscious attention, but . . . concentrating deeply on the plot permutations that were sounding hollowly within the cavern of my skull" (*The Early Asimov*, p. 183).

In "The Callistan Menace" the eighth expedition to Jupiter's moon Callisto is seeking to discover what destroyed the first seven. The ship has a beryl-tungsten hull where the earlier ones had had hulls of steel. It has a boy stowaway (hence Asimov's original title). It has the souvenir vitri-rubber space suit of the dead hero PeeWee Wilson, though everyone's suits are now of the modern-design steel. The souvenir suit is made usable as a way of keeping everyone's minds off their troubles. Change any one of these items and the story will not work. Make the vitri-rubber suit full-size or fail to refurbish it, give PeeWee Wilson a steel suit, make the ship's hull steel, let the men have new-style aluminum suits—tinker anywhere with these givens and the story falls apart.

But with exactly this combination of circumstances, the Callistan menace can be gigantic four-foot-long one-foot-thick slugs which project magnetic fields which in turn are intensified to lethal proportions by steel. The men exploring the surface of Callisto inside their steel space suits and outside the nonsteel spaceship are threatened. No one can do anything except the boy, who can use PeeWee (see the preplanning?) Wilson's refurbished nonsteel suit to save the men and the mission.

Asimov has also worked out a way to tell us all about the Callistan menace before it appears, so that the story will not have to be slowed down with explanations during the action-packed climax. About midway through the story, as an example of the kind of talk-fests the crew had, Asimov has one zoologically-oriented crewman tell the others about "a little slug-like thing found only on Europa . . . The Magnet Worm. It's about six inches long and has a sort of slate-grey color. . . . It kills by some sort of magnetic field. . . . The presence of iron more than quadruples its strength" (*The Early Asimov*, p. 15). Chekhov once remarked that if a short story writer mentions a shotgun hanging on the wall, somewhere in the story it must be taken down and fired. Asimov knew this instinctively. The Magnet Worm is not merely exotic detail for its own sake. It is part of the exposition of the story.

Asimov admits that the story accepts the science fiction conventions of the day rather than the thinking of scientists. Though as a science student Asimov knew better, he still gave Callisto lakes of water, an oxygen atmosphere, and plant and animal life. Accuracy of scientific content became important later. Early on, he was writing as the market demanded.

The inaccurate science does not ruin the story. Some people might object to the boy-hero-who-saves-the-day, but in this particular story a boy hero is justified by the necessity of having someone small enough to fit into the undersized space suit. And the small space suit is justified because it particularizes the story's hero: were it larger, anyone could have used it, instead of this one particular person who is the only one in the story the right size. There may also be some melodramatic qualities in the story, e.g., "I wheeled in dismay and remained petrified at the sight before my eyes." Still, on the whole, the story is lightly handled. Take, for example, the reaction of the captain to the discovery of the stowaway: "For half an hour the Captain shot off salvo after salvo of the very worst sort of profanity. He started with the sun and ran down the list of planets, satellites, asteroids, comets to the very meteors themselves. He was starting on the nearer fixed stars when he collapsed from sheer nervous exhaustion." This is an effective parody of years of science fiction cursing "by the big sun of Mercury!" "by the oceans of Venus!" "by the rings of Saturn!" The story is finished at its next to last paragraph, but Asimov allows himself a nice, light, jauntily optimistic closing:

> Callisto was a shrinking blue ball on the televisor—an ordinary unmysterious world. Stanley Fields [the boy stowaway], honorary Captain of the good ship *Ceres*, thumbed his nose at it, protruding his tongue at the same time. An inelegant gesture, but the symbol of man's triumph over a hostile Solar System.

Campbell rejected the story as being forced, as not going smoothly. He probably had in mind this awareness, which the story forces on its readers, that everything has been thoroughly thought out beforehand. Everything is carefully explained. Readers' objections and questions are taken into consideration and answered rather obviously. Campbell would not object to doing these things, but he would object to their being done so close to the surface of the story. As Campbell said, Asimov needed experience. One learns to write by writing. Even so, for only his second story, Asimov shows that he has already learned how to plan ahead and how to look at a story from the reader's point of view. "The Callistan Menace" is a much better second story than anyone has a right to expect from an eighteen-year-old. One can see the promise that Campbell saw.

Except for an aura of pulpish melodrama which clings primarily to the emotional, irrational character of Mark Brandon (for example: "Mark Brandon whirled and ground his teeth at him. 'I'm glad you feel happy about that,' he spat out viciously"), "Marooned Off Vesta" is a nicely told problem story. Its difficulty lies not so much in the story itself as in the situation with which the story opens. If we can accept that initial situation in which our heroes find themselves, then the story itself reads well and is entirely acceptable.

Interestingly enough, especially in this his third story, Asimov has taken what for other writers would be an episode in an adventure story and raised that episode to the level of an entire story. Two issues of *Amazing* earlier than "Marooned Off Vesta," for example, Frederick Arnold Kummer, Jr., had an action-adventure story called "The Treasure of Asteroid X." In it an intrepid spaceship captain is hired by a wealthy industrialist with a beautiful socialite daughter to take them in search of a century-old pirate's treasure hidden on a lost asteroid. The industrialist has an old map that "others" have been willing to kill for. Despite the opposition of these others, they find the treasure, the spaceship captain is now rich, and the socialite daughter has fallen in love with him.

A routine story except for one episode. The captain, Chance, the industrialist, Bronson, the daughter, Stella, and two others, Davis and Houck, are at one point locked in a cabin on a spaceship. The aluminum door is an inch thick. They must escape or die, but how?

> Chance studied the cabin. It contained a bunk, a clothes press, a chair, a wash stand . . . nothing that would help in the forcing of doors. There were instruments, also, as was customary in the captain's quarters . . . a speed indicator, a sidereal compass, a big mercury barometer for showing the air pressure within the ship, since a drop in the pressure might indicate a leak in the hull. Chance stood still, his eyes on the barometer. Mercury . . . and water available in the tap on the wash stand. . . .
>
> "I've got it!" He whirled about, snatched the barometer from the wall. "Houck, fill that tumbler with water! Here, Davis, help me break this barometer!"
>
> The others, watching, saw Chance snap off the end of the instrument, drip mercury through the keyhole into the lock.
>
> "Now!" he snapped. "The water!"
>
> Houck handed him the tumbler and Chance poured a stream of water into the lock.
>
> "See here," Bronson began. "Just what . . ."
>
> "The mercury removes the oxide film on the aluminum," Chance said patiently, refilling the tumbler. "In contact with water the metal shows its true nature and reacts rapidly, giving off hydrogen." He pointed to the bubbling water. "As a result the aluminum breaks down into aluminum hydroxide, a white powder. Watch!"
>
> Eyes fixed on the lock, they waited. Long minutes passed. Again and again Chance refilled the tumbler. Slowly the entire lock began to erode, leaving only a white dust.
>
> "Now!" Chance reached down, turned the knob. The lock grated, rattled brokenly, and the doors swung open.
>
> "Free!" Bronson cried. "Thank God!" [Pp. 68–69]

Thank, rather, Chance's scientific knowledge.

In "Marooned Off Vesta" Asimov never tells us why Warren Moore and Mark Brandon were on board the *Silver Queen* during its ill-fated trip through the asteroid belt, though it would have been easy to manufacture a story based on their reason. Give them, for example, a place they have to be by a certain time—or else! And then let the accident impede their progress. The problem would be to arrive at point X despite being marooned. The marooning would be a mere episode in the conflict of reaching their destination.

Instead, Asimov leaves out the before and after. The conflict is not good guys versus bad guys in some rush for a lost pirate's treasure. It is man's reason, as represented in Warren Moore, versus man's emotions, as represented in Mark Brandon. The theme of the story is that a calm and rational use of the scientific method, allied with some hard scientific data, is more useful in the saving of oneself than wave after wave of emotion. As Brandon puts it to Moore, "How can you think straight at a time like this?" And as Moore says later, "I know how you feel. It's got me, too. But you mustn't give in to it. Fight it, or you'll go stark, raving mad" (*Asimov's Mysteries*, p. 127).

The problem is that in this particular story the deck has been so carefully stacked during Asimov's preplanning that the theme almost becomes "Know the scientific method, for it can save your life in a few very carefully rigged situations."

Consider the situation. The space liner *Silver Queen* has collided with an asteroid and broken up. Three survivors—perhaps the only three—find themselves in orbit around Vesta. Question: Considering Vesta's very small gravitational field, what are the chances that any remnant of the *Silver Queen* would be captured by Vesta at all, much less go into a stable orbit? Question: What are the chances that the remnant's axis of rotation would point toward Vesta? Question: What are the chances that the entire ship's water supply would not only remain intact but be part of the remnant our heroes find themselves on? Question: What are the chances that Michael Shea (the third survivor) would have closed all the valves on the ship's water system immediately before the collision so that none of the water would be lost before Moore recognized its significance? It is all far too improbable. Yet change any of these items and the story falls apart. No matter how much Moore knew about science, he would be unable to save them. The situation is too unusual to carry the theme of the story. Instead, it argues against that theme. Still, given this very carefully arranged initial situation, the story in "Marooned Off

Vesta" follows naturally and well. Asimov has done a good job of concealing the story's main difficulty.

In fact, the story itself follows a classic science fiction pattern and (as was implied earlier) may have been among the first to do so. The hero's life is threatened and that threat must be removed. The reader is presented in natural conversation with all the relevant data. The hero solves the problem, but the solution is not immediately passed along to the reader. Instead, he acts on that solution. We have all the data he did plus his subsequent actions to help us solve the problem. Can we do it? (The excerpt from the Kummer story follows exactly this pattern, too.) Moore dons the only space suit available and goes outside the wrecked fragment. With the only heat-ray available he laboriously burns a hole in the water tank exactly where the axis of rotation comes through it. Then he goes back inside to answer questions.

The water is exhausting from the ship like a rocket, he explains to his puzzled comrades—and to us.

> "We'll land in five or six hours, probably. The water will last for quite a long while and the pressure is still great, since the water issues as steam."
>
> "Steam—at the low temperature of space?" Brandon was surprised.
>
> "Steam—at the low pressure of space!" corrected Moore. "The boiling point of water falls with the pressure. It is very low indeed in a vacuum." [Pp. 139–40]

Both "The Callistan Menace" and "Marooned Off Vesta" show definite signs of having been very carefully thought out beforehand. This preplanning was directed largely at the plot of "The Callistan Menace" in an effort to make plausible each event as it happened, and in "Marooned Off Vesta" so that the eighteen-year-old Asimov could use the solution he had recently learned in a chemistry class. In his first extant story and in his first published story, the second and third he wrote, we can see Asimov as a meticulous builder, a shaper of stories.

Kate Wilhelm has suggested that in her experience beginning writers tend to fall into two groups: storytellers and wordsmiths. "The drive of the story pushes the storyteller into clumsy phrases, purple prose, redundancies, but he has a story complete with beginning, middle, end. Things happen and there is a resolution. The wordsmiths often have collages of beautiful sketched images, and little else" (*Clarion I*, pp. 14–15). What deficiencies these first two Asimov stories have are clearly at the level of word-phrase-sentence rather than plotting. We may recognize that Brandon's whirling, spitting viciously, exploding, shouting, and lip-curling are all done in pulp idiom for a pulp audience, but understanding why they are there does not negate their presence. This tendency toward pulp language was imprinted in Asimov early, and in some ways he has not yet gotten over it. Asimov, surely a storyteller rather than a wordsmith, appeals to us for what he says—the story—rather than for the way he says it—the style. And this has been true since "The Callistan Menace" and "Marooned Off Vesta."

From the beginning of his career Asimov has known how to use conversation for exposition. That is, the characters in talking to one another convey to the reader the background information necessary to the story. The first third of "Marooned Off Vesta" is an outstanding example of this, and we have elsewhere noted the way he slips in to "The Callistan Menace" the information about the Magnet Worm so necessary for the end of that story. "Trends," the first story Asimov sold to Campbell, also shows us his ability to present data dramatically, to give us exposition through dialogue. The problem is that in "Trends" the material so presented is broad cultural history rather than a specific initial situation. As a result, the characters are made to lecture one another about social, political, and scientific developments from the Mad Decades of the twenties and thirties through the "present" of most of the story to the early twenty-first century. "Trends" is not so much fiction as the fictional disguise for an idea that could have been better made in nonfictional terms. As a work of fiction it is not a good story. But it is a good idea.

At the time of writing "Trends" Asimov was supplementing his income with a National Youth Association job that paid him fifteen dollars a month to do some typing, and he was doing the typescript on someone else's book on social resistance to technological change. In "Trends" a brilliant scientist and a few friends construct a rocket to the moon—actually, two such rockets, one in public which is destroyed, one in private which succeeds—and they do it in the face of public disapproval whipped up by religious fanatics and the newspapers. The idea was not Asimov's, but it was the idea that sold the story to Campbell. The major trend in history for centuries had run in favor of scientific research and discovery. The trend in the opposite direction since the Mad Decades was too short to be anything significant and in fact could be reversed, as it was by our hero's successful circumnavigation of the moon.

The sweep of the story forces Asimov into using a rather complex narrative point of view. The story focuses on two major events: the abortive moon launch of July 15, 1973, and the later successful one in the summer of 1978. There are summaries of events before 1973, of events from 1973 to 1978, and of the public reaction since 1978. To get it all in, Asimov chose to use a friend and co-worker of the scientist as his first-person narrator, and to have his narrator speak from the vantage point of the first decade of the twenty-first century. Thus, so far as the narrator is concerned, the events are long past. Yet the two launch days are presented as if they were happening right now in front of us. We as readers are asked to be present at them and to participate in them, even though they are really reminiscences of one who had lived through them all and could summarize events when he had to. Asimov tries to get dramatic closeness and dramatic distance simultaneously, and it doesn't quite come off.

The awkward narrative point of view, the tendency of the characters to lecture one another on subjects they already know (though we readers don't), the tendency of the narrator to summarize more and more as the story goes along—these things hurt the story as fiction. Using hindsight, we can see important things in it for a survey of Asimov's career. We see Asimov's penchant for putting his exposition in dramatic conversation rather than in tedious introductory paragraphs. We see his attitude toward religion as an enemy to scientific progress. And we see his interest in history and in the trends and cycles of history. (Notice that in this story an individual can terminate historical trends through his actions. This is not to be his position in the Foundation Series.)

Of these three important early stories, the best is probably "Marooned Off Vesta," despite its rigged initial situation. It shows a fine use of expository dialogue, it concentrates on one action with a well-defined beginning, middle, and end, and it dramatizes a serious theme: reason and science are more valuable to man's preservation than emotion. "The Callistan Menace" deserves admiration for its close plotting, but it lacks a theme that has any connection with you and me. "Trends" is by far the weakest piece of fiction of the three. It is saved only by the presence of an interesting idea, though that idea is only tangentially important today. Today people are anti-space program on social rather than religious grounds. But the mere idea that anyone could be anti-space program for any reason was novel in its time and for its science fiction audience.

Since Asimov's reputation as a science fiction writer was built on two series, the Robot Stories and the Foundation Series, it should not be surprising that from the beginning he was thinking in terms of doing series. In his fifth written and fifth published story, "Ring Around the Sun," Asimov's heroes are called Turner and Snead. Following the example of Campbell's own Penton-Blake stories, Asimov intended to do a series of Turner-Snead stories. He also intended "Super Neutron," his thirty-first written and seventeenth published story, to be the first in a series. He never got around to writing the second story in either of these aborted series.

Frederick Pohl did ask for a sequel to "Half-Breed," Asimov's fourth published story, and Asimov obliged with "Half-Breeds on Venus." And Campbell went along with Asimov's suggestion that he do a sequel to the second story Asimov sold to Campbell, "Homo Sol," but Campbell rejected "The Imaginary" when he saw it, and both these series never got beyond the second story.

Asimov, however, was not to be denied. He saw very practical values in the writing of series. "For one thing, you had a definite background that was carried on from story to story, so that half your work was done for you. Secondly, if the 'series' became popular, it would be difficult to reject new stories that fit into it" (*The Early Asimov*, pp. 42–43). Toward the end of this initial period in his career, two stories appeared in successive issues of *Astounding* (April and May 1941). They were "Reason" and "Liar!" They featured Asimov's robots. One was a Powell-Donovan story, the other a Susan Calvin. Together, they fixed in the science fiction audience's mind the idea that Asimov was doing a series of robot stories. Add to these two the earlier "Strange Playfellow," or "Robbie," and Asimov had, after two years' work, established a successful series.

Some of the stories that Asimov was writing here before "Nightfall" deserve attention, whether they were part of attempts to begin series or not. For one thing, scattered through these early stories are some interesting ideas or "gimmicks." For example, in his second published story, "The Weapon Too Dreadful to Use," an ancient Venusian language is described:

> "It is a dead language and I know little more than a smattering. You see, it is a color language. Each word is designated by a combination of two, and sometimes three, colored dots. The colors are finely differentiated, though, and a Terrestrial, even if he had the key to the language, would have to use a spectroscope to read it." [*The Early Asimov*, p. 88]

"The Secret Sense" features a Martian *portwem*, an organlike "musical" instrument which could "form any conceivable pattern of electric current." Asimov gives his Martians the ability to perceive things that Earthmen cannot, and the *portwem* organizes into aesthetic patterns sense experiences unavailable to us. As one Martian puts it to an Earthman,

> "But what do you know of beauty? Have you ever known what it was to witness the beauty of the naked copper wires when an AC current is turned on? Have you sensed the delicate loveliness of induced currents set up in a solenoid when a magnet is passed through it? Have you ever attended a Martian *portwem?*" [*The Early Asimov*, p. 173]

Actually, "The Secret Sense" is a very interesting story, but it was rejected by all the markets and Asimov finally had to give it away to get it published. (He later asked for—and got—five dollars for it in order to avoid the charge of giving stories to some magazines while selling them to other, competing magazines.) Perhaps the difficulty was that the story was based on art rather than action, and editors felt it wouldn't appeal to the male teen-aged market. Or maybe it was the unsympathetic hero. He is self-centered, vain, and spoiled. At one point in the story he describes himself as "an aesthete." When finally a Martian invites him to participate in a once-in-a-lifetime (for an Earthman) *portwem* at which he can, through drugs, experience once what Martians can experience anytime, the Martian acts out of desire for revenge. And we agree with him. The hero deserves to be punished for his badgering and bullying and downright bad manners. Yet when the *portwem* is over, we are asked to share the Earthman's sense of loss and to pity him. The shift from unsympathetic hero to intense emotional and aesthetic experience leaves us on the side of the experience, and we cannot see his horrible deprivation at the end as his just deserts. We share too much in his loss. It is interesting that the secret sense which opens the way for an Earthman to a new and overpowering sensual experience is stimulated in this story by drugs, the bane of modern society. This helps give the story a contemporary feel that it probably lacked when it first appeared thirty years ago. (As a sign of the times, by the way, it is also interesting to notice that the logos for "The Secret Sense" reads "by Isaac Asimov, author of 'Homo Sol,' 'Trends,' etc." Those were the only two Asimov stories that had appeared so far in *Astounding*. It is easy to see where the audience and the prestige were.)

Two other stories from this period that were very significant for Asimov's future writing career were "Black Friar of the Flame" and "Homo Sol." Asimov has evidently taken enough kidding about how bad "Black Friar of the Flame" was, because in *The Early Asimov* he is moved to write a defense of it. He points out that it looks forward to the Foundation Series in featuring a man-on-many-worlds universe and in using for the first time the planets Trantor and Santanni. (The hero's name in "The Weapon Too Dreadful to Use" was Frantor.) "Black Friar" also looks forward to *Pebble in the Sky*, he suggests, in patterning its background roughly on the historical antecedent of Judea under the Romans.

The story was also significant—for better or for worse—in that it broke Asimov of the habit of making repeated revisions in a story. He began "Black Friar" as a story called "Pilgrimage" in March of 1939 and revised it six times (including an intermediate title change to "Galactic Crusade") before it was accepted three years later. He has since decided that so much polishing is bad economics, and he no longer does it. This clearly helps him turn out more salable material in quantity, but it may also hurt his quality, since he composes at the typewriter. What happens if a story takes a wrong turn at the typewriter? It may still be salable, but it may not be as good as a rethinking and a rewriting might have made it. (I would instance "Reason" in the Robot Stories and "The General" among the Foundation Series as stories that went wrong at the typewriter and desperately needed thoroughgoing revisions which they didn't get. More of them in their proper place.)

"Homo Sol," one of the best of Asimov's stories, is even so another example of a story that went wrong, though here both Campbell and Asimov are responsible. This was the nineteenth story Asimov wrote, the seventeenth he submitted to Campbell, and the second Campbell took. But Campbell asked for and got two consecutive revisions, and Asimov tells us, "He inserted several paragraphs, here and there, without consulting me, in the final version" (*The Early Asimov*, p. 203). In answer to my request for more details, he wrote:

> About Homo Sol. The overall revision that Campbell had me make was the thesis that the human race is somehow superior to all the other intelligences. Even so I didn't do it sufficiently for him. Joselin Arn's speech on page 129 of the magazine was in part written by Campbell after he accepted the story. It was also his idea to add the Zeus and Demeter bit, which I did, but under (silent) protest. Campbell didn't do that often, but he did it sometimes. [Personal letter, August 8, 1972]

And in the margin of this letter he has written: "Also the bit about Asiatics being less emotional than Europeans and Africans more emotional. That was *his*."

In "Homo Sol" the men of Sol by mastering an interstellar drive have made themselves eligible to be the 289th members of the Galactic Federation (made up of humanoids from oxygen-atmosphere, water-chemistry worlds). But they turn down the first offer tendered them, much to the consternation of the Galactic Council. Tan Porus, one of the top psychologists of the federation, goes to Sol to see what went wrong and to correct matters (leaving behind one of the most fascinating squids you'll ever read about). He discovers that the psychology of Earthmen is completely different from any of the 288 races already in the federation. Earthmen react in masses rather than as individuals. As a result, they have better teamwork and get more done more quickly than anyone else. (Tan Porus acting as an individual cannot solve the squid problem after months of work. The inference to be drawn is that a team of co-operating individuals could solve it—but individuals only co-operate that fully on Earth.) Earthmen are particularly adept at converting innocent scientific devices into awesome weapons of destruction. Eventually, they could take on and defeat the entire federation.

Problem: how to get Homo Sol into the federation where they can be controlled. That is, how to neutralize the threat of this alien psychology.

Tan Porus manipulates a worldwide panic which disrupts Earth's economic patterns. Then he sends in a trade mission to set things right, i.e., to restore order on Earth and to get the Earthmen into the federation. And how does he know the trade mission will succeed? Because its one hundred male members all look like Zeus and its one hundred female ones all look like Demeter. "The Earthmen would be putty in the hands of their own personifications of storm and motherhood come to life. In two hundred years—why, in two hundred years, we could do anything" (*The Early Asimov*, p. 201).

As Asimov's letter (quoted earlier) tells us, this is Campbell's solution, and it is absurd. Since it postulates our development of an interstellar drive, the story clearly takes place in our future. Zeus and Demeter have no emotional power for us now, and will have none for our descendants. Earthmen would neither recognize nor be "putty in the hands" of mythological figures thousands of years out of date. The story has gone wrong. But since it was Campbell who added the Zeuses and the Demeters, it has gone wrong in Campbell's hands. Campbell was trying to sharpen Asimov's more general—and vague—solution: "The passive panic paralyzed industry, and the terrestrial government is faced with revolution. . . . Offer them Galactic trade and eternal prosperity, and do you think they'd jump at it?" Asimov had not bothered to explain exactly how Tan Porus had caused the panic in the first place, and he is perfectly willing not to tell exactly how Tan

Porus would go about ending it. Campbell's Zeuses and Demeters are meant to supply such specifics. Where Asimov preferred to be vague, Campbell preferred to be wrong.

It is a great compliment to the rest of the story that this ending can be considered merely a flaw in it rather than fatal to it. The character of Tan Porus, the problem with the squid, the quality of the writing—here Asimov is speaking in his own voice, as it were—all make "Homo Sol" strong enough to survive that ending and remain one of Asimov's best stories.

But what Asimov learned about Campbell's likes and dislikes as a result of "Homo Sol" and its revisions was to have momentous consequences for his later writing. He discovered that Campbell wanted Earthmen to be unique and in some way (to be determined by the individual story) superior to the other races in the universe. Asimov felt that superior technology or intelligence should win; Campbell felt Earthmen should win in the face of all odds. Asimov solved the problem by removing alien races from his stories. In order to continue to sell to Campbell without compromising his own views, Asimov "invented" the humans-only Galaxy. That's why there are no aliens in the Foundation Series.

I think Asimov and his readers lost more than they gained as a result. Larry Niven's "Known Space" is more interesting as a backdrop for stories than Asimov's Galaxy, because the presence of aliens in "Known Space" offers more variety and more opportunity for the construction of different physical forms and societies for consciousness to house itself in. The Foundation Series is less richly textured than it would have been with aliens, as well as less accurate. That Asimov has the imaginative power to create interesting aliens is demonstrated by the second half of his recent novel *The Gods Themselves,* which features trisexual nonhumanoid aliens living on a world in a parallel dimension. It might be argued that one of the by-products of Asimov's humans-only Galaxy was a concentration on the theme of politics. But I would give up some of the human politics to get at the more imaginative context. Besides, politics involves learning to get along with people who are different. A galaxy full of different races has more, not less, opportunity for significant political action.

To summarize Asimov's writing career before "Nightfall": The first three stories he wrote were "The Cosmic Corkscrew" (now lost), "The Callistan Menace," a very well plotted story, and "Marooned Off Vesta," which had a highly improbable initial situation but was well written and contained a significant theme. Asimov's ambition was to become a steady contributor to Campbell's *Astounding*, but he sold only two of his first nineteen stories there. Frederick Pohl gave Asimov early practical encouragement by buying seven of his early stories. He wrote two stories for which he intended to write sequels, "Ring Around the Sun" and "Super Neutron," and two stories for which he did write sequels, "Half-Breed," leading to "Half-Breeds on Venus," and "Homo Sol," leading to "The Imaginary." Still, it was with "Reason" and "Liar!" that he finally got a successful series going. "The Secret Sense" is an interesting and contemporary story, "Black Friars of the Flame" looks forward in some minor ways to Asimov's later work, and "Homo Sol," besides being one of Asimov's better stories in its own right, is very significant in Asimov's decision to write stories set in a humans-only Galaxy.

Before writing "Nightfall" Asimov had written thirty-one stories and sold seventeen (four more would sell eventually). "Marooned Off Vesta," perhaps "The Callistan Menace," and "Homo Sol," along with the robot stories "Reason" and "Liar!" were the best he had done so far. His own assessment of his career to this point is "Looking back on my first three years as a writer, then, I can judge myself to be nothing more than a steady and . . . hopeful third-rater" (*The Early Asimov*, p. 336).

Then, on March 17, 1941, he began to write "Nightfall," his thirty-second written story, his sixteenth published, and the story that established him as a frontline science fiction writer.

Science fiction readers and writers are unanimous in their respect and admiration for this story. In 1968–69, for example, the Science Fiction Writers of America voted "Nightfall" by a wide margin the best science fiction short story ever written, and in 1971 the readers of *Analog* in an informal poll expressed similar feelings. Whenever the magazines poll their readers for favorite stories, "Nightfall" is at or very near the top. For the average reader Asimov and science fiction are synonymous; for the science fiction reader Asimov and "Nightfall" (along with the Robot Stories and the Foundation Series) are synonymous. Whenever

I use "Nightfall" in the classroom, it is inevitably the students' favorite story in the course.

Yet Asimov professes himself to be ambivalent about the story's fame. He feels that the story shows a bit too much its pulp heritage, especially in its language, its characters, and its plotting. He also feels that he has written better stories since, perhaps many better stories. (He usually cites as his favorites from among his works "The Ugly Little Boy" followed by "The Last Question," though in *Before the Golden Age* he calls "The Last Question" "my personal favorite of all the short stories I have ever written" (p. 726).) In *Nightfall and Other Stories* he writes as follows:

> I must say, though, that as time passed, I began to feel some irritation at being told, over and over again, that "Nightfall" was my best story. It seemed to me, after all, that although I know no more about Writing now than I knew then, sheer practice should have made me more proficient, technically, with each year. [P. 1]

He decided to bring out a collection that began with "Nightfall" and contained nineteen other stories in chronological order, so "now you can see for yourself how my writing has developed (or has failed to develop) with the years. Then you can decide for yourself why (or *if*) 'Nightfall' is better than the others." This looks as if the purpose of the collection *Nightfall and Other Stories* is, at least partly, to destroy the reputation of "Nightfall."

But Asimov couldn't really bring himself to do that. The result is a collection of stories that he had not seen fit to anthologize before. There are no stories from the forties, the period immediately following "Nightfall" and during which he was composing the Robot Stories and the Foundation Series. Three quarters of the stories are from the fifties, which he had already culled over for *The Martian Way, Earth Is Room Enough,* and *Nine Tomorrows.* The result seems to be that Asimov wants us to compare "Nightfall" with stories that he himself did not really think of as his best. This is a good indication of his ambivalence toward "Nightfall."

Let's turn to the story itself. It is headed by a quotation from Ralph Waldo Emerson's essay "Nature," the first paragraph of the first chapter (also called "Nature"). The remark is an exclamation designed by Emerson to show the powerful effect nature would have on man if it weren't so familiar: "If the stars should appear one night in a thousand years, how would men believe and adore, and preserve for many generations the remembrance of the city of God!" In effect, the story converts the exclamation point to a question mark (as was actually done in the editions of *Nightfall and Other Stories*) and answers the question "Under such conditions, how *would* man remember and adore?" Asimov divides men into two groups depending on their reaction. The great majority convert to the Cult and react by turning passive: it is God's will that the world should end, and they accept it as God's will. The minority, under Aton and the astronomers, try to do something about it. They react actively, rationally. And Asimov leaves no doubt in our minds as to which side he is on. It's "Marooned Off Vesta" in a different form: the hysterics of Mark Brandon versus the reason of Warren Moore, the religion of the Cultists and the masses versus the reasoned planning of Aton and the scientists. Asimov shows that Emerson was right—man would believe and adore—but that man was wrong to do so. He should think rather than merely believe.

Let's move on to the problems Asimov sees in the story, the problems of language, characterization, and plotting. The pulpish quality of the writing can be illustrated by its first two sentences (italics mine).

> Aton 77, director of Saro University, *thrust* out a *belligerent* lower lip and *glared* at the young newspaperman in *a hot fury.*
> Theremon 762 took that fury *in his stride.*

Note that the diction Asimov uses is not simply strong. It is extreme and trite. The thrust-out lower lip, the glaring, and the hot fury are overly familiar to us all, as is taking something in stride. No matter how interesting the content may be, there is no originality or interest in the language.

Very soon after this, "Beenay 25 thrust a tongue's tip across dry lips and interposed nervously." This reuse of "thrust" indicates a paucity of vocabulary. Then "the director turned to him and lifted a white eyebrow." The lifted eyebrow is trite. Follow Aton's actions for a moment: "The director . . . shook it [a newspaper] at Theremon furiously. . . . Aton dashed the newspaper to the floor, strode to the window and clasped his arms behind his back. 'You may leave,' he snapped over his shoulder. He stared moodily. . . . He whirled. 'No, wait, come here!' He gestured peremptorily. . . . Aton gestured outward." An extreme example of this stereotyped pulp diction can be found toward the end of the story: "Theremon cried out sharply and muttered through a blinding haze of pain. 'You double-crossing rat!'" In the pulps any crying out was done sharply, the hero always muttered, a haze of pain was always blinding, and for some reason all rats were double-crossing.

Though the general quality of the writing has this pulpish triteness about it, some flashes of interesting language do get through. In the paragraph immediately following "You double-crossing rat!" we find, "then there was the strange awareness [still pulpy] that the last thread of sunlight had thinned out and snapped." Contrary to what happens in reading the greater part of the story, the interest here is almost solely in the language rather than in what is being described. (Have you ever seen any threads of light snap at sunset?)

And later, "Thirty thousand mighty suns shone down in a soul-searing splendor that was more frighteningly cold in its awful indifference than the bitter wind that shivered across the cold, horribly bleak world." That "shivered" is exactly right here, it is far from trite, and the whole sentence—the thought and the language combined—stimulates the reader. We have hints here of an Asimov who is a writer and knows how to manipulate language rather than simply an Asimov who knows his pulp idiom and how to write salable stories in it.

The characters tend to be pulpish, too. Writers for mass circulation media as old as the pulps and as new as TV quickly realized that certain professions are easier to write stories about because their practitioners can legitimately ask questions dredging up information the reader or the viewer needs to know. A detective, a physician, or a lawyer may ask what you were doing the night before last, but who would believe a plumber who asked the same thing? The point here is not that lawyers are inherently more interesting than plumbers. It is that stories about lawyers are easier to write than stories about plumbers, because the exposition is easier.

Another profession very popular in the pulps, on the radio, and on early TV—though not used so much anymore, perhaps because it has become trite through overuse—is the newspaper reporter. It is perfectly legitimate for a reporter to hear about something interesting and to go out to get the facts. And it is perfectly legitimate for the reader's-listener's-viewer's ignorance of "what happened" to be satisfied while the reporter learns these facts. Theremon is a reporter who goes to the observatory to have questions answered. As Aton and Sheerin answer them, we learn about the setting, the Cult, the conflicts, the eclipse. In other words Asimov in this story makes use of the age-old expository device of the inquiring newspaper reporter. Note how Theremon recedes in importance as the need for exposition diminishes.

Aton is another trite, conventional, unindividualized character. The extent of Asimov's characterization of him is to classify him as an astronomer—and you know how they are: "Astronomers were queer ducks, anyway, and if Aton's actions of the last two months meant anything, this same Aton was the queer-duckiest of the lot."

Only Sheerin comes across as an individual, with his high spirits and his gregarious willingness to help Asimov tell Theremon and us all we need to know to understand the story. He has curiosity. He leaves the Hideout in order to be "where things are getting hot" because he wants to see the legendary "Stars." He has courage. Sheerin leads the way down the dark staircases to bolt the doors against the invading mob from the city. Most important, he has hidden whiskey. "Tiptoeing to the nearest window, he squatted, and from the low window box beneath withdrew a bottle of red liquid that gurgled suggestively when he shook it. 'I thought Aton didn't know about this,' he remarked."

On the whole, the characters are not people but rather labels for the different parts of the story machine: a newspaper reporter who asks our questions for us, an observatory director who answers some of them, a jolly little tub who answers the rest when the director must get back to work. They exist not as people in their own right, but as counters to keep the story moving forward. This is the pulp attitude toward characterization. The story is the thing.

Despite the fact that the story is almost entirely conversation, it has a helter-skelter quality about it. One scene tends not to flow into the next, but to be interrupted by the next. In the first scene shift, Sheerin and Theremon simply walk into an adjacent room for some expository conversation. This ends with a "sudden hubbub that came from the adjoining room." This second scene ends in midsentence when "from somewhere up above there sounded a sharp clang, and Beenay, starting to his feet, dashed up the stairs with a 'What the devil!'" It turns out that a religious fanatic, Latimer, is destroying photographic plates. The interrogation of Latimer is interrupted by Theremon's reaction to the onset of Beta's eclipse: "'Look at that!' The finger he pointed toward the sky shook, and his voice was dry and cracked. There was one simultaneous gasp as every eye followed the pointing finger, and, for one breathless moment, stared frozenly. *Beta was chipped on one side!*" Sheerin and Theremon's resultant conversation is interrupted by Aton's approach: "'You know why it didn't w—' [Sheerin] stopped and rose in alarm, for Aton was approaching, his face a twisted mask of consternation. *'What's happened?'"* A conversation between Beenay and Sheerin is then interrupted: "Sheerin's chair went over backwards as he sprang to his feet in a rude interruption. 'Aton's brought out the lights.'"

Then a pause. Silence. "After the momentary sensation, the dome had quieted." Then a gradual recognition of the "extraneous noise" of the townsmen coming to destroy the observatory. "The silence ripped to fragments at [Theremon's] startled shout: *'Sheerin!'* Work stopped!" Out of the silence Asimov has begun to build his story's climax.

The pace of "Nightfall's" plot, then, is sustained with a series of interruptions which account for the story's helter-skelter quality. There really is no story. There is instead a continuing revelation of a situation. The "story" is 95 per cent exposition via conversation. The development—the forward thrust of the reader's interest—takes place in the reader's understanding. When we know what must happen and why and what its effects will be, the inevitable happens and the story is over.

The initial physical situation in "Nightfall" is very similar to that in "Marooned Off Vesta" in one important way. Both stories rely on a physical arrangement whose occurrence in nature is so highly unlikely that we might as well consider it impossible. A planet cannot have an orbit stable enough for long enough to support life when that planet moves in the midst of six suns. It is highly improbable that a moon the size described would be detectable only once every 2,049 years. It is very unlikely that a race could develop cities—and an urban architecture—without having experienced darkness and developing artificial sources of light on a large scale. Here on Earth the planet Venus is often visible in the daytime, yet we are to believe that Lagash is in the center of a globular cluster of "thirty thousand mighty suns" which remain invisible until the exact moment of Beta's total eclipse.

Certain details are vague as well. For example, at the beginning of the story, yellow Gamma is just setting, and red Beta rides high in the sky. As a result, the light is described as orange. Later everything is bathed in the dim red of Beta alone. Note that we have been shown a range of colors from yellow through orange to red (and only two of the six suns were involved). Under these conditions, how can anything on Lagash be said to have *a* color? (Aton's eyebrows, you will recall, were described as white.)

Again, Yimot and Faro perform an experiment intended to simulate the appearance of stars in a dark sky in order to see what effect such an event might have on their psychology, but nothing happens. Despite Sheerin's assertions that he knows why the experiment failed, it turns out his explanation is wrong, and we are left holding a loose thread. And students are always asking, what happened to the people in the Hideout? We are left to assume that there are too few of them to change the shape of history (a theme developed at length in the Foundation Series), but we don't really know when we finish reading "Nightfall." They aren't taken into account by the ending.

In one sense the story ends too soon. It has been Aton's story if it has been anyone's. He has led the efforts to find out what is happening and to preserve that knowledge for the next cycle. He has established the Hideout to help some sanity survive. What is the result of these efforts on his part? It is as if "Marooned Off Vesta" were allowed to end with Warren Moore's "Aha! Why didn't I think of it before?" We are never told how Aton's efforts turn out. They are subsumed in the larger catastrophe. The extent to which we are not told these things is the extent to which we are left holding loose threads at the end of the story.

After accepting the story for publication Campbell introduced into it one minor flaw and one nice touch. The nice touch was Aton's incoherent speech four paragraphs from the end, "We didn't know we couldn't know, etc." The flaw was the opening phrase of a slightly earlier paragraph: "Not Earth's feeble thirty-six hundred Stars visible to the naked eye." The whole story had meticulously refused to recognize the existence of Earth, yet this phrase added by Campbell violates this important part of Asimov's narrative strategy.

An early critic of "Nightfall" has dealt with some of these problems, at least by inference. Ernest Kimoy, in adapting the story for broadcast on the radio program "Dimension X" in the early fifties, made two major kinds of changes in the story. One kind was made necessary by the shift in medium from printed page to radio, from eye to ear. The narrative voice, for example, must actually speak aloud on the radio, and in effect this adds another character—the narrative point of view—whom most of us forget about when we read.

But the more important set of changes for our purposes include those made in an apparent attempt to deal with what Kimoy may have seen as flaws in the story. Kimoy the practicing writer is in effect Kimoy the practical critic. For example, he, too, seems to realize that "thirty thousand mighty suns" would be visible long before Asimov permits his characters to see them, since he changes the phrase to "thirty thousand minute suns." He also drops the whole Yimot-Faro experiment. One might argue that this was due to limitations of time. "Dimension X" was only a half-hour program. Still, cutting the Yimot-Faro experiment shows that it was cuttable. Besides being inconclusive, it did not contribute anything essential to the story.

The most significant difference in the two men's treatment of the same story can be found in their handling of setting. Asimov sets the whole story in the observatory. Thus people must come to the observatory to express their points of view. For example, Latimer, the Cultist who came to smash the photographic plates, is then interviewed at some length. Some things we can only learn at second hand, as when Sheerin tells Theremon that a fifteen-minute-long amusement-park ride through a dark tunnel caused insanity. Kimoy, on the other hand, sends Theremon away from the observatory to interview people directly. In succession he talks with a priest of the Cult, Sheerin, a man in the street called Pallet, and an aged member of the Cult. The priest gives the information presented in the story by the captured Cultist. Sheerin actually takes Theremon to see and listen to a person driven insane on the amusement-park ride. The man in the street takes a very practical attitude toward the whole affair: the world may be ending but he's putting money in the bank just in case. And the old Cultist presents the opposite reaction: he has sold everything that he has and given it to the poor so that he can go to glory with the Stars.

As both men treat the story, it has a great deal of dramatic impact, but Asimov's is the stronger of the two. His single setting gives the story a more unified impact than the diversified interviews in the street. Whether it is accurate or not, the flashing forth of thirty thousand mighty suns staggers us emotionally. It may not be scientifically true, but it is dramatically true, and for a writer effect is what counts. Asimov first made it as plausible as he could. Then he made it right.

What is "Nightfall" about, and where does its compelling power lie? In his essay "Social Science Fiction" Asimov distinguishes between two kinds of fictional reactions to the French and Industrial revolutions: "Social fiction is that branch of literature which moralizes about a current society through the device of dealing with a fictitious society," and "science fiction is that branch of literature which deals with a fictitious society, differing from our own chiefly in the nature or extent of its technological development" (*Modern Science Fiction*, ed. Reginald Bretnor, p. 123). In the context of the essay it is clear that Asimov views social fiction as presenting an alternate society with the intent of criticizing contemporary society, whereas science fiction creates an alternate society for its own sake, to show us that things could (not *should* or *ought to*) be different, to accustom us to change. Elsewhere he distinguishes between science fiction and what he calls tomorrow fiction, in which the writer simply tries to show what life will actually be like in a few years. The point in both distinctions is that science fiction must present an alternate society for its own sake rather than comment on contemporary society or attempt to show accurately where we are going.

"Nightfall" presents an alternate society for its own sake. It obviously is not an attempt to show what life will be like a few years from now, so it is not tomorrow fiction. And though it contains a few satirical touches directed at commonly held contemporary assumptions—for example, Beenay's notion that life as we know it could not exist on a planet revolving about a single sun—still it does not attempt to make us feel in our guts that air pollution is evil or that violent hoodlums have a right to their own identities. "Nightfall" is not social fiction.

There is no obvious connection between the characters in "Nightfall" and ourselves. They do not live on Earth past or future, and they are not the remnants of a human colony that ran into trouble. At the same time, we are given no reason to picture them in our imaginations as anything different from ourselves. They have arms and eyebrows. Or at least Asimov uses the language worked out to describe human beings in describing his aliens. Perhaps this is Asimov's use of the "doctrine of accommodation" that Milton scholars talk about, wherein Milton describes his angels—fallen and unfallen—as if they were shaped like us and collected sense data like us, though in fact they are not and do not. Milton simply accommodates the angels to human conceptions. Perhaps Asimov's aliens are really alien, but he has accommodated them to our concepts of ourselves so he can talk about them.

Fundamentally, though, it doesn't make any difference. "Nightfall" is about the relationship between consciousness and its environment. The physical apparatus in which that consciousness is embodied is irrelevant. Human-shaped or alien-shaped, the consciousnesses on Lagash are what they are because they developed under six suns and a nightfall that comes once every 2,049 years. Their psychology is different because their environment is different.

"Nightfall" has the powerful effect it does because it convinces us that that's the way we would be under those different circumstances. "Nightfall" embodies a cosmic conception: what we are and the way we think are determined by the accident of the environment into which we are born. It figures forth an alternate world and society for its own sake. But that world is not totally irrelevant to our own. It has lessons for us, too. Consciousness, regardless of the environment that shapes it, is sacred. The people of Lagash are our brothers. When they are destroyed, we are destroyed, because we share consciousness. John Donne wrote, "No man is an island, entire of itself; every man is a piece of the continent. . . . Any man's death diminishes me, because I am involved in mankind." "Nightfall" expresses the same sentiments, only on a universal rather than a planetary scale. The sacredness and dignity of life is the message of Donne's Seventeenth Meditation, Asimov's "Nightfall," and science fiction.

Second Period

"Nightfall" through ". . . And Now You Don't"
(1941–50)

Order Written		Order Published
32	"Nightfall"*	16
33	"Not Final!"*	18
34	"Legal Rites"	45
35	"Robot AL-76 Goes Astray"ʳ	20
36	"Foundation"–"The Encyclopedists"*ᶠ	24
37	"Runaround"*ʳ	21
38	"Bridle and Saddle"–"The Mayors"*ᶠ	25
40	"First Law"ʳ	98
41	"Time Pussy"*	23
42	"Victory Unintentional"ʳ	26
43	"Author! Author!"	139
44	"Death Sentence"*	29
45	"Catch That Rabbit"*ʳ	30
46	"The Big and the Little"–"The Merchant Princes"*ᶠ	31
47	"The Wedge"–"The Traders"*ᶠ	32
48	"Dead Hand"–"The General"*ᶠ	34
49	"Blind Alley"*	33
50	"Escape!"*ʳ	35
51	"The Mule"*ᶠ	36
52	"Evidence"*ʳ	37
53	"Little Lost Robot"*ʳ	38
54	"Now You See It"–"Search by the Mule"*ᶠ	39
55	"No Connection"*	40
57	"Grow Old with Me"–*Pebble in the Sky*	50

58   "The Red Queen's Race"*   41

59   "Mother Earth"*   42

60   ". . . And Now You Don't"—"Search
by the Foundation"*ᵗ   43

        * Bought by Campbell
        ʳ Robot Story
        ᵗ Foundation Series

cape!" The last two stories in *I, Robot* involve Susan Calvin only indirectly: in "Evidence" she is largely the shrewd bystander to a political drama, and in "The Evitable Conflict" she listens as another party discusses the four great computers that govern the economies of the world. The movement of *I, Robot* is best put by Susan Calvin herself: "I saw it from the beginning, when the poor robots couldn't speak [1998: "Robbie"] to the end, when they stand between mankind and destruction [2052: "The Evitable Conflict"]" (p. 218).

Asimov's creation of a frame tale and the rearrangement of the stories to fit it certainly imposes a greater unity on *I, Robot* than it would possess merely as a collection of robot stories, and the book is surely the better for it. There is, however, a more complicated factor that came to unify *I, Robot,* the Three Laws (or Rules) of Robotics. These laws were worked out by Asimov and Campbell during a conversation in Campbell's office on December 16, 1940, while Asimov was in the process of writing his third Robot Story, "Liar!" The first story in which all Three Laws made any difference was the fifth Robot Story, "Runaround." In other words, in the first four of the Robot Stories the Three Laws of Robotics either did not exist as yet or were not all that important.

Even after the Three Laws came into being, the most significant continued to be the First: "A robot may not injure a human being, or, through inaction, allow a human being to come to harm." Alongside this First Law the Second and Third Laws— "A robot must obey the orders given it by human beings except where such orders would conflict with the First Law" and "A robot must protect its own existence as long as such protection does not conflict with the First or Second Law"—pale into insignificance. The transcendence of the First Law should not be surprising, since that law is simply a specific instance of Asimov's scientific optimism. Asimov is not now and never has been an "antiscience" fiction writer. He believes that science has made available to us the knowledge that may yet save us. His robots are symbols of man's technological and scientific progress and are therefore to be admired; characters who are antirobot are antiprogress and are therefore reactionary villains—or at least ignorant. In other words, Asimov does not have what he calls elsewhere "a Frankenstein complex," a fear of the products of man's intelligence.

His fourteenth written and ninth published story, "Robbie," the first story in *I, Robot,* is a straightforward, conventional story bent into something strange and interesting by Asimov's personal interests and by his aiming it for the science fiction market. As is the case in most of Asimov's stories, "Robbie" is told by an omniscient narrator who limits himself largely but not exclusively to one character—here, Gloria Weston, eight-year-old daughter of Grace and George Weston. Clearly we are meant to sympathize with her, to yearn with her for the return of her friendly robot. But what does she do to earn our sympathy? She behaves more like a spoiled brat than a delightful child. For what is she rewarded by having Robbie returned to her?

The problems with Asimov's having chosen Gloria as the narrative focus go deeper than our hesitation to accept her as sympathetically as the story line demands. Actually, Gloria has nothing to do in the story. She is not the problem-solver, the conflict-resolver, and by another writer and for another market the story would have been told completely differently.

It would have been told focusing on Mr. Weston. After all, he is the only character in it who is presented with a problem that he solves through his own actions. He is caught between his nagging wife ("You listen to me, George") and his whining daughter ("I want Robbie. I want you to find me Robbie") when all he wants is to be left alone so he can read his paper. He makes three attempts to solve this problem, the third of which is successful. First he tries to substitute a dog for Robbie. Then he tries a holiday in New York. Finally he arranges the tour of the factory where they find Robbie. This does not make a noble hero of him. He has functioned at the level of "Oh, give the kid her lollipop so she'll shut up and leave me alone." But clearly it is his story, and it would most likely be told that way except for the writer and the market he was writing for. When the story is told from Mr. Weston's point of view, the importance of the robot is considerably reduced. Gloria could just as easily have been deprived of a bicycle or a pony. But Asimov is interested in the robot and in the one character who shares that interest. And the science fiction market-audience was also interested in that robot.

Because it so clearly demonstrates how a standard mainstream story can be redone in science fiction terms to suit the writer and his market, "Robbie" is an interesting story. But it is not a particularly pleasant one. Notice, for example, its negative, stereotyped depiction of family life: the weak, passive husband who must be forced to act by stronger willed females; the nagging wife who is motivated by what the neighbors will think; the spoiled child, isolated from the rest of humanity, reduced to trying to get her way through tears and tantrums.

At one point in the story, Asimov has Mr. Weston say to his wife, "You *know* that it is impossible for a robot to harm a human being; that long before enough could go wrong to alter that First Law, a robot would be completely inoperable." Obviously Asimov has in mind here only physical harm. How much psychological harm has the isolation and pampering of Gloria caused? Hasn't the robot, in helping to make Gloria what she is, harmed her? In the Three Laws of Robotics, what does the word "harm" mean, and how can a robot be expected to interpret it?

Following "Robbie" in *I, Robot* are the three Powell-Donovan stories. At first glance they may seem all of a piece. In all three stories the two field engineers for U. S. Robots are placed somewhere out in space with a new-model robot which is not performing correctly. Their job: find out what's wrong and fix it so that the robot can go into production. In all three the initial exposition is done via conversation between two of the characters. There follow several unsuccessful attempts at solving the problem before a last-gasp success.

But examined more closely the three stories differ markedly from one another. Take the initial exposition, for example. In "Runaround" Asimov sets up his story by having the excited (and excitable) Mike Donovan burst in on the calm, cool, and collected Gregory Powell and tell him the problem; in "Reason" Powell lectures the necessary background at a robot he's just finished assembling; and in "Catch That Rabbit" Powell lectures Donovan. The best handled exposition is in "Reason," because it is a logical and necessary part of the story: the robot and the reader both need to know the information that is being exchanged. The exposition in "Runaround" is not quite so good: we are obviously being led into the story, and we know it won't start until we've been fed enough data. There is not enough development along with the exposition. In "Catch That Rabbit," the poorest of the three stories on other grounds as well, the exposition is very weak. As Powell is talking, Donovan breaks in to say, "I know that—" to which Powell replies, "I know you know it." He barely manages to leave unsaid, "But the readers don't, so I've got to tell you anyway." So the expositions are similar in that in each two characters give us the necessary background through conversation, whereas they differ in plausibility and appropriateness—and therefore in quality.

Still, these are minor differences. More importantly, "Runaround" is a well-told story with only one major flaw, "Reason" could have been one of the great science fiction stories had its possibilities been developed, while "Catch That Rabbit" is simply fluff.

"Runaround" was the first Robot Story Asimov wrote after the exact formulation of the Three Laws of Robotics, and it is the best example of the Robot Story that actually uses all Three Laws. "Speedy" has become hung up between the Second and Third Laws. It has been ordered by a human being to approach a selenium pool on Mercury, and therefore it must do so, according to the Second Law. But the selenium pool is potentially dangerous for its continued operation, and therefore, according to the Third Law, it must protect itself by staying away. So Speedy spends its time circling the pool, trying to obey both laws simultaneously. The problem for Powell and Donovan is clear: Within the Three Laws of Robotics, how can they reassert their control over Speedy and thereby save their lives? It is a problem that the agile reader can solve for himself. Since the First Law transcends the other two, Powell puts himself in danger and Speedy must come rescue him, thus making himself available for reprogramming.

"Runaround" is a neat intellectual puzzle worked out in fictional terms and a very good story. Except perhaps for one thing. An earlier attempt at setting up a mining colony on Mercury had left behind some earlier model robots, which are so designed that people can ride about on their shoulders. What does the inclusion of these robots add to the story beyond a certain bizarre quality? In fact, their presence actually retards the development of the

story. When Powell risks his life in order to make the First Law operative and bring Speedy to his side, one of these earlier robots also blunders out to save him, and Powell is put in the situation of trying to shoo off one robot while attracting the other. These robots form an artificial complication and could easily have been left out of the story.

On the other hand, "Catch That Rabbit" does not use any of the Three Laws. The problem for Powell and Donovan here is simply that robot model DV-5 ("Davie") has a flaw in the circuit by which it controls the other robots. The solution is not to be found in the Three Laws. A minor adjustment in the circuit, and he's all right again. The cave-in which momentarily traps our heroes has nothing whatever to do with the story. It is certainly a flaw, because action for its own sake is never justified in a story.

In "Reason" religion is the anomaly developed by the new-model robot. The conflict in the story seems to be "Can a robot with religion still perform its assigned function?" When the answer turns out to be yes, Powell and Donovan, having spent the greater part of the story worrying, heave a sigh of relief, decide to let Cutie have his religious impulse, and leave for Earth. The problem has been allowed to degenerate into a nonproblem.

This story exists in what we might as well call two different versions. Its first appearance was in *Astounding* for April 1941. In preparing it for inclusion in *I, Robot* Asimov made nearly two dozen changes. One of them rectified an error that should not have been allowed to stand, even in the magazine version. There, the robots, their attention diverted by a religious ceremony, allow the energy beams to Mars to be cut off. Clearly, this runs counter to the eventual solution to both versions of the story —that religion is not, after all, a crippling defect; it's merely irrelevant—and so Asimov wisely drops it from the book version.

"Reason" was written before Asimov had worked out the Three Laws of Robotics. In his revision he tries to incorporate them into the story, despite the fact that one of the story's major elements is in clear-cut violation of the Second Law. Cutie and the other robots lock Powell and Donovan out of the control room and refuse to obey direct orders from human beings. The question that arises is "In view of the Second Law, how can a robot disobey a direct command?" Asimov works very hard to answer that question. He explains it this way:

> Obedience is the Second Law. No harm to humans is the First. How can he keep humans from harm, whether he knows it or not? Why, by keeping the energy beam stable. He knows he can keep it more stable than we can, since he insists he's the superior being, so he keeps us out of the control room. It's inevitable if you consider the Laws of Robotics. [P. 75]

As in "Runaround" the solution is intended to lie in the fact that the First Law transcends the Second.

But is this solution satisfactory? Remember that Cutie does not believe in Earth or in hordes of people on Earth. To what extent, then, can keeping the energy beam aligned be the same for him as keeping human beings safe? The phrase "whether he knows it or not" is crucial. Cutie is obeying the Master rather than the First Law. Note that the Laws of Robotics do not take into account disobeying the Second Law in order to obey the Master. Asimov simply has not succeeded in giving an adequate explanation of the robots' disobedience.

The story is disturbing for other reasons. Where exactly is the space station? Is it plausible for the station to be positioned in such a way that Cutie never sees the sun? Most importantly, where did Cutie's religious impulse come from in the first place? Asimov implies that Cutie was the first robot complex enough to reflect upon and ask questions about itself—to be conscious, in other words. But when I asked him, "Did you then—do you now —think of your robots as conscious?" his reply was "Yes, I do think of my robots as conscious." Therefore, even the robots in the stories before Cutie were complex enough to be conscious, and Cutie's religious impulse is not to be accounted for in this way.

In short, Asimov has raised the question of the religious needs of artificial consciousnesses, and then ignored it. Cutie develops a need for religion—and Asimov constructs a story assuring us that he can keep his dials aligned anyway. The initial situation of "Reason" is very promising, but the story that follows from it is disappointing.

Not counting a brief scene written in to "Robbie" when *I,*

Robot was put together, "Liar!" is the first story in which Susan Calvin appeared. We are told in the frame tale that the action is set in the year 2021 and that Calvin was then thirty-eight. Since the newspaper reporter's interview with her is supposed to take place in 2057, the story becomes a flashback to a Susan Calvin thirty-six years younger.

The narrative point of view is what might be called external omniscient. That is, we are given a series of seven scenes each of which has a different mixture of the five main characters, and we are never allowed to share anyone's thoughts. The narrative point of view, then, is "external" because we are presented only with what can be seen and heard, and it is "omniscient" because we are not limited to viewing via any one person. It is a very dramatic story in that we are present at each scene merely as observers, and all the data pass through our eyes and ears.

The technical problem the characters must solve is established immediately. By the third short paragraph we know that thirty-three RB model robots had been routinely produced, while the thirty-fourth had somehow developed telepathy. The problem: How? In a Powell-Donovan story Herbie would have irritated Donovan for a while, some assigned task would have been interfered with temporarily, but eventually Powell would adjust a circuit and Herbie would be normalized so the task could be completed, as in "Catch That Rabbit." Or, as in "Reason," Herbie would have remained telepathic in a mine on Ganymede where his anomaly wouldn't interfere with his shoveling.

But in "Liar!" Asimov permits the technical problem to become secondary to a human problem. By the time the story is over, no one knows or cares why Herbie became telepathic. That initial difficulty is transcended. "Liar!" is about people and the relationships among them—their hopes, fears, ambitions, love. The robot in the story is a device for intensifying and developing these human relationships and emotions. It is instructive of Asimov's interests and taste that "Liar!" is the story in *I, Robot* that he likes least.

There are two major candidates for the central character in this story: Herbie, since he is the one who causes things to happen, and Susan Calvin, since what happens to her and inside of her and as a result of her is what becomes most important in the story. Note that "Liar!" is basically a story about human vanity. Susan Calvin is vain enough to believe that Milton Ashe loves her. Peter Bogert's vanity finds expression in his ambition to become director. And Alfred Lanning is vain in his confidence concerning the superiority of his mathematical procedures over Bogert's. Herbie feeds the vanity of each by telling each what he wants to hear. This is why Herbie could be considered the central character in the story.

Eventually, Susan Calvin attacks Herbie with a paradox with which his positronic brain cannot cope, and he shorts out. She does this in order to cover up her blunder in thinking that Milton Ashe could love her. She protects her own vanity at the cost of Herbie's life. Because of her reactions, motivations, and actions, Susan Calvin could be considered the story's major character. In any event, by the time one gets to the end of the story, the initial technical problem has been forgotten. The human problems have swept it away.

It is necessary to give some further thought to Susan Calvin's treatment of Herbie at the end. "Bogert's face was bloodless, 'He's dead!' 'No!' Susan Calvin burst into body-racking gusts of wild laughter, 'not dead—merely insane. . . . You can scrap him now —because he'll never speak again'" (p. 116). One's attitude toward Asimov's robots will probably determine to a large extent what one thinks about this. If you consider them as complicated machines (as Asimov does), then her action was no worse than unplugging a coffeepot. But if you consider them artificial people (Asimov tells us that they are conscious, remember), then she has willfully driven another character insane in order to protect her vanity. In "Liar!" Susan Calvin is not the calm, rational, in-control person she becomes later. She is much more a human being like each of us, and she is driven to desperate action by circumstances beyond her control. Her atypicalness certainly contributes to Asimov's dislike of this story, since in her later form Susan Calvin is one of his favorite characters.

"Liar!" is an extremely efficiently told story. There is not a wasted sentence, phrase, or word. The plotting is masterful. Asimov moves his characters in and out with smooth assurance. They are kept separate when the story demands it, put together when the story demands it. "Liar!" is a polished masterpiece—and only

Asimov's fifteenth published story. "Nightfall" would be his six-teenth. Clearly he had early reached a high level of competence and was ready to become a "standard" in the field. Unfortunately, no one pays much attention to individual Robot Stories. They are all grouped together as if they were equal in quality. Every-one knows "Nightfall" by name, but "Liar!" is known only by its context. It deserves a better fate.

The other Susan Calvin stories in *I, Robot* (that is, the remain-ing four stories) are to varying degrees less successful than "Liar!" This is largely because they are all what might be called external stories. They do not concern themselves with the interior prob-lems of specific people, as "Liar!" had done. Instead, they show the working out of external problems.

"Escape!" (like *I, Robot*'s last story, "The Evitable Conflict") is a computer story rather than a Robot Story. There is no conflict in it. Powell and Donovan are put aboard an experimental hyper-space ship, Susan Calvin programs the computer that controls the experiment, and Powell and Donovan are whisked away. They can do nothing. Susan Calvin can do nothing. Everyone simply worries until the computer returns Powell and Donovan. It's the computer's story, not any human being's. And Asimov makes no attempt to get inside the computer's consciousness to examine its motivations, problems, conflicts. Thus the story is rather bland.

"Escape!" is most notable because it brings the team of Powell and Donovan into the same story with Susan Calvin, and because it contains a surrealistic passage in which Asimov tries to convey the chaos of consciousness in hyperspace. The story line forces him into experimental writing like "The white thread that was Powell groveled backward before the advancing shout" and "It all exploded into a rainbow of sound that dripped its fragments onto an aching brain." This is not Asimov's normal idiom.

Susan Calvin appears in "Evidence," but she is a minor char-acter. The story really belongs to Stephen Byerley, whom many people suspect of being a robot. Byerley is running for the elected office of mayor. His opponents try to use the robot issue to defeat him, since robots are forbidden by law to hold public office. In the key scene of the story, Byerley punches a human being in the mouth, thereby demonstrating that he need not obey the First

Law and that therefore he is not a robot. As a result, he is elected mayor and goes on to become Regional Co-ordinator and finally first World Co-ordinator. But we are given to understand that the human being Byerley punched was also a robot and the punch proved nothing. It merely secured his election. Byerley is a shrewd robot governing people illegally.

This story contains two very interesting features. First it tackles a big question. It probes the legal status of robots, i.e., of artificial consciousness. And it takes a side here. Mankind should not discriminate against his own creations. A child of man's mind deserves just as much legal consideration as a child of his body. Future laws prohibiting the equality of men and robots wouldn't make sense, Asimov is demonstrating, because robots could govern not only just as well as but probably better than men. In one place, Susan Calvin remarks of Byerley, "Actions such as his could come only from a robot, or from a very honorable and decent human being. But you see, you just can't differentiate between a robot and the very best of human beings." Note that the robot is not simply another man. He is "the very best of human beings." Elsewhere, in a passage too long to quote here, Asimov has Susan Calvin compare the Three Laws of Robotics with man's ethical and moral systems. The first sentence of the passage reads, "The Three Laws of Robotics are the essential guiding principles of a good many of the world's ethical systems." The robots are perfected men, or even non-imperfected, unfallen men. Asimov fails to probe the theological dimension that this could open up. He just isn't interested in it.

A second feature that deserves some consideration here concerns one of the minor characters in the story. While the present of "Evidence" concerns Byerley's attempts to evade the charge of being a robot, someone in the past had to make him. That someone was the real Stephen Byerley, about whom we are told the following: "Mr. Byerley's past is unremarkable. A quiet life in a small town, a college education, a wife who died young, an auto accident with a slow recovery, law school, coming to the metropolis, an attorney." Stephen Byerley has a secluded, crippled teacher-friend whom he calls John. Byerley's political enemy Quinn says of John, "Your crippled teacher is the real Stephen Byerley. You are his robot creation. We can prove it. It was he

who was in the automobile accident not you." Our interest is
caught by this cripple, his wife who died young, his accident, and
the willpower that helped him re-create himself so that, at least
vicariously, he could live a full life. Yet, frustratingly, this extremely interesting person is used merely as a plot device: he
creates the robot Byerley and he builds the decoy Byerley hits.
"John" Byerley's story would be a much more powerful one than
Stephen's. But John is not a robot, and Asimov does not write
about driven, passionate people.

"Evidence" is better than most of the other Robot Stories because it takes up an issue that is surely destined to become more
and more significant, the legal and ethical relationship between
man and artificial consciousnesses. Furthermore, in the crippled
Byerley Asimov has created a character that touches a nerve of
human compassion. One wishes Asimov would write an account
of John Byerley's life.

"The Evitable Conflict" is a remarkable story in several ways.
It clearly expresses Asimov's confidence in technology. Lurking
in the story is the tacit assumption that most people would side
with the Society for Humanity in its objections to a world controlled by computers rather than by men. Asimov argues the other
side. On the one hand, the Society for Humanity is gently de-
rided—its importance continually de-emphasized—as the conversation between Susan Calvin and Stephen Byerley develops.
On the other, the ability of the computers to control the economies of the world better than men is demonstrated. And not only
the economies of the world but—through these economies—the
destiny of mankind:

> Perhaps an agrarian or pastoral civilization, with less culture
> and less people, would be better. . . . Or perhaps a complete
> urbanization, or a completely caste-ridden society, or com-
> plete anarchy, is the answer. We don't know. Only the Ma-
> chines know, and they are going there and taking us with
> them. [P. 218]

Men have never been in control of their history. Desiring peace
and health and happiness, they have gotten war, suffering, and
misery. Only the Machines (read *Computers*) can fulfill man's
desires. To be against the Machines—to be against science and

technology—is to be against the best interests of humanity. Ironically, the Society for Humanity is really a society against humanity.

"The Evitable Conflict" also shows us for the first time some new dimensions in Asimov as a writer. We have seen already how Asimov has always known how to use conversation for the exposition of his stories. Here we see him successfully substituting conversation for a story. There is no action at all in "The Evitable Conflict." Seated by a fireside sipping tea, two people assimilate the data one of them has collected. The story is really a dramatized essay, and one can understand Asimov's later remarks about stopping the writing of fiction because he wanted to say things straight out, unencumbered with the necessity to create characters, plots, and dialogue. The veneer of fiction is very thin on this story.

We also see Asimov tinkering here with a fictional resource he doesn't tap very often, symbolism. (I am speaking here of symbolism appropriate to a single story. If one accepts the robots in toto as symbols of technology, then any robot story has that sort of symbolism in it.) The story contains four flashbacks, each reshowing us an earlier conversation with each of four Regional Co-ordinators from whom Byerley collected his data. Each conversation begins with a description of a map, and those maps symbolize their particular regions. For example, and most obviously, on Byerley's fourth and last visit he sees a map of the Northern Region:

> There was almost an ostentatious symbolism . . . in the fact that of the official Regional maps Byerley had seen, this one alone showed all the Earth, as though North feared no competition and needed no favoritism to point up its preeminence. [P. 211]

Furthermore, the tone of the story—its mature placidity and confidence—surely reflects Susan Calvin's age and experience. In the sense that it is her attitude and mood that control the mood of the story, it is her story. Asimov does not often show us such an ability to empathize with a character and to saturate a story in that character's sensibility.

Even the language of the story shows us an Asimov who can

write interesting prose as well as workable prose. For example, while visiting the Tropic Region Byerley is made to notice "the bright, bright sun and the quick, drenching showers. Even the squawking of the rainbowed birds was brisk and the stars were hard pinpoints of light" (pp. 205–6). The repetition of "bright" to intensify the sunlight, the pairing of "quick" and "drenching" to present efficiently the distinctive quality of the rainfall, and the consistency of the clustered (and perhaps trite) "hard," "pinpoints," and "sharp" are all bits of good writing, and the "squawking of the rainbowed birds" is brilliant. Language is strongest when it says something quickly, clearly, and efficiently—in other words, when it is poetry. "The rainbowed birds" is poetry. One wishes Asimov's market and audience loved language enough to put the pressure on him to develop this potentiality in his writing.

The Rest of the Robots (1964)

The Rest of the Robots contains eight short stories. The first, "Robot AL-76 Goes Astray," is notable largely for its slapstick humor, something that Asimov does not indulge in in print very often. (Humor, yes. Slapstick humor, no.) It is an amusing bit of fluff with an ending that is both unexpected and vaguely unsatisfactory. In its misguided attempt to do the work it was designed to do, Robot AL-76 invents a Disinto (a mining device which normally "eats up energy like so many electronic hogs") which runs on two flashlight batteries. Unfortunately, the robot has been ordered to forget everything, so the secret is lost. But why? Why not simply ask it to redesign another such machine? If it did it once, it can do it again.

The story demonstrates a persistent problem in Asimov's early Robot Stories—as well as in some of the later ones. The stories seem to take place in the present Asimov was living in rather than in the present his characters were living in. The world of "Robot AL-76 Goes Astray" is the world of the late 1930s, with a robot factory thrown in. In other words, in the early Robot Stories Asimov does not develop his settings. This is also clear in "Robbie" and in "Satisfaction Guaranteed." As a result, these stories about robots are curiously dated.

"Robot AL-76 Goes Astray" was chosen by Asimov to be included in the 1949 Leo Marguiles and Oscar J. Friend anthology

My Best Science Fiction Story. This might lead one to think that Asimov thought more highly of it than he did of such early stories as "Homo Sol," "Reason," or "Nightfall," and it might also lead one to suspect that deep down inside he prefers humor to straight fiction. But in a letter to me he remarked, "My selection of 'Robot AL-76 Goes Astray' . . . was made under the condition that I *not* select a story from *Astounding* and the title *My Best Science Fiction Story* was placed on the book without my knowledge and to my chagrin for I most definitely did *not* consider 'AL-76' my best." Therefore no conclusions can be drawn from Asimov's having placed this story in that Marguiles-Friend collection—except that by 1949 his reputation was such that his inclusion was considered desirable.

"Victory Unintentional" hinges on Asimov's ability to put together a natural sequence of events and conversations in which the question of whether ZZ One, ZZ Two, and ZZ Three are human or not cannot be allowed to arise. The story becomes a tour de force in avoiding the obvious. The opening page and a half is exceptionally well done. The unusual situation seizes our imagination, and the range of conditions under which the robots can continue to function is clearly demonstrated to us. Asimov is relatively successful at concealing the key question (are these creatures human in the eyes of the Jovians?) so that the ending strikes us as surprising and inevitable and right, all at the same time. In a sense, the ending is flawed by the problem's being solved not by the activities of the protagonists, but by a misunderstanding on the part of the Jovians. The title, "Victory Unintentional," reflects this *deus ex machina* conclusion. The story shares very clearly one of Asimov's basic attitudes: these robots are much superior to human beings. The Jovians could never have had their egos so effectively destroyed by mere people.

"First Law" is a piece of irrational nonsense in which Mother Love is made to transcend the First Law of Robotics even though robots come off an assembly line and not out of a mother's womb. It is presented, however, as Mike Donovan's tall tale told in a taproom, and as such it may work for some people. But Campbell rejected it, and it sat in Asimov's files for fifteen years before it was finally placed. The most significant thing about it is the playful attitude it reveals Asimov as having toward his now-sanctified

Three Laws. Perhaps Campbell rejected it partly as bad for the public image of Asimov's Robot Stories.

"Let's Get Together" is a Cold War espionage story dated by references to people, events, and attitudes important when the story was written, e.g., "dating back to the days of Eisenhower and Khrushchev." By the time he wrote this story, Asimov had become interested in detective and mystery fiction—as he still is— and "Let's Get Together" reflects that interest. *The Caves of Steel* and *The Naked Sun* had already been written, as had about a third of the stories later collected in *Asimov's Mysteries*.

In his headnote to "Satisfaction Guaranteed" Asimov remarks upon "the unusual quantity of mail from readers, almost all young ladies, and all speaking wistfully of Tony—as though I might know where he could be found." And no wonder! Tall, dark, handsome, extremely personable and competent, Tony is TN-3, a product of U. S. Robots' assembly lines. Susan Calvin has placed him illegally in the home of Larry and Clair Belmont so that U. S. Robots can obtain data needed for when robots are finally permitted to work on Earth among ordinary people. Larry leaves on a business trip, and Tony and Clair are left alone for the major portion of the story. "Satisfaction Guaranteed" chronicles their developing relationship.

Because the First Law of Robotics states that "A robot may not injure a human being, or, through inaction, allow a human being to come to harm," Tony cannot stand by and permit Clair's insecurity and self-doubts to gnaw away at her. He teaches her interior decorating and good grooming so that she can entertain without feeling inadequate. He treats her with respect and is interested in her problems. He is the perfect male (especially in comparison with her clod of a husband). In very understated and indirect ways Asimov indicates to us that Clair, without her own knowledge and approval, is sexually attracted to Tony. Her greatest frustration comes to be her love for Tony, a love that he, a robot, cannot return.

The solution we are given is that Larry returns home to find a new, beautiful, and confident Clair, and that once Tony is shipped back to the factory, Larry and this new Clair will live happily ever after. This cannot work. It was Tony and not Larry who awakened in Clair her potentialities as a woman. The bland substitution of Larry for Tony simply cheapens her. Besides, the new Clair would not put up with Larry's condescension and boorish behavior. The marriage must be doomed.

But the inadequate ending of the story, dictated by its market and audience, is not what is important in the story. What is important is its demonstration that a little kindness and attention can help the loneliest person achieve a new kind of life. At its core, "Satisfaction Guaranteed" is about human loneliness. Asimov's usual theme of the superiority of the robots is here stated in human rather than technological terms. As a result, the story struck a nerve of human compassion in its readers, and the wave of mail flowed in. It may be seriously flawed in its ending, but it does raise the issue of the sexual relationship of man and robot, and it has a sympathetic, real, developing human being in Clair Belmont. "Satisfaction Guaranteed" is surely one of Asimov's best early stories.

Asimov fails to convince me that the basic premise of "Lenny" is sound, and so I cannot think very highly of this story. As Susan Calvin states that premise, "We make every effort to make a robot as mentally like a man as possible. Eliminate what we call the adult functions and what is naturally left is a human infant, mentally speaking" (p. 116). When an LNE robot comes off the assembly line with its adult functions accidentally canceled out, what can it do but croon "da, da, da, goo" and stick its thumb in its mouth? But to me a robot is a machine. When its programming does not take effect, one is left with an unprogrammed robot, not an infant robot. Even infant behavior could only be the result of programming. And I think Susan Calvin is demeaned when, at the end of the story, we see her fetching a baby rattle for a robot calling, "Mommie, I want you. I want you, Mommie."

"Galley Slave" also shows an expository technique different from what Asimov had used in his earlier Robot Stories. Normally, for example, a Powell-Donovan story begins with the erratic behavior of a robot being presented to us, and we share Powell and Donovan's attempts to understand and rectify that behavior. Here, however, a robot is on trial for some unspecified crime. For more than half the story we are wondering not only how Susan Calvin will succeed in defending the robot but also what it is the robot has been charged with. Personally, I am not certain that this deliberate withholding of vital information from the reader is a legitimate technique for arousing curiosity. Perhaps Asimov feared that if the reader knew that from the beginning the charge was poor proofreading he wouldn't continue the story. It's not a crucial enough issue. Still, Asimov has decided that he can ask his readers to side with his robot and Susan Calvin without specifying anything about the issue. This demonstrates clearly his serene confidence in his robots—and in his readers' acceptance of his robots. I suspect that anyone coming for the first time to Asimov's Robot Stories through "Galley Slave" would be bewildered and confused by the first half of the story. "What's going on?" is not after all an irrelevant question, and it is unfair to force the reader to ask it in quite this fashion.

As the reader gradually comes to understand what the story is about, a curious thing is likely to happen. Finally we learn what the robot is accused of, finally we learn who framed him and why —and strangely our sympathies begin to shift. Viewed in one way, the story is of Susan Calvin's attempt to preserve the reputation of U. S. Robots; viewed another way, it is about Simon Ninheimer's attempt to preserve the dignity of human scholarship. Since Ninheimer is involved with humanity and Calvin with machinery, we come to side with Ninheimer. And the story is richer for this ambiguity. It is no longer an easy "Hooray for the robots and boo for those against the robots." Instead, here is the recognition that with each technological gain something is lost. We may get to our destination more quickly in an auto or an airplane, but we no longer hear the birds sing. A complexity such as this one in "Galley Slave" indicates that Asimov does not always see things with the unbounded optimism he is usually credited with. He is a better writer because of it.

The protagonist of "The Last Question" is no individual human being but humanity itself. The conflict is between man (and his creations) and the universe. The universe is running down and will eventually stop. Since it is man's habitat, when it goes, man goes. So man develops more and more complex computers (read "robot") to which he puts the question How can the universe's tendency toward entropy be reversed? Six times in six widely separated futures the answer returns, insufficient data. Finally—on the seventh day, as it were—when mankind has been literally absorbed into the data banks of the ultimate multidimensional computer, and when the universe has finally run down, the mankind-computer solves the problem and sends out its first message implementing the solution, "Let there be light!"

This story makes several assumptions and suggestions. First, it assumes that the history of the universe is cyclical, that having reverted to an energyless state it can be restarted. Second, it suggests that for the next cycle beyond ours, the motivating force behind that restart will be mankind. And third, it hints at the possibility (by analogy) that God is a combination of a sentient race and its machinery left over from a previous cycle. If one views the story as presenting not a cyclical but a circular image of the history of the universe, then man-plus-technology becomes his own creator, man is his own God—literally.

Fascinating paradoxes abound here, and Asimov has certainly tackled some big questions. What could be bigger than the relationships among man, his environment, his extensions of himself via technology, and God? "The Last Question" is a thought-provoking story rather than a solution-offering story. In some ways it can best be read as a fable saying that if mankind will only identify himself and his own best interests with the machine, he can accomplish anything. Technological man is godlike, his potential unlimited. Asimov's optimism is clearly to the fore in this story.

I have saved till last my remarks on "Little Lost Robot" from *I, Robot* and "Risk" from *The Rest of the Robots* because I think these two stories taken together yield an interesting set of insights into Asimov's attitude toward language and into his prose style.

In "Little Lost Robot" a frustrated engineer tells an overly helpful robot to "go lose yourself"—so the literal-minded robot does just that, and the problem becomes how to identify one robot hiding out among sixty-two of his identical brethren. It is a clever, well-written story. But perhaps more clearly than any of the other Robot Stories, "Little Lost Robot" betrays a basic problem with Asimov's Robot Stories. Note that the robot, whose name is NS-2, or Nestor, triggers the story by taking literally a human command. "Go lose yourself" means "Go away." It does not mean "Go hide." In other words, Asimov has his positronic robots able to listen to and speak English without understanding it. Asimov has said that he found many stories in the sixty-three words of the Three Laws of Robotics. Actually, "Runaround" and the revised "Reason" are the only Robot Stories that play the Three Laws game. An equally fertile source of story ideas is the encounter between a literal-minded robot and a figure of speech. Imagine, if you will, a robot receptionist who is ordered to give a certain client the cold shoulder—and comes up with a new principle of refrigeration. Or a robot who hears that a certain human being will come to grief if he gets any farther out in left field— so he spends the rest of the story trying to keep that human out of all fields entirely or in right fields only.

In "Risk" a robot is told to pull back firmly on a lever. Now, "firmly" for a robot means the exertion of much more force than "firmly" for a human. So the robot bends the lever and louses up the experiment. Even literal words—if they are relative ones— can generate stories. We can think of such stories ourselves. A valet robot which breaks down when told to draw a hot bath. "Hot" for a robot would be death for a human, so he has been given a direct order he cannot follow. Or a robot with a minor malfunction that would clear up at 750° F. and a human who tells that robot to make itself comfortable.

The point of all this is that Asimov occasionally makes use of language problems of two types to get his stories going. One type is the literal robot given a figurative order, as in "Little Lost Robot"; the other is a robot given an order containing a term that means something different relative to a robot than it means relative to a human being, as in "Risk." Yet it seems to me that these difficulties are of such a major order that the robots could never have been permitted out of the factory until they were corrected. The linguistic defects of the robots are so great as to render them unworkable. In the stories Asimov constantly treats the symptoms rather than the disease.

All this, I think, gives us an interesting insight into Asimov's attitude toward language. Asimov is extremely literal-minded himself. He permits the robots to go into production with the crippling defect outlined above because he doesn't realize himself how figurative our language really is. For him such unfortunately imprecise phrases as "Go lose yourself" or "Pull the lever back firmly" would be chosen extremely rarely. In both these cases Susan Calvin herself must be called upon to solve the problem, so extraordinary does Asimov take them to be.

We can carry this line of argument still further. Asimov's literalness shows up not only in his plotting but also in his sentencing—in his "style," if you will. Asimov is perhaps overly sensitive on this matter of his style (or lack of one). In *Nightfall and Other Stories*, for example, he writes, "I wasn't at all sure that I could manage style, or that I even knew what style might be. It was only a few months ago, indeed, that a reviewer, referring to me in her review of one of my books, said, 'He is no stylist.' I wrote at once to ask what a stylist was, but she never answered, so it looks as though I'll never find out." When I wrote to him asking what he thought his major weakness was, he replied, "My weakness is that I have no 'style,' no 'poetry,' no 'imagery'—and I don't consider that a weakness." Literally, logically, that statement would singe a positronic brain: "My weakness is lack of x" and "Lack of x is no weakness" are logically incompatible statements. But the meaning is clear to a human brain: Asimov has had it thrown up to him so often that lacking "poetry" and "imagery" is the equivalent of lacking a style that he's tired of hearing it. Besides, as he surely knows, lack of poetry and imagery does not mean lack of style. It means a style that lacks poetry and imagery. That is, a style in which a man with an overly literal attitude toward language can most naturally and easily express himself.

Asimov, of course, does not feel that he is as literal-minded, as nonfigurative, as I have here drawn him. He wrote to me,

> I must deny that I am very literal-minded. Not at all; I am hated by all who meet me because nothing will keep me from punning and playing with words on even the most solemn occasions and that is impossible for a literalist.

But it seems to me that there is a great difference between puns and metaphors. In fact, I suspect that puns are exactly the kind of wordplay a literalist would be most likely to engage in.

When I asked him what he felt was his greatest strength as a writer, he replied, "The reader always knows exactly what is happening and why. Even if not all of the motivations are at the moment clear, he has every security that they will be made clear. He also knows that my phraseology will be lucid and that everything in the story will be self-consistent and that it will all end up logically." Clarity, lucidity, consistency, logic. These are the hallmarks of Asimov's style. Before Asimov we had the prose of A. Merritt, Clark Ashton Smith, and H. P. Lovecraft; for years after Asimov we had the prose of . . . Asimov.

Today, Thomas Disch, Samuel Delany, Harlan Ellison, R. A. Lafferty, and Roger Zelazny are giving us alternatives to Asimov. Still, one fact remains: For twenty-five years it was Asimov's style that dominated science fiction. To call him no stylist is to be inaccurate. To react against his style is the normal course of literary development. To ignore his stylistic contributions to science fiction, contributions that were firmly made in the Robot Stories, is to do a great disservice to perhaps the most influential stylist that science fiction has had.

The Foundation Series

(in order published)

FOUNDATION (1951)
24 Part II: The Encyclopedists (Salvor Hardin)
    May 1942: "Foundation"
25 Part III: The Mayors (Salvor Hardin)
    June 1942: "Bridle and Saddle"
31 Part V: The Merchant Princes (Hober Mallow)
    August 1944: "The Big and the Little"
32 Part IV: The Traders (Limmar Ponyets)
    October 1944: "The Wedge"

FOUNDATION AND EMPIRE (1952)
34 Part I: The General (Bel Riose)
    April 1945: "Dead Hand"
36 Part II: The Mule (Ebling Mis)
    November, December 1945: "The Mule"

SECOND FOUNDATION (1953)
39 Part I: Search by the Mule (Bail Channis)
    January 1948: "Now You See It . . ."
43 Part II: Search by the Foundation (Arcadia Darell)
    November, December 1949; January 1950:
    ". . . And Now You Don't"

Written for FOUNDATION
55 Part I: The Psychohistorians (Hari Seldon)

NOTE: The date given is that of the issue of *Astounding* in which the story was originally published. The succeeding title is the original magazine title.

CHAPTER THREE

Asimov's Foundations I

Three of the books that Asimov published in the early fifties were
Foundation (1951), *Foundation and Empire* (1952), and *Second
Foundation* (1953). These three books are often referred to as
the Foundation Trilogy. The term "trilogy" is somewhat misleading, however, because it implies a completed unit composed of
three novels, and I have actually heard some people refer to one
or another of the three books as novels. Actually the three
volumes contain eight previously published stories of various
lengths plus one new story, and these nine stories taken together
do not form a unified, completed work. Asimov himself tends to
refer to it as the Foundation Series rather than the Foundation
Trilogy, because really it is an open-ended series of stories that
just happened to get printed all together in three books. I prefer
the term "series" also, partly because it is more accurate, and
partly because it admits of the possibility that Asimov could yet
write more Foundation stories.

The Foundation Series was yet another product of the symbi-
otic relationship that existed between Asimov and Campbell.
Here is Asimov's account of the generation of the series:

> The Foundation Series had its origin in 1941, in the course
> of a subway ride [on August 1] to see John W. Campbell,
> Jr., editor of *Astounding Science Fiction*. In those days, I
> visited him frequently and always brought with me the plot
> of a new s.-f. story. We discussed it and I went home and
> wrote it. Then he would sometimes accept it and sometimes
> not.
>
> On this subway ride, I had no story idea to present him
> with so I tried a trick I still sometimes recommend. I opened

a book at random, read a sentence, and concentrated on it till I had an idea. The book was a collection of the Gilbert and Sullivan plays which I just happened to have with me. I opened it to *Iolanthe* and my eye fell on the picture of the fairy queen kneeling before Private Willis of the Grenadier Guards.

I let my mind wander from the Grenadiers, to soldiers in general, to a military society, to feudalism, to the breakup of the Roman Empire. By the time I reached Campbell I told him that I was planning to write a story about the breakup of the Galactic Empire.

He talked and I talked and he talked and I talked, and when I left I had the Foundation Series in mind. It lasted for seven years, during which I wrote eight stories, ranging in length from a short story to a three-part serial. [*Opus 100*, p. 220]

The first story written in the Foundation Series—called "Foundation" in the magazine and "The Encyclopedists" in the book—was submitted to Campbell on September 8, 1941, and accepted on September 15. The first story in which the Three Laws of Robotics were explicitly formulated, "Runaround," was submitted October 20 and accepted October 23. And the second-written Foundation story—"Bridle and Saddle" in the magazine and "The Mayors" in the book—was submitted *and* accepted on November 17.

The fall of 1941, therefore, saw the publication of "Nightfall" (September issue), the formulation of the Three Laws of Robotics, and the writing of the first two stories in the Foundation Series. Surely it is no hyperbole to say that in the fall of 1941 a minor writer named Isaac Asimov novaed into one of the brightest stars in the science fiction sky. He has not faded since.

Asimov did not write the Foundation Series with an eye to its eventual hard-cover publication as a unit. Sufficient unto the day were the wages thereof. Each story—and each check—was an end in itself. ("I wrote each story with no thought at all for the morrow," he once wrote me.) For this reason, I think it best to examine each story separately before discussing the series as a whole. With only two exceptions, one minor and one major, the stories appear in the three collections in the same order that they appeared in *Astounding*, which means that going through them in the order given in the Table of Contents is the same as going through them in the chronological order of their publication. The minor exception is that "The Merchant Princes" and "The Traders,"* Asimov's forty-sixth and forty-seventh written and thirty-first and thirty-second published stories, are reversed in the book for greater continuity. The major exception is that the first story in *Foundation*, "The Psychohistorians," was written in 1950 exclusively for that collection, and it never appeared in magazine form. This means that the first story everyone encounters when reading the Foundation Series in hard cover or paperbacks was actually the last one written.

With this proviso in mind, let us work our way through the individual stories in Asimov's Foundation Series.

Foundation (1951)

When I asked Asimov about the genesis of "The Psychohistorians," this was his reply:

> The first part of FOUNDATION, the "Psychohistorians" was added at the last minute at the request of Martin Greenberg of Gnome Press who was the original publisher of the Trilogy. He wanted some introduction since he felt the first Salvor Hardin story would be too abrupt otherwise. I wrote it specifically for the book and never offered it to anyone. (I agreed to do it because by that time, eight years after the first story was written, I felt the writing thereof to be a little roughhewn and I welcomed a chance to let the reader begin with several thousand words of something a little more polished—just to get him started right.) [Personal letter, April 30, 1973]

Greenberg's notion that the first Salvor Hardin story, "The Encyclopedists," "would be too abrupt" without some preparation is an interesting one. Evidently the readers of *Astounding* had not found the isolated first Salvor Hardin story too abrupt.

* I shall refer to the stories by their book titles only from here on. See the chart on p. 59 for the corresponding magazine titles.

But there is a difference between eight separate stories published intermittently over eight years and a collection of those stories that one can sit down and read as a unit. Greenberg was recognizing that the whole had become greater than its parts and that, twenty years ago at least, a narrative whole required a beginning, a middle, and an end. Since starting with "The Encyclopedists" gave him too much a sense of starting in the middle, he felt a beginning was needed. Note, by the way, that Asimov seems to have disagreed with Greenberg on this point: he agreed to add the story not to ease a feeling of abruptness, but to put before the reader a better written piece of writing "just to get him started right."

The major problem with "The Psychohistorians" stems from Asimov's having written it as an introduction to an already-written series of stories. Alone among the Foundation stories, it does not stand alone. It is too obviously dramatized exposition. It reads more like chapter one of a novel than the first story in a series. It is an introduction to something else more than it is something of its own. Taken on its own terms, however, as dramatized exposition, it is a story worthy of study. Since it is so expository, a discussion of it is also a presentation of most of the assumptions behind the Foundation Series.

In "The Encyclopedists" the great Hari Seldon, originator of the Seldon Plan, had been dead for fifty years. What Asimov decides to do in "The Psychohistorians" is to go back to the time toward the end of Seldon's life when he began to implement his Plan. In a sense the whole series is about the gradual working out of the Seldon Plan, so going back to its beginning is also going back to the beginning of the series. It is supplying the beginning that Greenberg felt was necessary.

But Seldon cannot himself be the narrative-point-of-view character. For one thing, for the readers of the already-written stories he had become almost a mythological character. It is bad enough having to bring him onstage and reveal that he was only human after all. That man who "was old and almost bald and . . . walked with a limp" simply can't be Hari Seldon! This is an emotional mistake from the reader's point of view even if it was necessary from the storyteller's. For another thing, Hari Seldon always seems too much in control of events around him, too much the

manipulator who always gets what he wants. Where's the conflict, the uncertainty, the wondering how it will all turn out? Not
in Hari Seldon.

Instead, Asimov chooses you and me—or, at least, our Galactic
Empire equivalent: someone who does not know what is going on
but who learns, and through whom we learn, in the course of the
narrative. Gaal Dornick has just received his Ph.D. in mathematics and comes to Trantor, capital world of the Galaxy, in order to
join a "mysterious Seldon Project." We are not to inquire too
closely into why he would join the Project without investigating
more carefully what it does or intends to do. (Strangely enough,
science fiction in this pre-Manhattan Project period made fre-
quent use of super-secret scientific government projects. I suppose this was an unspoken awareness that the age of the genius
puttering in his basement was about to be replaced by the well-
organized research and development team.) We are also not
meant to inquire too closely into Gaal Dornick's character, though
I guess those who believe in such stereotypes as the absent-
minded professor will also believe in the hayseed Ph.D. just into
the big city of Trantor from the provinces.

While reading "The Psychohistorians" we learn the following
things. First, the series is set thousands of years in the future
when mankind has spread through the Galaxy and established
a Galactic Empire governed by the Emperor residing at Trantor
in the center of the Galaxy. Second, no mention is made—here
or elsewhere in the series—of aliens, by which method Asimov
effectively excludes them from his series and creates a humans-
only Galaxy. He excluded them, as we have already seen (p.
18), because he wanted to sell his stories to Campbell, and he
and Campbell disagreed about human-alien relationships.

Third, Hari Seldon has single-handedly developed a new
science called psychohistory, defined as "that branch of mathematics which deals with the reactions of human conglomerates
to fixed social and economic stimuli." Implied in this science are
two assumptions: (1) "that the human conglomerate being dealt
with is sufficiently large for valid statistical treatment" and (2)
"that the human conglomerate be itself unaware of psychohistoric
analysis in order that its reactions be truly random" (p. 14). This
definition and its two assumptions are as central to the Founda-

tion Series as the Three Laws of Robotics are to the Robot Stories.

Fourth, using this science, Hari Seldon has come to understand that the 12,000-year-old Galactic Empire is falling and that the process of decay will be completed in another 500 years. Furthermore, nothing can be done to avert the Fall. It is too late. The Empire is too massive. Seldon also sees that following the Fall will come 30,000 years of confusion, barbarism, and human misery until the formation of the Second Galactic Empire. Seldon's Plan is an attempt to reduce that dreadful period to a mere thousand years and thus save humanity 29,000 years of suffering. This is what Gaal Dornick learns that the Seldon Project is seeking to accomplish.

The major episode in the story is Seldon's (and very incidentally Dornick's) trial for treason on the grounds that predicting the Fall would hasten the Fall by undermining the confidence of the people in their government. Therefore, the very act of prediction is antigovernment. The fifth major block of material grows from the results of this trial. Seldon causes the Project—or Foundation—to be exiled to the barren planet of Terminus at the outer edge of the Galaxy, there (as he explains to Dornick) to put together an encyclopedia of all man's knowledge so that during the Interregnum this knowledge will not be lost and civilization will be more quickly restored. Seldon also tells Dornick that a Second Foundation "will be established at the other end of the Galaxy . . . at Star's End." But in the tradition of Asimov's own Jefferson Scanlon in "Half-Breed" and Heinlein's D. D. Harriman in "The Man Who Sold the Moon" and "Requiem," Hari Seldon is too old to participate directly in the fulfillment of his dreams, and the story ends with Seldon's words "I am finished." Finished in the sense of having accomplished what he set out to do, and finished in the sense that he has lived out his life.

These, then, are the five major things established by "The Psychohistorians": a decaying Galactic Empire based at Trantor, a humans-only civilization, psychohistory and its two assumptions, the Seldon Plan for reducing the Interregnum from 30,000 to 1,000 years, and the establishment of two Foundations, at opposite ends of the Galaxy, as the initial steps in that Plan. For the First Foundation, with its enormous task of compiling an encyclopedia of all knowledge, Asimov had in mind the Library at Alexandria, founded about 300 B.C. after the death of Alexander the Great and during the breakup of his empire. Of the Second Foundation Asimov casually and surprisingly remarks, "At the start I had no conception of the Second Foundation at all. It was merely a reserve in case I needed it" (personal letter, April 30, 1973). Again, the Foundation Series was conceived of as a series of complete stories using the same background and not as the chapters in a novel. Sufficient unto the day, etc.

In "The Psychohistorians" Asimov has introduced his readers to most of the major elements they will be encountering in the series. This certainly satisfies Greenberg's reasons for wanting it written: to avoid the abruptness of starting it in mid-Plan with "The Encyclopedists." (One suspects, by the way, that another story was needed to fill out the volume to a standard length anyway.) But what of Asimov's stated reason: to present the starting reader with a more finished piece of writing? My personal feeling is that "The Encyclopedists," which would have come first, is a better piece of writing than "The Psychohistorians." Let me explain.

I have already mentioned that "The Psychohistorians" is dramatic exposition rather than story. It is preparation for storytelling, not storytelling. It is incomplete without the rest of the series.

It lacks a human being with whom the reader can clearly and easily identify. Gaal Dornick is the trite country-boy-in-the-big-city welded improbably onto a Ph.D. in mathematics. Besides, he is too passive a figure to care about. What of importance and interest is he trying to accomplish? The only other candidate for central character, Hari Seldon, is too busy explaining his Plan to be human, and the story is told in such a way that his Plan is his personal problem. Whether it works or not does not seem to matter very much to Seldon. In a story that introduces a series about relieving the human race of 29,000 years of misery, nothing seems important to the characters on an individual basis. They are counters used to help Asimov convey information; they are not people. "The Psychohistorians" is clearly not a human-centered story.

It also has too many settings—or too many little scenes, depending on how you want to look at it. This jumping about gives the

story a herky-jerky feeling. It is a patchwork of snippets. It does
not flow smoothly.

The story contains at least one major contradiction. When Asimov early in the story wants to emphasize the tyrannical nature
of the galactic state, he remarks of the trial, "Press and public
were excluded and it was doubtful that any significant number of
outsiders even knew that a trial of Seldon was being conducted"
(p. 22). Yet later he has Seldon make the following apparently
clinching argument: "The tale of my interrupted trial will spread
through the Galaxy. Frustration of my plans to lighten the disaster will convince people that the future holds no promise to
them. . . . Have me killed and Trantor will fall not within five
centuries but within fifty years" (p. 30).

Perhaps by less "roughhewn" and "more polished" Asimov was
speaking of style rather than story construction. Even here the
story is in no way superior to the others in the series. For example,
it is often pointed out that verbs are the heart of a good prose
style. Yet Asimov's language is noun-centered, interested in
things, not processes or actions. Here are the verbs, the heart of
one's style, from the first paragraph of "The Psychohistorians":
"was," "was," "had seen," "is," "had seen," "had lived," "circled,"
"was," "see," "was." "Circled" is the most vigorous, complex
verb here, and it is used in the context of a planet that "circled
a star," surely not a sprightly new use of the word, especially for
science fiction readers.

So "The Psychohistorians" is dramatic exposition, not a story,
and is therefore incomplete in itself; it lacks a sympathetic central
character; it has too many little scenes; it is flawed in having at
least one major contradiction; and stylistically it does not make
use of its verbs to help convey data. As an individual story, it is
not all that good. As the beginning of the series—that is, in context—it does its job.

The next two stories, "The Encyclopedists" and "The Mayors,"
were the first two Foundation stories to be written. They are
linked in at least two major ways. First, the central character in
each is Salvor Hardin, mayor of Terminus. Second, "The Encyclopedists" ends with the assertion that the solution to the problem
facing Hardin is "Obvious as all hell!"—without telling the readers what that solution was. They had to wait till the next issue of

the magazine—and the second story in the series—to find out. Another similarity, not so important, is that at the ends of both stories Hari Seldon appears by three-dimensional recording in the Time Vault to ratify the actions taken by Salvor Hardin. "The Encyclopedists" and "The Mayors" are clearly companion pieces.

In these two stories one of the major difficulties with "The Psychohistorians" is avoided. Unlike Gaal Dornick, who stands off to the side with his hands in his pockets while the prosecutor gets Hari Seldon to explain the premises of the Foundation Series to us, Salvor Hardin, the narrative-point-of-view character in both stories, is also the problem-solver in them. In both he successfully manages to maintain the independence of Terminus in the face of external threats from its immediate neighbors, especially Anacreon.

Asimov characteristically begins his stories by naming his main character and having him do something in the very first sentence. Also characteristically, he will tell his whole story—or at least the great majority of it—solely through the eyes of one particular person, what I am calling the narrative-point-of-view character. The opening of "The Encyclopedists" is therefore slightly unusual. The first two words identify a character, all right, "Lewis Pirenne" (and surely the name of the great French economic historian Henri Pirenne was somewhere in Asimov's mind here), but Lewis Pirenne is not the central character in the story. Salvor Hardin does not enter until the fifth paragraph, at which point the narrative point of view comes unstuck from Pirenne and fastens itself on Hardin for the rest of this story and much of the next one. The first four paragraphs establish the personality of Hardin's political enemy as well as prepare the stage for Hardin's entrance.

Some other minor things nag at the reader in this story. For example, in that first scene Hardin arrives in Pirenne's office to keep an appointment he had made earlier. But as the conversation develops we are never told exactly why he originally scheduled the appointment. Hardin passes to Pirenne two bits of news, first, that "two hours ago" the Governor of Anacreon had assumed the title of King, and second, that in two weeks an envoy from Anacreon would be arriving on Terminus. Either of these could have been the subject of the appointment, in which case it would have had to be made within the last two hours. Yet Pirenne does not seem to be that accessible a person, and the leisurely quality of the opening conversation does not imply an emergency situation. One feels that Hardin had made the appointment some time before to talk about something else (what, we are never told) and now has taken advantage of the opportunity to discuss more immediate issues. The context of the conversation, in any event, seems vague to me.

Another example of a minor difficulty: As Rodric, the envoy from Anacreon, rides from the spaceport to Cyclopedia Square, he remarks to Hardin, "You have a great deal of unexploited land here, mayor. You have never considered dividing it into estates?" (p. 44). And later Hardin assumes at least twice that Anacreon's real intentions relate to "the parceling up of Terminus into landed estates" (p. 50). This is obviously correct and one of Asimov's givens in the story. Yet at one point Rodric suggests payment of taxes first in gold, chromium, or vanadium, then in manufactured goods, and he is genuinely surprised to discover that neither is available on Terminus. Land is his third suggestion for payment. This conversation violates the given that Anacreon was after land as its original intention. As such it is a flaw in the story.

On the positive side, "The Encyclopedists" contains an excellent example of Asimov's attitude toward the subject matter of his science fiction in general and especially of the Foundation Series in particular. Rodric had fought in the recently concluded war between Anacreon and Smyrno, and at dinner he "monopolized the conversation by describing—in minute technical detail and with incredible zest—his own exploits as battalion head. . . . The details . . . were not completed until dinner was over. . . . The last bit of triumphant description of mangled spaceships came when he had accompanied Pirenne and Hardin onto the balcony" (p. 45). This is a summary of the traditional action-adventure science fiction of the time. Note that Asimov presents it in such a way as to make us critical of it: it is the boring account of a man of mere action, and it isn't worth going into in detail.

When we are permitted once again to hear the actual words of the conversation, Rodric is saying, as transition from the account of "mangled spaceships," "And now . . . to serious matters." For Asimov, action for its own spectacular sake is not a serious matter. I remember reading somewhere that people who really know their science fiction know it's about politics, not science. This remark is certainly true of the Foundation Series. "Serious matters" means decision-making, bargaining, coming to understandings, talking around a table. The atomic bomb would not have been used without the decision being made to use it. For Asimov, that decision-making is more significant than the flash, thunder, and destruction that followed. In the Foundation Series he gets behind—under—action to the causes of action. He moves us from the arena of activity to the understanding of the significance of that activity. The Foundation Series, with its endless series of people sitting around tables talking, deciding lines of action, is about politics.

Let me move to another observation that "The Encyclopedists" gives rise to, this time about the Foundation Series rather than about Asimov's science fiction generally. Put bluntly, in the Foundation Series Asimov has too strong a tendency to conceal relevant data. As a result, the endings of the stories too often seem like rabbits pulled out of hats. A friend of mine once called the series a series of exercises in *deus ex machina*. One reason for this is admittedly the given of the Seldon Plan: Let history have its way and everything will turn out all right. Don't do anything and live happily ever after. (Surely this is another sign of Asimov's reaction against the more traditional swashbuckling blood-and-thunder space opera.)

But there is a second reason for this *deus ex machina* feeling, and that is the concealment of relevant data. Usually in a story a central character will be presented with a problem, he will make a series of attempts to solve that problem (this series being called the conflict), and then finally he will solve it. In "The Encyclopedists" Hardin recognizes the threat posed by Anacreon, "outright annexation and imposition of its own feudal system of landed estates and peasant-aristocracy economy upon" Terminus (p. 60). He spends some time collecting data from Rodric and from Dorwin, envoy from the Empire, and he also spends time nagging at and arguing with Pirenne and his friends.

But what is he doing to solve the problem? Nothing, so far as we are told. Despite the fact that Hardin is our narrative-point-of-view character, we aren't even allowed to see what he's *thinking* about doing much less what he *is* doing. This is most obviously stated at the ends of two of the sections of the story. At the end of the second section Hardin begins to ponder what he has learned from Rodric: "'Back to oil and coal, are they?' he murmured—and what the rest of his thoughts were he kept to himself." And thus does Asimov conceal them from the reader. At the end of the third section Hardin begins to contemplate Hari Seldon's ability to "unravel human emotions and human re-actions sufficiently to be able to predict broadly the historical sweep of the future. And that meant—hm-m-m!" In neither case are we allowed to follow Hardin's thinking from data to planning.

Taken as a device to heighten reader interest—More is going on here than meets the eye; read on, read on—this technique is effective. We have already seen how in a story like "Marooned Off Vesta" Asimov follows the standard pattern of presenting a hero with a problem, letting the reader be with him as he accumulates data, having the hero assert that he has solved the problem (without revealing yet to the reader what the solution is), having the hero act on the solution he has worked out so that the reader has both the data the hero had and the hero's actions to use as clues in working it out himself, and finally letting the hero reveal that solution to us. The game is in trying to work it out when at least part of the time the answer is known to a character but hidden from the reader.

The blackout technique that Asimov uses in "The Encyclopedists" is similar to, yet different from, this standard pattern. The difference is that so far as the reader can tell Hardin makes no attempt to solve the problem. He identifies it. He upsets others because they are doing nothing. But nowhere are we shown or told what he is doing either. Defining conflict as I have—the series of attempts by the central character to solve the problem—one can see that the element of conflict has been omitted from the story. In "The Encyclopedists" the conflict itself is concealed from the reader, not merely (as in "Marooned Off Vesta") the solution to the conflict.

As a result, when we find that Hardin's line of action was the correct one, our impression is that Asimov has pulled a rabbit out of a hat. We had not even been allowed to see that Hardin had a line of action, so the solution seems *deus ex machina*. Early in the next story, "The Mayors," Hardin presents the solution that he worked out to the problem in "The Encyclopedists":

> What I did . . . was to visit the three other kingdoms, one by one; point out to each that to allow the secret of atomic power to fall into the hands of Anacreon was the quickest way of cutting their own throats; and suggest gently that they do the obvious thing. That was all. One month after the Anacreonian force had landed on Terminus, their king received a joint ultimatum from his three neighbors. In seven days, the last Anacreonian was off Terminus. [P. 85]

Where in "The Encyclopedists" are we told that Hardin was thinking of making these trips? None of this is in the story. The events leading up to the resolution of the story have been excised from it.

What saves "The Encyclopedists," besides the clarity of Asimov's writing, is the vivid imaginative shock we get in the last scene, followed immediately by that wonderfully audacious flinging-down-of-the-gauntlet ending. The prerecorded appearance of Hari Seldon in the Time Vault is a breathtaking, awe-inspiring, even reverential moment. There is something ceremonial, grand, and inevitable about it. Overwhelmed by this, we are not likely to object to Hardin's apparent inactivity—or, better, to Asimov's concealing of Hardin's activity. And when we are challenged with "the solution to this first crisis was obvious. Obvious as hell!" without being told what that solution is . . . well, the problem has become ours, not Hardin's, and we no longer care about his lack of attempts at solving it. We are finally told, here in the last paragraph, that Hardin had figured it out and acted long ago. But by then it is too late for us as readers. Emotionally, we no longer care about Hardin as problem-solver. Having already forfeited conflict, the story by its end has also disposed of central character—and replaced him with the reader.

"The Encyclopedists" is an audacious, highly irregular, and nonconventional story in the ways I've tried to point out above. It represents, I think, Asimov at his most innovative and experimental, and the experiment was certainly worth making in the first story written in such a revolutionary series as the Foundation Series turned out to be.

The two things that I have tried to emphasize in my discussion of "The Encyclopedists"—Asimov's reaction against traditional, action-adventure science fiction and his excision of conflict from the story (the two, of course, being closely related)—can also be seen, though to a lesser degree, in "The Mayors." "The Mayors," for example, makes a great deal of a Salvor Hardin saying mentioned in "The Encyclopedists": "Violence is the last refuge of the incompetent." In the context of the science fiction market of the thirties and forties, this can only be taken as negative criticism of much that was being written and published in the field. The heroes of the space operas were constantly being victorious in spectacular battles featuring all sorts of fantastic weapons and super-weapons of the future. The technology of future warfare was a staple in science fiction. And Asimov rejects it all!

The young radical, Sef Sermak, seems to stand for the traditional reaction of science fiction heroes. When Hardin explains to him the precarious political balance that succeeded the removal of the Anacreonian fleet from Terminus thirty years before, Sermak asserts, "That was the time to begin all-out preparation for war," to which Hardin replies, "On the contrary. That was the time to begin all-out prevention of war" (pp. 85–86). Remembering that Asimov wrote in the fall of 1941, one wonders how much of Seldon's ability to avoid violence was wishful thinking on the part of Asimov. The United States was on the verge of World War II and could have used a successful Salvor Hardin.

One final example will, hopefully, clinch the point. Hardin is speaking. "The temptation was great to muster what force we could and put up a fight. It's the easiest way out, and the most satisfactory to self-respect—but, nearly invariably, the stupidest" (p. 85). Thou shalt not behave like the hero of a space opera.

In "The Mayors" the problem once again facing Hardin is how to save Terminus from an invasion by Anacreon. Once again we are not told or shown what Hardin is thinking or doing to solve this problem, though he is not quite so passive as before. We get a few hints that he is at least working on the problem. For example, when Hardin leaves to attend the coronation of

Leopold I on Anacreon, he gives his lieutenant, Yohan Lee, orders to "announce, officially, that on March 14th next, there will be another Hari Seldon recording, containing a message of the utmost importance regarding the recent successfully concluded crisis" (p. 112). He doesn't confide his plans to Yohan Lee or to us, but obviously he's got something up his sleeve. On his trip he "made flying visits to eight of the larger stellar systems of the kingdom of Anacreon, stopping only long enough to confer with the local representatives of the Foundation" (p. 113). Again, we are not told why. In a story over fifty pages long we must rely on hints such as these two that the central character is doing something to solve his—and his planet's—problems. Asimov has omitted the conflict from "The Mayors" almost as thoroughly as he did from "The Encyclopedists," and I think for the same reason: he wanted to avoid the melodrama of the standard science fiction space opera. I mention this lack of conflict merely as an observation. Whether it is a "good thing" or a "bad thing" for Asimov to have done is up to the individual evaluator.

However, I do see some bad things in "The Mayors." For example, toward the beginning of each Foundation story Asimov had to work in a passage of background information for those readers who had not happened to read the previous stories. In "The Mayors" Hardin is made to lecture that background at Sef Sermak. At one point, Sermak shrugs his shoulders and remarks, "Of course, I know what you did" (p. 85), to which Hardin replies, "I'll repeat it anyway," because the readers don't. This is expository dialogue at its most obvious, and Hardin's stated reason for repeating it—"Perhaps you don't get the point"—is not really adequate.

Still, overobvious exposition is a minor flaw and can easily be overlooked. I'm not sure that two other problems that arise can be so easily tucked away. Following Hardin's long conversation with Sermak (from which I have been quoting) is a long conversation between Hardin and Poly Verisof, High Priest of Anacreon and a Foundation agent. In it Hardin remarks, "The Foundation, as he [Hari Seldon] says, was established as a scientific refuge—the means by which the science and the culture of the dying Empire was to be preserved through the centuries of barbarism that have begun, to be rekindled in the end into a Sec-

ond Empire" (p. 94). This certainly is the reason that Asimov
gives eight years later in "The Psychohistorians," but we have
also been told that this is a cover story, a fake.

And who should know that it is fake better than Salvor Hardin?
He was present in the Time Vault at the end of "The Encyclopedists" when Hari Seldon appeared and said, "The Encyclopedia
Foundation, to begin with, is a fraud and always has been! It is
a fraud in the sense that neither I nor my colleagues care at
all whether a single volume of the Encyclopedia is ever published" (p. 73). Why, after this, the Foundation continues work
on the Encyclopedia is not made clear. "The Psychohistorians"
presents a scientifically oriented Foundation. "The Encyclopedists" labels that a fraud and replaces it with a politically oriented
Foundation. It is not a matter of both being correct: "The . . .
Foundation . . . is a fraud," Seldon himself has said. It's an
either/or, not a both/and, situation. One feels that Asimov's
Foundations are shifting under him. (Remember his remark, "I
had no conception of the Second Foundation at all"? His conception of the First does not seem all that firm, either.)

Probably, as the early stories in the series took shape, Asimov
intended to abandon his scientific Foundation for his political
one. But later, as the Second Foundation developed into one
based on nonphysical science, the First Foundation, to balance
it, redeveloped its scientific basis but with the emphasis now on
the physical sciences rather than the original encyclopedia of all
science and culture. Since these developments took place over
years of writing the series and under the pressure of producing
individual stories, I doubt that Asimov was consciously manipulating the shifts.

Whether the Foundation is scientific or political, real or fake,
is one problem not cleared up in the story. Another arises a bit
later in the same conversation between Hardin and Verisof.
Hardin is speaking of the next crisis that was building. "I've got
the idea—just a notion—that the external and internal pressures
were planned [by Seldon] to come to a head simultaneously.
As it is, there's a few months' difference" (p. 96). The internal
pressure referred to is the coming election with the opposition
furnished by Sermak, and I have no quarrel with it. But the external pressure is the expected attack by Anacreon once the

Foundation finishes repairing an ancient Empire ship which Anacreon had found. How could Seldon's mathematics have predicted the finding of that ship and how long it would take the Foundation to repair it? I think Asimov's extrapolation of the gas laws into psychohistory—you can't predict the movements of individuals, since they move entirely at random, but you can predict the behavior of large masses of individuals quite accurately —is here being incorrectly applied to a unique random occurrence. That Empire ship drifted into the Foundation Series from space opera and cannot be accounted for by the laws of psychohistory.

Generally Asimov is very good at anticipating such readers' questions in the course of his stories. Hardin, for example, seized his political power in a coup at the end of "The Encyclopedists." Yet much is made in "The Mayors" of that saying of Hardin's previously referred to, "Violence is the last refuge of the incompetent." Yohan Lee is made to voice the obvious objection: "There was a time when you and I put things through violently, in spite of your slogan about what violence is" (p. 87), and Asimov works in his answer through Hardin: "Our own little putsch was carried through without loss of life, you remember. It was a necessary measure put through at the proper moment, and went over smoothly, painlessly, and all but effortlessly." Nonviolently, not violently.

The key element in the story is the religion of science which the Foundation had established on Anacreon. As one becomes more and more aware of the resentment toward that religion on the part of Wienis, the Prince Regent of Anacreon, one gradually begins to wonder why he ever let it be established in the first place. One might argue that it was Wienis's brother the King who had made the original decision and thus Wienis was stuck with it. But Wienis, we are given to understand, has always been an especially powerful person. So the nagging question is still appropriate, and Asimov has an answer for it. Hardin explains, "In their anxiety to cement forever total domination over their own people, the kings of the Four Kingdoms [including Anacreon] accepted the religion of science that made them divine" (p. 128). Wienis would not complain about this. Asimov is usually ahead of his readers.

It will be remembered that the framework for the Foundation Series, as well as for "Nightfall" and the Robot Stories, was worked out together by Asimov and Campbell. Campbell's influence on specific stories (e.g., "Nightfall" and "Homo Sol") has also been noted. His influence seems to have been especially strong in "The Mayors." Here is Asimov's account of it: "The religiously-disguised technology of the second Salvor Hardin story was one of Campbell's pet notions and he talked me into it over some considerable resistance on my part" (personal letter, April 30, 1973). There would be no "The Mayors" without the religion of science, and it was Campbell's idea rather than Asimov's.

Finally, Asimov, in discussing science fiction mystery stories, has noted a complaint that others brought to his attention. "I was told that 'by its very nature' science fiction would not play fair with the reader. In a science fiction story . . . the author would have his detective whip out an odd device and say, 'As you know, Watson, my pocket-frannistan is perfectly capable of detecting the hidden jewel in a trice'" (*Asimov's Mysteries*, p. x). And a moment later he says, "You don't spring new devices on the reader and solve the mystery with them." Now it seems to me—and obviously to Asimov, too—that any story that conjures up a gadget in order to resolve its problem is playing unfair games with its readers. I have tried to show specifically how two of Asimov's stories—"The Encyclopedists" and "The Mayors"—achieve surprise endings by suppressing the efforts of Salvor Hardin to resolve the stories' conflicts. In "The Mayors" one of the efforts Hardin makes is to have that recently found Empire ship fitted out in ways not known to Wienis or to us. Forty-four pages into the story, during the climactic scene, Wienis croaks at Hardin, "You can't stop my fleet. They're on their way, Hardin, with the great cruiser you yourself ordered repaired, at the head." Hardin replies, "Yes, the cruiser I myself ordered repaired —but in my own way. Tell me, Wienis, have you ever heard of an ultra-wave relay? No, I see you haven't" (p. 122). The readers haven't, either. This "ultra-wave relay" is a pocket-frannistan if I've ever seen one.

In "The Mayors" there is so much else going on that we notice, wince once, and forgive such tricks. This cannot be said of

"The Traders," to me the weakest of all the Foundation stories. On the next-to-the-last page of this twenty-page story, Limmar Ponyets, the story's central character and problem-solver, explains that he was successful because Pherl, the story's villain, "had never heard nor conceived of a microfilm-recorder" (read pocket-frannistan). "The poor sap had never seen three-dimensional color-sound images in his life" (p. 154). That the world of the story contains such devices is not at issue. That their existence was concealed from the reader is. Conjuring up frannistans is another method Asimov uses—and perhaps the least legitimate —that gives the Foundation Series that peculiar feeling of *deus ex machina*, of rabbits appearing out of hats.

The fifth and last story in *Foundation*, "The Merchant Princes," was the longest and most ambitious of the Foundation stories to that date. Four stories followed it, and all were longer. So "The Merchant Princes" is a pivot between the short Foundation stories and the long ones.

In "The Merchant Princes" Asimov continues to avoid using the conventions of traditional action-adventure space opera. For example, after Hober Mallow becomes mayor and institutes his unpopular foreign policies, his Minister of Education and Propaganda, Ankor Jael, is made to object, "Your only plan of battle is to retire without a battle. . . . You openly proclaim a stalemate. You promise no offensive, even in the future," and Mallow responds, "It lacks glamor?" "It lacks mob emotion-appeal." "Same thing" (p. 220). It lacks the blood and thunder so typical of much science fiction at the time. Its appeal is to the intellect rather than to the emotions—or, perhaps better, it is to the emotions through the intellect rather than through physical activity. Mallow's later remarks on Hari Seldon and the Seldon Plan can also be applied to Asimov and the Foundation Series: he "did not count on brilliant heroics but on the broad sweep of economics and history" (p. 222).

Unfortunately, "The Merchant Princes" continues to show Asimov's reliance on the conjuring up and use of pocket-frannistans. Here it is called "a Visual Record receiver" (p. 211). Mallow goes to the planet of Korell for two reasons, first, as a master trader to open up a new sales territory, and second, as an agent of the Foundation to try to discover where the Empire of Korell was

getting the atomic weapons with which it had presumably captured three Foundation ships. While there, he returns to an angry
mob an Anacreonian priest seeking sanctuary aboard Mallow's
ship.

Later, when Mallow decides to run for a spot on the Council,
his political enemies bring him to trial for abandoning that priest,
not because it was illegal, but because it would discredit Mallow
among the electorate. He takes the stand in his own defense and
describes something he did that we have never been told about,
"an action as yet unmentioned, because unknown": "I set up a
Visual Record receiver, so that whatever happened might be preserved for future study" (p. 211). He has recorded the key scene
and can now use it in the courtroom.

But that is not all. In the original scene the priest throws up his
arms when he learns he is to be evicted, and "there was a momentary, tiny flash that came and went in a breath" (p. 174). In
the replay the priest again "lifted his arms in a mad, final curse
and a tiny flash of light came and went" (p. 212). Mallow causes
the record to be stopped and that flash of light enlarged. "The
light had become a set of fuzzy, glowing letters: KSP," for
"Korellian Secret Police" (p. 214).

Mallow gives his explanation: "That . . . is a sample of tat-
tooing, gentlemen. Under ordinary light it is invisible, but under
ultraviolet light—with which I flooded the room in taking this
Visual Record, it stands out in high relief."

Asimov makes some attempt to render plausible Mallow's making of the Visual Record in the first place: he wanted to preserve
this key scene for future study so that perhaps he could come to
understand it better. But Asimov's hiding the fact of the recording from us until he pulls it out of the hat at the trial is less fair.
Least acceptable of all is Mallow's flooding of the room with
ultraviolet light at the time he made the recording. No reason
for his doing this is given or suggested. He does so because much
later he has to be able to read the tattoo it renders visible. His
action can only be explained by reference to the exigencies
of later plot twists, and it is not in itself plausible or probable.
(And wouldn't other optical effects reveal the presence of the
ultraviolet light to everyone in the room?)

More than the other stories in the collection *Foundation*, "The Merchant Princes" raises in its readers a nagging question. The second assumption behind psychohistory was "that the human conglomerate be itself unaware of psychohistoric analysis in order that its reactions be truly random" (p. 14). Yet "The Merchant Princes" begins with the remark "It may be another one of Hari Seldon's crises," and the response is "As a general rule, politicians start shouting 'Seldon crisis' at every mayoralty campaign" (p. 159). Later, much is made of one of the character's not knowing what a Seldon crisis was. In other words, knowledge of the Seldon Plan and Seldon crises was generally disseminated among the people of the Foundation. They are Hari Seldon's Chosen Race, and they believe in their destiny among the stars. In what sense, then, is the human conglomerate of the Foundation unaware of psychohistoric analysis?

I remember more than twenty years ago the mother of a friend of mine reading the Foundation Series with a great deal of delight and amusement. I had thought it entertaining but not funny, and I asked her about it. "Oh, but the style, the wordplay," she insisted. "Asimov can be so delightfully ironic." I think I see now what she meant. At one point in "The Merchant Princes," for example, Asimov plays the following game with the connotations of words: "The Commdor referred to his dwelling place as a house. The populace undoubtedly would call it a palace. To Mallow's straightforward eyes, it looked uncommonly like a fortress" (p. 179).

More subtly, perhaps: The Commdor at first refuses to consider trade with the Foundation because "my people will not take commerce which sparked in crimson and gold" (p. 178), by which he meant a commerce clothed in the trappings of the Religion of Science. But two pages later, Mallow wins the Commdor to a trade agreement by putting a necklace of pebbles around the neck of a girl who had just been given a force-field cloak: "each pebble, as it entered the luminescent field, became an individual flame that leaped and sparked in crimson and gold." Despite his earlier statement the Commdor does indeed accept "commerce which sparked in crimson and gold."

In "The Merchant Princes" is a scene that has always stood out for me, and I have been agreeably surprised in talking with other readers to learn that it has stood out for many of them, too. It is the whole of Section 10 of the story, beginning on page 187. It is the account of Hober Mallow's visit with Onum Barr of Siwenna in search of information concerning the Empire and its present status. I believe that what is so impressive about this passage is the human dignity of Onum Barr combined with Asimov's quiet understatement of that dignity. The first paragraph sets the tone, which is sustained admirably throughout:

> Onum Barr was an old man, too old to be afraid. Since the last disturbances, he had lived alone on the fringes of the land with what books he had saved from the ruins. He had nothing he feared losing, least of all the worn remnant of his life, and so he faced the intruder without cringing.

Because the scene begins from Barr's point of view—and one of Asimov's favorite techniques is to present scenes from the points of view of minor characters—even when that scene shifts to the more objective "Barr said, Mallow said," the reader seems to be participating with Barr rather than Mallow. It is Onum Barr's scene. For some reason, Asimov is always good with older people. (See, for another example, Joseph Schwartz in *Pebble in the Sky*.) He seems to respect—almost to revere—them, and they come across with strong, quiet dignity.

When, in the first scene of the next story, "The General," Asimov tries to repeat the scene, he is not so successful. For one thing, Ducem Barr is a scholar who has pieced together data rather than an old man who has grown in wisdom by living. For another, Bel Riose is more belligerent and forceful than Hober Mallow. Riose cannot underplay his role and let the other have center stage. The Mallow-Barr conversation is one of the highlights of the series, and there is nothing quite like it elsewhere in the three books.

Foundation and Empire (1952)

Foundation and Empire and *Second Foundation* each contain two rather long stories. The first of these four, "The General," has always seemed to me to be a story that went wrong in the typewriter and that needed a thorough rewriting which it didn't get. The reasons for its going wrong and for its not getting the rewriting are probably both temperamental with Asimov and generic with his market. Let me explain.

"The General" is the story of Bel Riose, the last great general of the Empire under the last great Emperor, Cleon II. In its magazine appearance it was called "Dead Hand" because the conflict in the story is between the dead Hari Seldon and Bel Riose. Seldon's Plan implied the continued growth and success of the Foundation until the Second Empire was established, while Riose wanted to stop the Foundation because his allegiance was to the still-extant First Empire. Which would win? Foundation or Empire? Hari Seldon or Bel Riose? As Ducem Barr explains at the end of the story:

> "Only the combination of strong Emperor *and* strong general
> . . . can harm the Foundation; a strong Emperor cannot be
> dethroned easily, and a strong general is forced to turn out-
> wards, past the frontier . . . But . . . the Emperor is strong
> because he permits no strong subjects. . . . Riose won vic-
> tories, so the Emperor grew suspicious. . . . It was the *suc-
> cess* of Riose that was suspicious. So he was recalled, and
> accused, condemned, murdered. . . . There is not a conceiv-
> able combination of events that does not result in the Foun-
> dation's winning. It was inevitable; whatever Riose did,
> whatever we did." [P. 77]

This is both the strength and a large part of the weakness of the story. Whatever the characters did, the result was inevitable. This makes the doings of the characters useless, and fiction is largely about characters and what they are and do.

There are two points to be made here. The first concerns Lathan Devers, trader and agent for the Foundation, who allows himself to be captured by Riose. Unlike Salvor Hardin, who never seemed to do anything yet eventually turned out to have done the right things without our being told of them, Lathan Devers is always attempting to do something and he is always failing. He tries, for example, to open a wedge between Riose and the Em-peror's ambassador Brodrig, but succeeds only in causing Brodrig to desert the Emperor for the general. Later, Devers and Barr escape to Trantor where they try to see the Emperor in order to convince him that Riose is a traitor, but they fail and end up fleeing Trantor for their lives. We follow all this activity in some detail, and it turns out to have been froth. The Foundation was going to win no matter what anyone did. So their activities were a waste of their time and ours.

The second point has to do with alternate subject matter for the story. If activity is useless and irrelevant and time wasting, where does the story lie? Not in what people do, but in what they are. The central character in "The General" is the general, Bel Riose. Yet he does not appear in the last twenty-one pages of the story! What is important, enduring, tragic, is the overwhelming of Riose by forces outside his control. This is a perennial and important issue: the individual man versus his physical and social and economic environment. We want to know about Riose's reaction to this eternal human dilemma. What is his reaction to his recall? On what grounds does he defend himself at his trial? What is the face-to-face relationship between Riose and Cleon II? How does he endure his imprisonment, and with what thoughts? Here is where the important human story is located. Instead, we leave him forever, knocked unconscious during the melodramatic escape of Devers and Barr, and we follow their useless and unsuccessful antics for the rest of the story.

The story went wrong in the typewriter partially because of Asimov's unwillingness to tell a character-centered tale, partially I suspect because he guessed his market and audience wouldn't be interested, and partially because he was more interested in the Seldon Plan's inevitability than in an individual who wasn't even a member of the Foundation. The story is not a tragedy but a piece of popular fiction, because it avoids the deeper and more fundamental questions that it might have raised. It does not end with the soul-disturbing destruction of Bel Riose, an extension of you and me, but with another comfortable and reassuring victory for Hari Seldon and the Foundation. For these reasons I use a phrase as strong as "went wrong in the typewriter." I think the story should have followed the decline and fall of Bel Riose instead of the escape and flutterings about of Lathan Devers and Ducem Barr.

Asimov got the idea for Bel Riose and what happened to him from the historical precedent of Belisarius as Belisarius is presented in Gibbon's *Decline and Fall of the Roman Empire* and, more importantly, in L. Sprague de Camp's *Lest Darkness Fall*, a science fiction novel by a good friend of Asimov's. But one must be careful about what "got the idea" means in such instances. Damon Knight has accused Asimov of merely copying history and therefore of not writing science fiction in the Foundation Series.* Asimov has defended himself by arguing that history does repeat itself in large sweeping ways and that therefore it is perfectly legitimate to plot stories of the future by referring to the past.†

I do not find their discussion on this particular point very useful. I have read Gibbon's account of Belisarius and I have reread *Lest Darkness Fall*. Asimov has not slavishly copied either one. As he himself puts it, "I used history as a guideline to keep me from using ridiculous misinterpretations of what can happen, given people and their way of behaving" (personal letter, April 30, 1973). One of the canons of fiction has always been (see Aristotle's *Poetics*) that the action be probable, and Asimov likes to use history as an indication of what is probable, of what can happen because something similar has happened. Given Asimov's inherent interest in history—in college he almost majored in history rather than in chemistry—it is not surprising that he uses history this way.

Besides getting his idea for Bel Riose from the historical Belisarius, his "notion of the Mule as someone who destroyed an apparently inevitable sweep of victory, which was then reconstituted after his passing, was based on Tamerlane's disruption of the march of the Ottoman Empire—which resumed after Tamerlane's death" (personal letter, April 30, 1973). The Mule figures strongly in the second story in *Foundation and Empire* and in the first in *Second Foundation*, and I have never heard of anyone's reading those stories and exclaiming, "Why, he's merely copying Tamerlane!"

The important thing is that "get the idea for" does not mean "copy slavishly." In fact, the most important reference of the term

* "Asimov and Empire," *In Search of Wonder* (Advent Publishers, 1967).
† "Social Science Fiction," Reginald Bretnor, ed., in *Modern Science Fiction* (Coward-McCann, 1953).

"idea" is not to individuals like Bel Riose or the Mule or even to the specific actions they perform. It is rather to the general historical context in which they participate. Belisarius was the successful and extremely loyal general building a reputation away from court and ruined by the malicious rumors of jealous courtiers and the frightened insecurity of a suspicious and overly careful Emperor. So was Bel Riose. Tamerlane stopped the historical inevitability of the growth of an empire momentarily. So did the Mule. It is the general context, not the specific person or plot, that Asimov got from history. The charge that he was copying history rather than writing fiction simply doesn't hold up. Besides, a writer must get his ideas somewhere. Why is the result fiction if the idea comes from an expression on someone's face at the grocery store or from a paragraph in *Scientific American* and not fiction if it comes from a history book?

CHAPTER FOUR

Asimov's Foundations II

We must now move on to the two stories featuring the Mule.

Three centuries had passed since Hari Seldon had established the two Foundations as part of the Seldon Plan. The First Foundation had survived four Seldon crises. The first crisis had come fifty years in to the Plan when Salvor Hardin had seized control of Terminus in order to defeat an invasion from Anacreon. The second came thirty years later when Hardin used the Religion of Science to once again repel a threat to the Foundation from Anacreon. In the third, seventy-five years after that, Hober Mallow used trade without its religious trappings in order to defeat the Republic of Korell in such a way as not to attract the attention of the distant, shrinking, but still powerful Empire. Forty-five years later, the Empire's greatest general, Bel Riose, despite poor leadership within the Foundation, had been defeated by the inevitable and Seldon-foreseen march of history. In all four crises the seemingly dangerous threats to the Foundation had dissipated due to circumstances beyond the control of individuals. The tide of history flowed in the Foundation's favor.

Asimov had so far written five *deus ex machina* stories in which the resolutions came about as historical movements rather than as the result of actions and desires on the part of individual human beings. As has been shown, occasionally the *deus ex machina* element was an illegitimately conjured up and used technological device like the "microfilm-recorder" of "The Traders" or the "Visual Record receiver" of "The Merchant Princes." But these are merely plotting problems. Thematically, Asimov had written five stories which showed that history will have its way with us, will we nill we.

And he came to feel that some variety, some change of pace, was needed. He was telling the same story over and over: Individuals don't count. So he created the Mule, an individual who did count. Three hundred years after Seldon instituted his Plan, the independent Traders were supposed to band together and revolt against the hidebound Foundation. When Seldon appeared in the Time Vault, it was to address himself to this problem. But the independent Traders, who had considered revolt earlier, had instead joined forces with the Foundation in the face of a common threat, the Mule. Of the Mule, Seldon says nothing. The Mule was an individual who could not be taken into account by the human-conglomerate approach of psychohistory.

With the Mule, two major things happen. First, an individual disrupts the Seldon Plan and conquers the Foundation. Second, the Second Foundation becomes significant, not as a force in the story whose efforts we participate in and share, but as the object of a search by both the Mule, who must find it to destroy it, and the Foundation, which must find it to help it defeat the Mule. "The Mule," then, has a standard and classical pattern: two groups in conflict with one another to achieve a goal.

The Mule is a mutant who has the ability to realign the emotional makeup of an enemy so that the enemy becomes a loyal supporter. For example, at a military trial mentioned relatively early in the story the Mule finds the opportunity to tinker with the psychic makeup of several generals of the Foundation. As a result, later in battle the generals defect to the Mule's cause and the result is victory for the Mule and defeat for the Foundation.

The outstanding example of this ability of the Mule's at a personal level is Captain Han Pritcher of Information (i.e., the Foundation's intelligence service). Though he begins as a very stubborn and individualistic opponent of the Mule, he is "converted" and becomes convinced of the rightness of the Mule's cause. In fact, he makes a convincing case for the Mule: "In these last seven years, he has established a new Empire. In seven years, in other words, he will have accomplished what all Seldon's psycho-history could not have done in less than an additional seven hundred. The Galaxy will have peace and order at last" (p. 204). This is so convincing that even the reader wonders how the Mule can be considered an enemy, a bad guy. His is

simply an alternate—and faster—route to the Foundation's eventual goal anyhow. Why not support the Mule?

The answer is given a few pages later by Ebling Mis, the
Foundation psychologist in charge of locating and warning the
Second Foundation: the Mule would "establish a distorted new
Empire upheld by his personal power only. It would die with his
death; the Galaxy would be left where it was before he came,
except that there would no longer be Foundations around
which a real and healthy Second Empire could coalesce. It would
mean thousands of years of barbarism" (p. 214). So the Seldon
Plan is to be protected and preferred, even if the Mule himself
is not a villain.

"The Mule" has always seemed to me to be one of Asimov's
most successful stories. For one thing, it continues to show that
curious ability Asimov has to come at a scene from the point of
view of a minor character in such a way that that character and
his concerns spring to life before us. One example of this has
already been mentioned in "The Merchant Princes" in the marvelous conversation between Hober Mallow and Onum Barr. In
"The Mule" perhaps the best example is the scene from the point
of view of Jord Commason (pp. 183–86). Less good as an example, because less fully worked out, but still representative of
the technique, is the scene in which Lee Senter watches the
Foundation ship land on Trantor (pp. 196–98).

This story also shows in a curious and perhaps playful way
Asimov's awareness that he is writing popular fiction. In popular
fiction—and especially in action-adventure space opera—ordinary,
everyday people like you and me are constantly finding themselves enmeshed in earth- and/or universe-rending struggles.
Insignificant people become significant ones. It's a good storytelling device because it makes it easier for the reader to identify
with the hero, and it makes daydreaming more fun. In "The
Mule" the bride and groom, Bayta and Toran, are on Terminus
just as the Foundation falls and on the planet Haven immediately
before it, too, is taken by the Mule. Bayta finally recognizes that
what has been happening to them is as melodramatic as a work
of fiction: "Such things don't happen in real life. You and I are
insignificant people; we don't fall from one vortex of politics

into another continuously for the space of a year" (p. 219). Unless, of course, one is the heroine of a work of popular fiction.

Trying to identify the central character raises some interesting points about this story. As I have already suggested, in connection with "The General" especially, Hari Seldon can sometimes be considered the central character of individual stories. It is his thinking and planning that anyone who opposes the Foundation must defeat. But Seldon is clearly out of it in "The Mule," at least insofar as his connection with the Foundation is concerned. One might argue, along with Ebling Mis, that the Second Foundation was established by Seldon to handle such variations from the Plan as the Mule, but there is no evidence for this in the story and no evidence that the Second Foundation—and therefore Hari Seldon—is the agency that defeats the Mule in this story. (It will eventually be asserted by Asimov in "Search by the Foundation" that the Second Foundation did indeed help Bayta defeat the Mule, but I am sure that argument arose as an afterthought in a later story and should not be used as evidence here.) So Hari Seldon cannot be considered the central character of "The Mule."

I can see arguments in favor of three other characters in this connection. Ebling Mis has the task of locating the Second Foundation, so he does have a problem to solve. After spending weeks in the Imperial Library on Trantor, he does discover its location, so he is also a problem-solver. But his trying to solve that problem occupies a peripheral and relatively small part of the story, and we are given very few glimpses of his struggle. We are not allowed to participate in this particular conflict. Besides, we never learn what he has learned. The information is irrelevant to this particular story. Therefore, his locating that information cannot be what this story is about, and Ebling Mis is not its central character.

Bayta is the one who finally figures out what has really been going on, and it is she who prevents the Mule from learning the location of the—for him—dangerous Second Foundation. By the time the story is over, and in the context of the defeat of the Mule, she is surely the story's heroine, and she is so treated by future generations. But I think the key phrase here is "by the time the story is over." As we read the story we do not think of her as the one who is trying to accomplish something. She becomes the heroine by virtue of her role in those crucial final scenes, but she is not the central character of the story before then.

Only the Mule can be considered the story's central character. Having been kicked around by the Galaxy for twenty-two years, he decided to use his power to do some kicking of his own. Heredity and environment shaped him to be a seeker-after-power. "Through a pirate, I obtained my first asteroidal base of operations. Through an industrialist I got my first foothold on a planet. Through a variety of others ending with the warlord of Kalgan, I won Kalgan itself and got a navy" (p. 222).

Then he faced the Foundation, and that's where "The Mule" starts. His problem is how to defeat the Foundation. His solution was to ally himself to the Foundation agents sent to investigate him at Kalgan. He chanced to find Bayta and Toran, spies of the Independent Traders, before he found Han Pritcher, the agent from the Foundation. In the company of Bayta and Toran, along with Ebling Mis later, the Mule was able to be in the key places he needed to be: at the court-martial to "convert" the minds of military leaders and on Terminus and Haven to prepare their defeats.

Only, there turned out to be two Foundations instead of one. Having defeated the First, he still had to find and defeat the Second. He accompanied Ebling Mis to the Library on Trantor and helped him seek the Second Foundation by intensifying Ebling Mis's thought processes. At the end it is the Mule versus Bayta for the knowledge in Ebling Mis's mind—and Bayta wins.

I recite all this not to retell the story, but to show that only the Mule has been in control and solving problems throughout. "The Mule" has more dramatic unity when seen from his point of view than from that of any other character. The Mule is present at and/or responsible for all the key events in the story. He is clearly its central character, as the title itself indicates.

Asimov has here taken on a fearful task of authorial prestidigitation. He has decided to tell a 150-page story from a series of points of view other than that of its central character, all the while concealing that central character from us. Just as he excised conflict from his Salvor Hardin stories, so here he has excised central character. In a sense this is a continuation of the technique that I have argued failed him toward the end of "The General": there the story became one about Devers and Barr, relatively unimportant side characters; here the story is about Bayta and Toran, Han Pritcher and Ebling Mis. Only when it's over do we realize it was really about the title character, the Mule, all along. If there are some minor plotting flaws (why, for instance, does Han Pritcher appear on Trantor in Chapter 24?) and if the characterization is sometimes deficient (Toran is such a nothing one wonders why Bayta ever married him, and Ebling Mis is simply Tan Porus of "Homo Sol" all over again), still Asimov has on the whole put the story together with great skill. And as with the Salvor Hardin stories, I think "The Mule" is experimental writing in that term's truest and best sense: the working out of narrative techniques that are most appropriate to the subject matter at hand. The Salvor Hardin stories and "The Mule" show us Asimov at his best, working on the frontiers of science fiction in both subject matter and writing technique.

Second Foundation (1953)

The second of the two stories about the Mule, "Search by the Mule," is not so successful as the first. I feel that "Search by the Mule" fails because it is too inner-directed. Or rather, its inner-directedness is not well done. Too much of "Search by the Mule" consists of accounts of what the Mule's motivations are, and Han Pritcher's, and Bail Channis's. The basic problem is that we are told what these motivations are rather than allowed to form our own judgments as a result of seeing and hearing the actions and speeches of the characters. Thus the story becomes mired down in the transmission of psychological information from Asimov to us. The information is not at fault, but the method of presenting it to us is. As a result, the story drags.

There are two other reasons why the story doesn't work: the Interludes and the tone of voice. This is the only Foundation story into which Asimov builds a series of Interludes, one after each of the six chapters except the fifth. Their function is clear. The basic conflict in the story is Mule versus Second Foundation. The actions of the Mule and his agents, Pritcher and Channis, are given in the chapters; the discussions by the Second Foundation are given, in briefer and briefer snippets, in the Interludes.

These Interludes allow us for the first time to be with members of the Second Foundation—yet only the first and fifth Interludes contain any information at all. All we get is a sort of choric commentary on what is already known from the main story. The first Interlude has a curious discussion of the death of Ebling Mis and who was responsible for it, and the last one ends the main story by bringing Bail Channis back to an awareness of his true identity. Strictly speaking, that material belongs in a chapter, not an Interlude. So the Interludes chop up the story with extraneous material which contributes nothing to the advancement of the story. They are useless.

At least two passages early in the story are written in a tone of voice Asimov has not used before in the series and will not use again. I have mentioned already the lightness, the irony, that often shows through in the style of the stories. We become aware of a personality behind the words, and we share that personality's wry evaluation of the things he comments on. Here, in these two passages in "Search by the Mule," Asimov's control of that personality breaks down. It no longer speaks from behind the tissue of the story, but it tears the tissue apart, steps through, and speaks in too outright a way.

The passages I refer to are the opening of Chapter 1, pages 3–4, and the first half of the First Interlude, pages 16–17. Let me give brief examples from each. From Chapter 1, following the introductory quotation from the Encyclopedia Galactica: "There is much more that the Encyclopedia has to say on the subject of the Mule and his Empire but almost all of it is considerably too dry for our purposes in any case." "Our purposes"? Who is speaking? To whom? "We therefore abandon the Encyclopedia and continue on our own path for our own purposes." Whose path? What purposes? And now from the First Interlude containing a meeting of the Second Foundation: "To us they are merely voices. . . . Nor . . . can we even consider an exact reproduction of any part of the session—unless we wish to sacrifice completely even the minimum comprehensibility we have a right to expect." And, following a description of the meeting, "Which is about as far as I can go in explaining color to a blind man—with myself as blind as the audience." These passages are the only ones in the series in which we are made aware of a speaking voice, and the second is the only one in which that voice refers to itself as "I." For two brief moments the compiler of the Foundation Series stands before us, the Encyclopedia Galactica (116th edition) at one hand, a complete knowledge of all "past" events and people at the other. No human compiler could know all these things. The "I" referred to can only be an omniscient being, a god—and to claim that the Foundation Series is narrated by God is absurd. The introduction of the author as an omniscient future narrator and compiler is a mistake.

"Search by the Mule" doesn't work because it is inner-directed by lecture rather than by example and event, because the Interludes are actually interruptions, and because an irrelevant and misleading narrative voice is introduced.

In one sense, and to a limited degree, I think Asimov's storyteller's instincts led him right in this story. The story features a Han Pritcher involuntarily "converted" by the Mule to his service and a Bail Channis voluntarily converted by the Second Foundation to its purpose. The Mule seeks to find and destroy the Second Foundation; the Second Foundation seeks to deceive the Mule into thinking he *has* found and destroyed it. Han Pritcher *becomes* convinced the Mule's aims are good and just. Bail Channis *becomes* convinced the Second Foundation is on Tazenda—or more precisely, on Rossem. The Mule *becomes* convinced he has destroyed the Second Foundation. All these things are changes inside people. Asimov's storytelling instincts told him this was an inner-directed story, and so we get those passages I have already discussed concerning the motivations of the Mule, Pritcher, and Channis.

Two final things demand attention, both of them, unfortunately, negative. The story is very tightly plotted, one must grant that. But it leaves the impression that it was written to demonstrate the writer's ingenuity rather than to tell a story. Toward the end, anybody could be a member of any organization for whatever reason Asimov conjures up. Stories that surprise are pleasing; stories that bewilder are not. "Search by the Mule" bewilders rather than surprises.

But the greatest charge to be made against this story has to do with its morality rather than its craftsmanship. The Second Foundation arranges things so that the Mule attacks Tazenda, believing it to be the location of the Second Foundation, and murders its entire population. Here is the justification given by the First Speaker of the Second Foundation:

> "The destruction of Tazenda was unavoidable. The alternative would have been a much greater destruction generally throughout the Galaxy over a period of centuries. We did our best in our limited way. We withdrew as many men from Tazenda as we could. We decentralized the rest of the world. Unfortunately, our measures were of necessity far from adequate. It left many millions to die." [P. 71]

Milton's Satan could not have argued the case better. Nor could Hitler, who had solved his Jewish Problem with the murders of millions of Jews. The First Speaker, Satan, Hitler—all stand together. And this story seeks to justify and condone the policies of the First Speaker.

I don't believe Asimov thought about these implications. I think he was writing a work of popular fiction and that he never thought of the population of Tazenda as real and to be sorrowed for. It was just a device, a way of convincing the Mule he had found and destroyed the Second Foundation, etc., etc. But fiction is the illusion of reality, and if the population of Tazenda doesn't count, neither do Seldon and his Plan, the First Foundation, Salvor Hardin and Hober Mallow and Ebling Mis and the whole Foundation Series. Asimov is here inadvertently preaching in favor of something I know he despises, as all civilized men must. Ends do not justify means. Methods of achieving goals are as important as the goals themselves. The sacrifice of the population of Tazenda is an atrocious act of inhumanity on the part of the Second Foundation. My own attitude toward the Second Foundation has never recovered from it. And I can only view it as a major flaw in the Foundation Series.

The last story in the Foundation Series as it now stands is "Search by the Foundation." In many ways, including the parallelism of the titles, "Search by the Foundation" is a second version of "Search by the Mule." Both alternate between scenes laid in the First Foundation and scenes laid in the Second, though in "Search by the Mule" the Second Foundation scenes are labeled "Interludes" and in "Search by the Foundation" they are simply alternate chapters. In the first version it is the Mule who must be tricked into thinking he had destroyed the Second Foundation, while in the second it is the Foundation itself. The Mule is convinced at least partially because he kills innocent millions on Tazenda, and the Foundation is convinced at least partially because it kills fifty volunteers on Terminus. (Note that the number of deaths necessary as the Second Foundation's earnest money has been drastically reduced, and those killed have become volunteers. Asimov didn't like the Tazenda affair, either.) The narrative-point-of-view character of both is a person whose mind has been tinkered with by the Second Foundation so that the testers of those minds could be convinced of the truth of what those minds thought: the Mule "knew" Bail Channis thought the Second Foundation was on Rossem because Channis's mind had been wiped clean and rebuilt by the Second Foundation, and Dr. Darell "knew" Arkady's mind was clear of Second Foundation trickery because the Second Foundation had controlled her mind while she was still an infant and before traces of that control would be left. And both stories end with a series of revelations as to where the Second Foundation really is. Therefore, I consider "Search by the Mule" to be a rough draft of "Search by the Foundation," and furthermore I consider the second story much the superior of the two.

As one indication of this superiority, consider the exposition—the presentation of relevant data about the past—in each story. In "Search by the Mule" the Mule lectures the background at Bail Channis and us, beginning with the justification, "You're a native of Kalgan, aren't you? Yes. Well, then, your knowledge of the Seldon Plan may be vague" (p. 14). In "Search by the Foundation" Arcadia (Arkady) Darell, a fourteen-year-old schoolgirl, is dictating for her class a paper called "The Future of Seldon's Plan." Both of these devices for inserting background material into the stories may seem overly obvious, but the Mule's lecture is something we endure for the sake of the story, while Arcadia's dictation is a delight in itself, partially because the paper with its data is constantly being interrupted so that it does not become dreary, partially because Asimov concentrates on characterizing Arcadia and he does a very good job of it. The exposition may not be inserted more subtly in this story, but it is more entertainingly done, and we get not merely exposition but also characterization at the same time. "Search by the Foundation" gets off to a very efficient, informative, and entertaining start, much better than the wordy and disjointed opening of "Search by the Mule."

Much of one's reaction to "Search by the Foundation" is determined by one's reaction to Asimov's portrayal of Arkady Darell. Many readers dislike the story because they dislike her. I am not one of them. Certainly she is a precocious schemer and manipulator. It might be extreme but not unfair to characterize her as a spoiled brat used to getting her own way. But the degree to which she is not an ordinary fourteen-year-old is the degree to which she is an individual in her own right. Characterization is the process by which an individual is shown to be different from the other members of its group. That Asimov has characterized Arkady—has succeeded in separating her from her group —is a strength, not a weakness. Besides, built into the story is a good and strong reason for her being the kind of individual she is. As the First Speaker eventually puts it, "She has been Controlled, and will be all the better for it, since her Control involved the development of a precocious and intelligent personality" (p. 223). Arkady Darell is one of Asimov's best characterizations, and "Search by the Foundation" is all the better for it. Despite all of its authorial lectures on the motivations of its characters, "Search by the Mule" does not have an interesting, alive human being in it. (Well, perhaps Han Pritcher.)

I have tried to indicate the superiority of "Search by the Foundation" over "Search by the Mule" on the representative grounds of exposition and characterization, at least characterization of the lead figures in the two stories. I will add here the assertion that the Second Foundation chapters in "Search by the Foundation" work—that is, they convey data and move forward the central concerns of the story—while the Interludes in "Search by the Mule" had not worked. Furthermore, the narrator keeps himself out of this story, as he had not in the first one. Furthermore, the Tazenda slaughter of millions has been lessened to the sacrifice of fifty, so the story quantitatively is less morally reprehensible. For a variety of reasons, of which these are samples, "Search by the Foundation" is a better story than "Search by the Mule."

Still, "Search by the Foundation" contains a major problem which I personally cannot reconcile and which damages the story irreparably for me. It is the characterization of the Second Foundation. I have admitted that the Tazenda affair taints my attitude toward the Second Foundation in that story, and I suppose that when I read the next story in the series that taint carries over. I think that I am supposed to be in favor of Hari Seldon's Plan, to want humanity to be spared 29,000 years of chaos and suffering, and to feel that what helps the Plan is good and what hinders it is bad. The Mule was bad because his reunification of the Galaxy could only last his lifetime, and his defeat was good because the Seldon Plan could be gotten back to.

But when I read the chapter of "Search by the Foundation" called "Seldon's Plan," I am horrified. First we are given a First Speaker—and in the sense of being given a problem that he attempts to solve and, after difficulties and complications, does solve, the First Speaker is the central character of this story, our hero, if you will—we are given a First Speaker who can contemplate thus: "For twenty-five years, he, and his administration, had been trying to force a Galaxy of stubborn and stupid human beings back to the path" (pp. 93-94)! Can we sympathize with such an attitude?

This would be bad enough, but then we learn some things about Seldon's Plan we had never heard before. It was not instituted merely to shorten the Interregnum from 30,000 to 1,000 years. It was also instituted to change the nature of the Second Empire. That is, the Plan was both quantitative—shortening the duration of the Interregnum—and qualitative—changing the nature of human civilization.

The First Speaker asks the Student through whom Asimov lectures his readers, "Do you think that any Second Empire, even if formed in the time set by Seldon, would do as a fulfillment of his Plan?" and the Student replies, "No, Speaker, I do not. There are several possible Second Empires . . . but only one of these is *the* Second Empire" (pp. 101-2). The description of "*the* Second Empire" is as follows:

"Conditions have been so arranged and so maintained that in a millennium from its beginnings—six hundred years from now, a Second Galactic Empire will have been established in which Mankind will be ready for the leadership of Mental Science. In that same interval, the Second Foundation, in *its* development, will have brought forth a group of Psychologists ready to assume leadership. Or, as I have myself often thought, the First Foundation supplies the physical framework of a single political unit, and the Second Foundation supplies the mental framework of a ready-made ruling class." [P. 101]

Seldon's Plan in its entirety, then, shortens the Interregnum *and* sees to it that humanity will accept "a benevolent dictatorship of its mentally best" (p. 101). It seeks to establish a "dictatorship" led by the Second Foundation. The First Speaker is seeking to become dictator of the Galaxy.

The First Speaker is being entirely accurate when he defines the conflict in the story by saying, "We have still a society which would resent a ruling class of psychologists, and which would fear its development and fight against it" (p. 102). And I know where this puts me.

So long as I as reader understand the Seldon Plan only partially, I could sympathize with it and use it as my touchstone of who and what was good and bad in the series: pro-Plan was pro-humanity and good, anti-Plan was antihumanity and bad. But now that I have been given this information about the Plan, I, as reader, become its implacable enemy. From now on, to be pro-Plan is to be a villain and to be anti-Plan is to be a hero. When in "Search by the Foundation" the Foundation is convinced by the machinations of the Second Foundation that the Second Foundation no longer exists, when Seldon's Plan has been put back on track after the dislocations caused by its encounter with the Mule, I see triumph for the Second Foundation and disaster for humanity. When the story ends with the gloating of the First Speaker, I do not feel exaltation. I feel only frustration at not being able to punch him in the nose.

What moves me even more is the end of the preceding chapter. Suspicious that Arkady has been an unwitting agent of the Second Foundation, Dr. Darell checks her brain waves for the telltale signs of Control. He doesn't find them because she was placed under Control as an infant, though of course he cannot know that. "Never in Darell's life had an analysis proceeded so slowly, cost him so much, and when it was over, Arcadia huddled down and dared not look. Then she heard him laugh and that was information enough. She jumped up and threw herself into his opened arms. He was babbling wildly as they squeezed one another" (p. 218). And in their happy babbling they and mankind have lost. Waiting ahead is the "benevolent dictatorship of the mentally best," the "group of Psychologists ready to assume leadership," the "ready-made ruling class." "Search by the Foundation" has turned the Foundation Series unwittingly (I think) into a tragedy of the highest order, because not simply one tragic hero but all of mankind must share in it.

Having worked our way through the individual and separate stories in the Foundation Series, we must now examine the unit that is created by placing those stories together. Some of the things that unify the series are obvious from the foregoing discussions: they all take place against the same backdrop of declining Empire and Seldon Plan, of Foundations and socioeconomic-historical movements. Characters and events in earlier stories are referred to in later ones. Sometimes the characters in one story are the descendants of characters in earlier stories; i.e., Arkady is Bayta's granddaughter and Ducem Barr is Onum Barr's son. The stories span nearly four hundred years of Galactic history, and Asimov carefully lets us know when each story takes place relative to the other stories. So the stories are obviously related to one another via background, assumptions, time scheme, characters, and events, all things that we have already discussed.

They are unified in other ways, too. For one thing, all the stories make use of quotations from the Encyclopedia Galactica, 116th edition, "published in 1020 F.E. by the Encyclopedia Galactica Publishing Co., Terminus, with permission of the publishers" (to be found on the first page of text of each of these collections). The year 0 F.E. would be the year the Foundation was established on Terminus. Hari Seldon died in 1 F.E. At the other end of the series, Arkady Darell was born 362 F.E., her role in the fulfillment of the Second Foundation's plans was played in 376 F.E., and she died in 443 F.E.

Note that the edition of an Encyclopedia Galactica used was

the 116th published in 1020 F.E. This means two things, one of
which is of some importance to us as readers. First, the first edition of the encyclopedia had to have been issued well before the
end of Seldon's thousand-year Plan. Second, and far more important, from the beginning of the series we are presented with
documentary evidence that the Plan was successful. We are looking back on those events, not forward to them. The suspense is
not whether the Plan will succeed, but how. In this way, the
quotations from the Encyclopedia Galactica add a great deal to
the series' tone of inevitability. Everything will turn out all right
because it has turned out all right.

Another element that appears in all the stories and helps unify
them is the obvious one of Asimov's style. James Blish has remarked that Asimov's style is "just what is required for a story in
which history is the hero and the fate of empires is under debate" because he writes "everything with considerable weight and
solidity, turning each sentence into a proposition, a sort of lawyer's prose" (*The Issue at Hand*, p. 30). This "praise" of Asimov
has a negative effect because it makes Asimov's style sound
heavier and more massive, more "ponderous" and more "porten-
tous"—i.e., dull?—than it is. In the same passage Blish explicitly
says that Asimov's style lacks a "lightness of touch." I have already
argued in favor of a "lightness of touch" in the Foundation Series
(see p. 81). Let me give one further example here. In "The
Encyclopedists" the Anacreonian envoy Rodric "proceeded in a
slow, ceremonious manner to Cyclopedia Square, cheered on
[his] way by a properly enthusiastic crowd." What is the effect
of that "properly"? When Rodric comments, Hardin replies, "In
our short history we have had but few members of the higher
nobility visiting our poor planet. Hence, our enthusiasm." And
Asimov adds the remark, "It is certain that 'higher nobility' did
not recognize irony when he heard it" (pp. 43–44). Either this
undercurrent of light irony is too light for Blish to notice, or when
he wrote he was remembering only the passages from the Encyclopedia Galactica. The Foundation Series is fun to read at a
stylistic level, too.

It has always seemed to me that there are two basic attitudes
one can take toward language. On the one hand, it is something
to look through, like clear glass, so you can see and understand

what is being held on the other side of it. This language disappears as you read, and you become immersed in the scene or idea the language is making available to you. This is the effect sought by writers like Asimov, who emphasize clarity, lucidity, simplicity. This is the language English departments try to help students write in composition courses. On the other hand, some writers are interested in the language itself. For them it is like a stained-glass window: you look at it not for what you can see through it, but for what it is in itself. This is the language that English departments approve of in their "great writers," figurative, metaphorical, ambiguous, rich. If Asimov the science writer and science fiction writer is primarily interested in language as a device for clear communication, he can occasionally strike off passages in which the language itself becomes attractive. For example, during Seldon's trial the prosecutor asks, "Is it not obvious to anyone that the Empire is as strong as it ever was?" To which Seldon replies:

> "The appearance of strength is all about you. It would seem to last forever. However, Mr. Advocate, the rotten tree-trunk, until the very moment when the storm-blast breaks it in two, has all the appearance of might it ever had. The storm-blast whistles through the branches of the Empire even now. Listen with the ears of psychohistory, and you will hear the creaking." [P. 27]

This is fine and effective writing, and in its own way it is as clear as the other type. It is interesting that this sort of language takes the fight out of the prosecutor. His immediate reply is given, we are told, "uncertainly," and after Seldon continues in the prophetic fit for another moment or two, the prosecutor replies with "a small voice in the middle of a vast silence." He has been put down by Seldon's vision of the future and by his ability to express that vision in words. Asimov shows proper respect for the wordsmith, though he himself is not one. (Please note that I am not making a value judgment here. I am simply noting two attitudes toward language and observing that Asimov is one of those writers who—to use my image again—prefers clear glass to stained glass.)

In addition to the Encyclopedia Galactica and style, a third element shared by all the stories in the series is Asimov's technique of presenting as different from our society only those things necessary to his stories. That is, even though the stories take place in a Galactic Empire setting hundreds of thousands of years in our future, very little seems to have changed so far as social patterns and human behavior go. Men still smoke around the conference table, and young girls still write nice little essays for their classes. Oh, the cigar and cigarette ashes are disposed of in disruptors rather than ashtrays, and instead of writing themes on paper, they are dictated into transcribers, but at core everything is the same—except for the Galactic Empire, the Seldon Plan, the two Foundations, the Mule, the essentials of the series.

Nagging at the edges of some of the stories are some important differences. In "The Mule," for example, much is made of Bayta and Toran's actually going to the bother of getting married. It's such an antiquated custom, no one does it anymore. Toran's father was notorious as a ladies' man, and evidently he had never bothered to marry Toran's mother. But Asimov does not tell us what has replaced marriage and the family as institutions for raising children, and he does show us Arkady Darell growing up in a family-unit home. The question of such social changes over hundreds of thousands of years just isn't gone into.

I call this a "technique" rather than a failure in imagination because I think that Asimov, in purposely letting daily living remain the same, has made it easier for us as readers to accept the changes that are crucial to his stories. Detailed descriptions of everyday life are not relevant to the Empire-making decisions and conflicts at the core of the series. Surely, language will have changed by the time the First Galactic Empire is ready to collapse, but all Asimov's characters speak rather colloquial English. It's easier for us to understand them. Just so, it's easier for us to understand them if their social patterns and daily lives remain the same. And it's easier for us to comprehend the Empire, the Plan, the Mule, etc.

Asimov's Jewish heritage is also evident in the Foundation Series. I have earlier referred to the populace of the Foundation as a "Chosen Race," one that is portrayed by Asimov as having confidence, in the face of millions and millions of Gentiles, in its destiny as the ultimate recivilizer of the Galaxy. In "Search by the Mule" the planet Rossem, with its snowy climate, its bearded village Elders, and its sturdy agricultural economy, looked enough like Russia and its Jews—Asimov was born in Russia, don't forget—that I wrote to him about it. His reply:

> Rossem and its people *do* sound like Russian Jews—not because there is any deep purpose to that but only because the *only* culture I am acquainted with, other than General American, is East European Jewish. Consequently, if I want a non-American culture I have a tendency to slip into Jewish. Preem Palver spoke with a straightforward Jewish accent, not only for that reason, but because by making him a comic character I (successfully, I think) diverted attention from him as the First Speaker. [Personal letter, August 7, 1973]

So the fact of Jewish elements in the Foundation Series is clearly established.

In his recent history of science fiction, *Billion Year Spree,* Brian Aldiss has made a brief remark about the Foundation Series that seems to me to be both shrewd and misleading: "It is a pity that his [Asimov's] largest milestone, the Foundation trilogy, was written before SF authors were able to think of their books as books, rather than as short stories or serials. . . . Conceived as one organic whole, the Foundation Series would have undoubtedly risen to greater majesty" (p. 269). Certainly Asimov did not think of the Foundation stories as a book or as three books. Certainly things grew, changed, evolved, as he wrote. I have mentioned the way the Foundation began as an Encyclopedia Foundation, changed into a political and religious one, and then became a center for physical scientists (pp. 75–76). I have quoted Asimov's remark that "at the start I had no conception of the Second Foundation at all. It was merely a reserve in case I needed it" (p. 67). I have shown how the Second Foundation was far in the background of the first six Foundation stories, how it was merely the object of parallel searches by the Foundation and the Mule in the seventh, "The Mule," and how it figured as protagonist in the last two stories. I have also tried to show that the Seldon Plan changed from simply shortening the Interregnum to shortening the Interregnum and establishing a Second Empire ruled by the elitist Second Foundation. I think it would also be appropriate here to say that I wrote to Asimov asking him about his conception of the Second Foundation, since it disturbed me so much. Here is his reply: "I don't have a clear feeling about the Second Foundation. That would have come in the later stories when I would set about thinking about it. Each story was written without reference to what was to come, so that the Second Foundation's ambivalent nature was left as it was" (personal letter, August 7, 1973).

All of this is in support of Aldiss's shrewd remark that the Foundation Series was written at a time when science fiction authors thought of their work solely in terms of the day and not in terms of one permanent hard-cover publication. But his evaluation and interpretation of this fact, at least in the case of the Foundation Series, is open to debate and disagreement. I'm not sure that "it is a pity" that Asimov was able to write and publish the series, even if only in a limited-audience magazine. And besides, what does "conceived as one organic whole" really mean? As I read him, Asimov stopped writing stories in the series precisely because he conceived of them as an organic whole. In *Opus 100* this is part of what he says on this point:

> But there are disadvantages to a series of stories. There is, for one thing, the bugaboo of self-consistency. It is annoying to be hampered, in working out a story, by the fact that some perfectly logical development is ruled out since, three stories before, you had to make such a development impossible because of the needs of the plot of *that* story. . . .
>
> Before I could write a new Foundation story I had to sit down and reread all the preceding ones, and by the time I got to the eighth story that meant rereading 150,000 words of very complicated material. . . .
>
> Furthermore, in designing each new Foundation story, I found I had to work within an increasingly constricted area, with progressively fewer and fewer degrees of freedom. I was forced to seize whatever way I could find without worrying about how difficult I might make the next story. Then, when I came to the next story, those difficulties arose and beat me over the head. . . .
>
> The eighth story had carried me only one-third of the way

through the original plan of describing one thousand years of future history. However, to write a ninth story meant re-reading the first eight. . . . [P. 221]

I fail to see the difference between Asimov's concern for "self-consistency" and Aldiss's "conceived as an organic whole." Perhaps the difference is merely temporal; but can't authorial conception extend over a period of months and years? It is the unity of the result that is at issue, not the length of the process of conception. *King Lear* is an organic whole whether Shakespeare conceived and wrote it in five years or five days. Perhaps something that grows over a period of time from a tiny seed is more organically whole than something conceived instantly and in its entirety.

Permit me briefly to play a game with the Foundation Series. Let's pretend that the series is a novel, and let's analyze some of the most rudimentary elements in it. The central character would be Hari Seldon (or "history," depending on where you want to put your emphasis, the person or the thing personified). The initial situation is Galactic Empire, capital on Trantor, humans-only Galaxy, etc., etc. The complication—the problem Seldon must solve—is the imminent collapse of the Empire followed by 30,000 years of human suffering and misery before the rise of the Second Empire. His solution is the Seldon Plan (including the Foundation on Terminus, the Second Foundation at Star's End, etc.), and the conflict is the series of episodes—stories—involved in the working out of this Plan over a period of a thousand years. The conflict intensifies with the appearance of the Mule, which throws the Plan almost completely off, and (so far as I am concerned) it changes radically with the redefinition of the Plan by the role Asimov decides to have the Second Foundation play. We participate in only the first four hundred years of the thousand-year Plan, but the successful conclusion is made clear by the very existence of the Encyclopedia Galactica, published in 1020 F.E. Viewed this way, the unity of the Foundation Series is clear.

What is lacking in the series as it stands? We know nothing of the first three hundred years of the history of the Second Foundation. Considering its location, there must be interesting stories to tell of it during the Fall of the Empire. And we know nothing of the last six hundred years of either Foundation. Since (in my eyes, at any event) the Seldon Plan and the Second Foundation have been compromised in the chapter "Seldon's Plan" from "Search by the Foundation," I would expect—hope—to see how the Foundation eventually defeats the Second Foundation and fulfills its sense of destiny. Perhaps the Second Empire develops earlier as a result of the Foundation–Second Foundation struggle in much the same way as man reached the moon more quickly as a result of the competition between the United States and the Soviet Union. Perhaps there is a Third Foundation Seldon never mentioned which co-ordinates the struggle between the two. And besides the fact that it produced the 116th edition of the Encyclopedia Galactica, we know nothing about the nature of the Second Empire. Is it Foundation- or Second Foundation-oriented? And perhaps, now that Asimov would be writing for an editor other than Campbell, aliens could be introduced. *That* would be a whole new ball game.

The point is that the Foundation Series was organically conceived and that it is unified as far as it goes. But it is not yet a complete work.

I must take up one other subject before finishing this chapter: the theme of the series. More of the series can be organized around one theme than any other, and that is the role of the individual human being in history. Put differently, it is the old, old question of free will versus predestination. Asimov clearly demonstrates in a variety of ways that the individual counts for nothing as a causal factor in historical movements. As Ducem Barr said of Bel Riose's struggle with the Foundation, "There is not a conceivable combination of events that does not result in the Foundation winning. It was inevitable; whatever Riose did, whatever we did" (p. 77). History is inevitable, predestined. The individual is out of it.

On the surface there appear to be at least two exceptions to this, Hari Seldon himself and the Mule. But the Mule had to be made a mutant in order to accomplish what he did in the face of the sweep of history. An ordinary—or even extraordinary—normal human being (like Bel Riose) could do nothing. And what actually does Hari Seldon do other than foresee events? To what extent can he be said to *control* them? Until the Second Foundation steps in to return history to the course foreseen by Seldon, the Plan is descriptive rather than causal. And even then, the Second Foundation seeks to return the course of events to Seldon's Plan; it does not seek to implement that Plan. The Plan is implemented as a result of the normal course of history. The theme from Salvor Hardin on has been "Hands off the Plan, and everything will be O.K." Neither Hari Seldon nor the Mule is a human being who influences greatly the broad sweep of history.

In fact, one comes out of it all wondering on what grounds Seldon foresaw a 30,000-year Interregnum. Once the Foundation is placed on Terminus—and Seldon even foresaw the great probability of that—everything else but the Mule was inevitable. Once again: The major theme of the Foundation Series is the insignificance of the individual human being in the broad movements of history.

I have found it necessary to spend as much time as I have on the Foundation Series because it is a pivotal group of stories in two different contexts. It is pivotal in the history of science fiction. As Donald Wollheim has pointed out, "The stories published before Foundation belong to the old line, the stories published after belong to 'modern' science fiction" (*The Universe Makers*, p. 37). My analysis tends to show that the Foundation Series was a reaction against action-adventure for its own sake, a substitution of nonviolence for violence, a turning from activity to the decisions to be made before activity. Asimov's Foundation Series demonstrated that science fiction could be about something other than vigorous physical activity and violence. In Asimov's particular case he made it about politics. Other writers have since chosen biology or anthropology or linguistics or religion. The Foundation Series enriched science fiction by opening up whole new areas of treatment and subject matter.

More importantly for *The Science Fiction of Isaac Asimov* the Foundation Series established and solidified Asimov's position as a front-rank, top-notch writer of science fiction—along with "Nightfall" and the Robot Stories, of course. Despite its flaws— and I have not ignored them or tiptoed carefully around them—I think the Foundation Series is the best thing Asimov has done.

Asimov's Novels

Pebble in the Sky (1950)
The Stars Like Dust (1951)
The Currents of Space (1952)
David Starr, Space Ranger (1952)
Lucky Starr and the Pirates of the Asteroids (1953)
Lucky Starr and the Oceans of Venus (1954)
The Caves of Steel (1954)
The End of Eternity (1955)
Lucky Starr and the Big Sun of Mercury (1956)
Lucky Starr and the Moons of Jupiter (1957)
The Naked Sun (1957)
Lucky Starr and the Rings of Saturn (1958)
The Death Dealers (1958)   Not science fiction
Fantastic Voyage (1966)   A novelization, not a
   novel
The Gods Themselves (1972)   Hugo and Nebula
   Award winner

CHAPTER FIVE

Asimov's Novels I

The United States entered World War II with horse-drawn artillery and double-winged airplanes. It came out with radar, jet planes, and the atomic bomb. A populace that had had to save its tin cans and tinfoil suddenly found itself with automobiles, airliners, and television. The impact of science and technology on the American way of life had become obvious and bewildering. One of the results of that impact was the burgeoning of science fiction after World War II.

The key year was 1950. The demand for science fiction had become so great that large-sized pulp magazines like *Wonder Story Annual* and *Fantastic Story Quarterly* reprinted old stories for the new audience. Two new digest-sized magazines, *Fantasy and Science Fiction* and *Galaxy,* introduced spectacular new writers like Alfred Bester. And the large publishing houses like Doubleday decided to issue hard-cover editions of science fiction novels and collections. Asimov's first published book, *Pebble in the Sky* (1950), was among Doubleday's first science fiction novels.

The history of *Pebble in the Sky* is an interesting one, and Asimov tells it in some detail in *The Early Asimov* (pp. 499–500, 560–63). Let me give its essentials. In the late forties Asimov was becoming restless under Campbell. For one thing, from 1943 through 1949, he had published fifteen stories, all of them in *Astounding,* and he had begun to have nagging self-doubts about being a "one-editor author." For another, Asimov has always been oriented toward hard science, and he disagreed with some of Campbell's editorial policies. For example, in thinking about "Search by the Foundation," I began to wonder if the mental powers of the Second Foundation might be related to "Dianetics," one of Campbell's enthusiasms at the time, and so I asked Asimov about it. After denying the connection, he went on to explain, "I was strongly opposed to Dianetics and to other enthusiasms which John Campbell worked up at about this time, and the decline in the number of my appearances in *Astounding* after the appearance of Dianetics had my unhappiness with the pseudo-scientific flavor of the magazine as one of its causes" (personal letter, August 7, 1973).

There may also have been working—though I have no direct evidence for this—the "Maxwell Perkins syndrome." Thomas Wolfe left his editor at Scribner's, Maxwell Perkins, because some critics were saying that Perkins was as responsible for Wolfe's novels as Wolfe was. Wolfe felt he had to prove he was his own man. Perhaps Asimov's fear that he was a "one-editor author" was related to this. After all, hadn't Campbell given him the Emerson quotation and the basic situation for "Nightfall"? Hadn't Campbell been at least as responsible for the Three Laws of Robotics as Asimov? Hadn't Campbell persuaded Asimov to do a Foundation *series* instead of one story? Hadn't Campbell's hardheadedness on human-alien relationships led to Asimov's celebrated humans-only Galaxy? Hadn't Campbell talked Asimov into "the religiously-disguised technology of the second Salvor Hardin story . . . over some considerable objection on my [Asimov's] part"? Could Asimov write successful science fiction on his own without Campbell?

In 1947 Sam Merwin, Jr., then editor of *Startling Stories*, told Asimov that that magazine intended to follow *Astounding*'s lead and publish some hard-science stories. Merwin then asked Asimov to write a forty-thousand-word "short novel" for *Startling*. As a result, Asimov spent the summer of 1947 doing the research for his doctoral dissertation and writing a short novel called at that time "Grow Old with Me."* After approving part of the final

* In a footnote, Asimov remarks, "This was inspired by Robert Browning's poem *Rabbi Ben Ezra* and was a misquotation—which shows you the level of my culture. The first line of the poem is 'Grow old along with me.'" Actually, "along" is in the line for the poet's purpose of euphony. For a prose writer who emphasizes clarity it is redundant: what is the difference in meaning between "with" and "along

draft in September, Merwin rejected the story in October on the grounds that hard science was to remain out at *Startling* after all, and to be acceptable "Grow Old with Me" would have to be entirely rewritten as an adventure story. Asimov tells us he "seized the manuscript and stalked out of the office . . . in an obvious rage."

The reasons for his anger are not far to seek. Asimov had invested considerable time and effort in the story that summer and fall. He had done so at Merwin's request. Campbell hadn't turned down one of his stories in more than five years. And this brings us to the crux of the matter. He had taken Merwin's request as a fairly safe opportunity to prove to himself that he was not a "one-editor author"—and he had bombed. He tells us "the rejection . . . sufficiently disheartened and humiliated me so that I withdrew from writing for nearly a year."

Asimov did take the story to Campbell, who also rejected it, but "he told me enough things wrong with the story to make me feel that perhaps Merwin had not been so arbitrary in rejecting it." Unfortunately, Asimov did not in this instance write down any of the criticisms Campbell made and he no longer remembers any (except for the minor one that its length demanded that it be printed as a two-part serial and it had no natural breaks in it).

So, disgusted, Asimov stuck the story in a drawer.

Re-enter, early in 1949, Frederick Pohl. Doubleday had decided to publish some hard-cover science fiction, and one of their editors, Walter I. Bradbury, approached Asimov about "The Mule." Asimov didn't take the matter seriously and let it drop. But Frederick Pohl, Asimov's agent now for a second brief period, convinced him to let Bradbury see "Grow Old with Me"— despite Asimov's protests that the story was "lousy" and "no good." Bradbury liked it well enough to pay Asimov an advance of $250 to expand it from forty to seventy thousand words. Asimov spent April and May of 1949 on the revision, but again he remembers no details of what he changed and added. He thinks it is practically a new novel, retaining only Joseph Schwartz and the Judeo-Roman background. He retitled it *Pebble in the Sky,* and on May 29 Doubleday accepted it for publication.

---

with"? Asimov's memory had simply canceled out a word that was useless according to the way he used language.

Frederick Pohl had encouraged the early Asimov by buying several of his stories when he was first breaking into the magazines, but Asimov feels that Campbell's criticisms were more helpful than Pohl's acceptances. Be that as it may, Asimov credits Pohl with getting him started in hard covers because of his role in the evolution of the twice-rejected "Grow Old with Me" into the published *Pebble in the Sky*. At two crucial periods in Asimov's career, Pohl was there, and he certainly deserves a great deal of credit for the development of Asimov the science fiction writer.

I do not think that the importance of the publication of *Pebble in the Sky* to Asimov's career and subsequent development can be overemphasized. In the eleven years before it, the years of "Nightfall," the Robot Stories, and the Foundation Series, he had earned $7,821.75 through writing. Eight years after it, he is earning so much more writing than teaching that he can quit teaching and become a full-time free-lance writer. If there is one key turning point in Asimov's career (aside from getting that first story published, of course), it is the publication of *Pebble in the Sky* and its opening up of the hard-cover book market.

That publication also marks the beginning of what I have termed the third period in his science fiction career. I decided to mark the end of this period with the publication of *The Naked Sun* in 1957 because that is one of Asimov's most famous and widely read novels and because it was in 1957 that he decided to leave teaching for writing. In 1958 the break was actually made, and also in 1958 he published the last of the Lucky Starr juvenile novels as well as his straight mystery novel, *The Death Dealers*. Only two of his fifteen novels, *Fantastic Voyage* (1966) and *The Gods Themselves* (1972), were published outside this period.

In the balance of this chapter and in the following chapter I want to examine in some detail all of Asimov's novels except *The Death Dealers* (because it is a mystery, not a science fiction novel), *Fantastic Voyage* (because it is a novelization of someone else's movie script and in that sense he is not to be held responsible for it), and *The Gods Themselves* (because it belongs in a later chapter, "The Most Recent Asimov"). With minor exceptions, which are made for obvious reasons, I want to take them up in chronological order. That is, I will begin with the three

early novels that are related to one another by their backgrounds
and by their having eventually been printed together in one volume as *Triangle* (1961): *Pebble in the Sky* (1950), *The Stars
Like Dust* (1951), and *The Currents of Space* (1952). Then I
want to move to *The End of Eternity* (1955) and the six Lucky
Starr juveniles published between 1952 and 1958. I will finish by
examining the two Robot Novels, *The Caves of Steel* (1954) and
The Naked Sun (1957).

Pebble in the Sky (1950)

Where the Foundation Series had been set against a background
of an old and declining Galactic Empire, *Pebble in the Sky* is set
in a young and healthy one. Hari Seldon established the Foundation in the 12,068th year of the Galactic Era, while the action in
Pebble takes place in 827 G.E. How far this is in the future of
A.D. 1950 is not made clear. At one point, one character remarks,
"The worlds up there have been existing all history long as far as
I know," and when he is asked, "But how long is that?" he replies, "Thousands of years, I suppose. Fifty thousand, a hundred—
I can't say" (p. 120). Elsewhere a character is made to think that
if he could prove that Earth was the original single-planet home
of mankind, "his reputation would be assured on every inhabited
planet of the Milky Way, on every planet that man had set foot
through the hundreds of thousands of years of expansion through
space" (p. 28). That this Galactic Empire is the same in both
Pebble and the Foundation Series is made clear not only from the
G.E. dating system but also by references such as the one to "the
Emperor's court at Trantor" (p. 24). Therefore, *Pebble in the Sky*
is laid in the same imaginary space-time continuum as the Foundation Series, despite certain minor discrepancies like there being 200 million worlds in *Pebble's* Empire and only 25 million
in that of the Foundation Series.

Except for two very brief opening scenes laid in contemporary
Chicago, the setting of the novel is the Earth of that far-distant
future. Large areas of that Earth are radioactive and therefore
"forbidden." Apparently in the far-distant past (i.e., our immediate future) an atomic war had been waged, though it is not clear
how a civilization that had destroyed itself via atomic warfare

could also spread humanity throughout the Galaxy. When I asked Asimov about this point, his reply was,

> I have no answer as to how a half-dead radioactive Earth could have colonized the Galaxy. I used to worry about it and made up my mind that if I were questioned, I would say that interstellar travel had come shortly before the all-out thermonuclear war and that the imminence of war hastened the colonizing ventures. As it happens, though, you are the first to ask. [Personal letter, September 26, 1973]

The extent of the forbidden areas has cut down on the amount of habitable land, and as a result a curious custom called the Sixty has evolved. In order to make room for the children of the next generation, people at sixty voluntarily submit themselves for euthanasia. As one character explains it, "It *must* be that way. Other worlds won't take us, and we must make room for the children some way" (p. 122). The reason the other worlds won't take them is that the radiation on Earth is popularly (among the other worlds of the Galaxy) thought to have caused Earthmen to be more disease-ridden than men elsewhere. They aren't safe to be around.

One would think, though, that sometime during the process of discovering 200 million habitable worlds, someone could have set aside one for Earthmen to emigrate to. In fact, this very solution to Earth's problem is suggested at the end of *The Currents of Space*, which, as we shall see, also refers to a far-future radioactive Earth. The planet Florina is being evacuated, and the suggestion is made, "Why can't we do for Earth what we're doing for Florina? . . . The Galaxy is big" (p. 216). This implies that there must be a planet for Earthmen somewhere. But the lead character responds, "No. . . . It's a different case. . . . We of Earth know that Earth was the original planet of the human race. . . . It's a planet that can't be abandoned; it *mustn't* be abandoned."

Though I find the reason given for the nonmigration more convincing in *Currents* than I do in *Pebble*, I still don't really believe in the Sixty. On an atomic-war-ravaged future Earth whose population is imprisoned by a lack of interstellar travel, the Sixty is perhaps possible. But I do not believe that everyone would volunteer to die at sixty if *any* alternative were available. For example, why couldn't all sixty-year-olds retire to another Earth-type planet? They could do so proudly, knowing that they had served their planet and continuing to their deaths to consider themselves Earthmen. No, for me the Sixty cannot exist in a Galactic Empire. Asimov is trying to give us two different futures: the cautionary tale of post-atomic-war horrors and the optimistic tale of unlimited human expansion throughout the Galaxy, and it seems to me that the two are mutually exclusive.

Asimov himself points out that the political situation in *Pebble* is patterned after that of Judea under the Romans (*The Early Asimov*, p. 143). The Galactic Empire is the Roman Empire. Trantor is Rome. Earth is Judea. The Emperor's representative has the title of Procurator of Earth. The garrison is manned by bored professional soldiers who are waiting to be transferred to a more attractive planet, etc., etc. Earthmen have a sense of their uniqueness: all humanity originated on Earth. And a sense of their destiny: one day Earth will rule the Empire. (Three uprisings have already been crushed.) "They face two hundred million worlds, each one singly stronger than they, and they are confident. Can they really be so firm in their faith in some Destiny or supernatural Force?" (p. 68). The Judea-under-the-Romans echoes are even louder in a remark made during a hearing before the Procurator: "I find no fault in this man" (p. 213). (The referent of "this man" is the *villain* of the story.)

Basically, *Pebble in the Sky* is about the discovery and thwarting of a plot by certain overly ambitious Earthmen to take over the Galaxy. The weapon to be used is germ warfare. Earth's scientists had developed an especially virulent strain of "Common, or Radiation, Fever," to which Earthmen were immune. Rockets carrying the virus were to be launched simultaneously from a single building near St. Louis, and enough of the Empire's 200 million worlds were to be infected that a plague would sweep across all humanity, leaving the disease-ridden Galaxy open for conquest by Earth.

Personally I love a good story in which a threat to the universe is staved off by the heroic actions of one stalwart individual. Such stories form the backbone of action-adventure science fiction. But the threat to the universe must be a convincing—or at least semiplausible—one, and I don't find this germ warfare threat all that convincing.

For one thing, there is no good reason why all the rockets had to be launched simultaneously, at zero hour (except, of course, for the excellent dramatic reason that a definite deadline that must be beaten makes for more exciting reading). The great and varied distances to be traversed meant that the rockets would not arrive all at the same moment anyhow. Why not send one rocket today, another day after tomorrow, several next week, timing the launches so that they would arrive at their targets all at once? Evidently, there was no orbital surveillance of Earth by the Empire, as the huge five-sided building outside St. Louis would have been easily spotted if there had been. And one shouldn't forget that the "rockets" would be making the greater parts of their trips through hyperspace, where they would be impossible to detect and trace. Granting the development of a control that would make this possible, surely the rockets could be brought out of hyperspace at varying distances from their targets so that simultaneous *attack* rather than *launch* could be achieved.

One also wonders how many rockets could be sent out against 200 million worlds from one building. Granted that the plot depended on the spread of the disease from world to world, still what percentage of worlds would have to be infected for the plan to work? Even 1 per cent of 200 million is, after all, 2 million rockets. From one building? All at once? Besides, space makes a much better quarantining barrier than mountain ranges, rivers, or politically decreed imaginary lines. With the superior communications implied in a Galactic Empire, wouldn't an effective quarantine be relatively easy to establish?

For at least these reasons, the threat of germ warfare does not convince as a plausible and imminent danger to the Galaxy. As with the radioactive Earth which causes the Sixty, I think this germ warfare element came out of a set of assumptions about the present and the immediate future that are incompatible with a Galactic Empire setting. The Sixty and germ warfare belong to an isolated Earth without interstellar travel, not to the Empire. Asimov has not succeeded in bringing together the near future and the far future.

The threat to the universe is, then, contrived. But what about the removal of that threat, the solving of the problem in the story? Here it is necessary to look first at the central character—or characters. For once again—and this time, I suspect, inadvertently— Asimov is trying something a bit different. He has taken the standard role performed by the hero of an action-adventure story and he has divided that role between two different characters. The actual problem-solver is Joseph Schwartz, a sixty-two-year-old Earthman from the twentieth century who has been propelled into the future by a freak accident and who finds himself saving the Galaxy. (Shades of Edmond Hamilton in stories like *The Star Kings* and *The City at World's End!*)

But once Asimov had this elderly Schwartz in that future civilization, he evidently found that he couldn't construct a novel with Schwartz as its action-adventure hero. Instead, Bel Arvardan, native of Baronn (Sirius Sector), archaeologist, citizen of the Empire, young, handsome, intelligent, decisive—Bel Arvardan is made the repository of the reader's hopes for a successful conclusion to the story. He speaks on equal terms with the Procurator, he pushes around the soldiers of the Empire, he becomes convinced of the reality of the danger to the Galaxy and promises to do what he can to allay it. Pola Shekt, beautiful daughter of the brilliant Earth scientist, Dr. Shekt, continually turns to him for comfort, reassurance, help—and we turn with her. Arvardan comes to dominate the novel as any good hero should, except that he fails in his attempts to convince the Procurator of the seriousness of the plot, and in the climactic scene he loses his temper, is rendered unconscious, and so misses the passing of the deadline. Heroes don't lose emotional control of themselves, at least not Asimov's heroes! It didn't happen to Warren Moore in Asimov's first published story, "Marooned Off Vesta." It didn't happen to Gregory Powell in the Robot Stories, and it only happened once to Susan Calvin, in "Liar!" Hari Seldon, Salvor Hardin, and Hober Mallow were always in control of themselves and of events. No, emotional reactions cloud the reason and make problem-solving difficult, as we can clearly see in the case of Bel Arvardan. So Pola's hopes and our own expectations are dashed at the end of *Pebble in the Sky*.

But once again Asimov has a rabbit (this time named Schwartz) safely hidden away in his hat. While Arvardan and the

Procurator and Pola and Dr. Shekt and practically everybody else in the novel are sitting around discussing the situation and getting Arvardan angry, Joseph Schwartz goes and gets in an airplane and bombs the building from which the rockets were to be launched. Interestingly and typically, Asimov keeps us listening to the useless conversation instead of letting us participate in Schwartz's heroics. The habits of the Foundation Series die hard. But in the Foundation Series the conversations were the action, and here the conversation is irrelevant to the story. I think Asimov was carried into that climactic scene by the momentum of Arvardan-as-hero and by the temperamentally congenial habit of presenting significant conversation rather than irrelevant action. Unfortunately, in this particular case, the conversation is irrelevant and the missed action is significant.

What is gained is the good storytelling effect of plunging the reader into despair: the deadline has passed and Arvardan has failed. But *voilà!* Joseph Schwartz has succeeded. As with Salvor Hardin in "The Encyclopedists" Schwartz has worked out a plan and put it into effect, all unbeknownst to us poor readers. And once again the ending has that *deus ex machina* feeling. So Joseph Schwartz, who had started out as our lead character and then faded into the background as Arvardan's more forceful (and conventional) personality took control, reasserts himself and saves the Galaxy.

Asimov has given Schwartz the problem-solving role of the central character, and he has given Arvardan the central character's ability to inspire confidence on the part of comrade and reader. One effect of this (besides the shock of switching heroes at the end) is to diffuse the unity of the story. Two characters are used to do what clearly one could have done: a younger Schwartz could have saved the Galaxy and won the girl. Here the heroics go to one and the girl to another. Dammit, when you've saved the Galaxy, you're supposed to get a girl. You've earned one. It's—it's traditional. It's the way things are. And there's that Asimov writing what sounds in summary like an action-adventure story but isn't really. The point is that *Pebble in the Sky* continues to show us an Asimov rebelling against—or at least ignoring—the conventions of an action-adventure genre.

His insistence on doing this accounts in large measure for his influence in the field.

A third effect of his separation of the role of central character
into two different characters is that it makes the story more complex, less a good guy versus the forces of evil. In a standard
action-adventure story one always knew that Captain Future was
the hero and that Crag, Ortho, and the rest were simply extensions of the good guy. But here, Schwartz is himself, an individual
with his own personality and problems. And so is Arvardan. And
Pola. And Dr. Shekt. They are each individuals trying in their
own sometimes muddled ways to do what each thinks best. No
one really organizes or directs their efforts. No one so to speak
symbolically sums them up as representatives of good. They are
what they are.

I have so far mentioned several things in the carpentering of
this novel which strike me as being rather roughhewn. The Sixty
and the germ warfare belong to an immediate-future cautionary
tale rather than an expansive Empire story such as this. The threat
against the universe—attacking 200 million worlds from a garage
in St. Louis—is not convincing. Substituting Arvardan for
Schwartz through much of the novel obscures Schwartz's role as
the hero of the story. There remain one or two more roughnesses
of this sort that need to be pointed out.

For one thing, the device by which Asimov removes Joseph
Schwartz from the twentieth century and deposits him on the
radioactive Earth of the Galactic Empire hundreds of thousands
of years in our future is, simply put, unbelievable. Now I know
that believability is really a property of the reader and not of an
event in the story, and that for the sake of the story some people
will accept anything. As Somerset Maugham once remarked,
"Plausibility is what you can get your readers to swallow." Still,
some people's throats are bigger than others, and this particular
time-travel gimmick sticks in mine.

At the Institute for Nuclear Research in Chicago a chemist is
making an electrolytic copper determination when his platinum
crucible of crude uranium begins to show a corona. A fellow
chemist dashes the offending material to the floor, where there is
"the deadly hiss of molten metal." Neither can figure out what
caused the uranium to melt, and one says, "It was below the

critical mass. Or, at least, below the critical masses we think we know. Yet uranium melts at about 1800 degrees centigrade, and nuclear phenomena are not so well known that we can afford to talk too glibly" (p. 11). Appropriately enough for a novel to be set on a radioactive Earth, the causal agent in the time travel is the little-understood and mysterious uranium.

What they eventually notice is that the inexplicably active little crucible of uranium had sent out a ray of some sort which drilled first tiny and then larger and larger holes in things as it radiated outward. "A beam expanding in a straight line could travel several miles before the Earth's curvature made the surface fall away from it sufficiently to prevent further damage, and then it would be ten feet across. After that, flashing emptily into space, expanding and weakening, a queer strain in the fabric of the cosmos" (pp. 12–13). Schwartz was standing in the path of this ray and was moved through time by it. The ray is supposed to have worked instantaneously: the initial chapter is even called "Between One Footstep and the Next." All matter—inorganic (the holes in the walls, part of a Raggedy Ann doll) and organic (Schwartz)—is affected. This must include the atmosphere. Yet no thunderclap is heard as the suddenly vacated space is filled. A minor matter, I suppose. More importantly, Schwartz is supposed to be walking along a suburban street with homes all around him. How reasonable is it that only a couple of tiny holes, part of a Raggedy Ann doll, all of Schwartz, and presumably a miles-long conical section of air was transferred in time— and no parts of any nearby buildings? Sorry, but I can't buy this time-travel gimmick.

Another difficulty arises when, in the future now, Schwartz is taken in by a husband and wife, Arbin and Loa, who are hiding her father, Grew, from the Sixty. They must decide what to do with Schwartz, and what they decide is so wildly implausible, so much done for the sake of the plot than because it's what normal people would normally do, that all I need do is quote the passage for its jury-rigged quality to become evident. Grew is speaking:

> "It so happens that the Institute for Nuclear Research has developed an instrument that is supposed to make it easier

for people to learn. There was a full-page spread in the
Week-end Supplement. And they want volunteers. Take this
man. Let him be a volunteer."

Arbin shook his head firmly. "You're mad. I couldn't do
anything like that, Grew. They'll ask for his registration number first thing. It's only inviting investigation to have things
in improper order, and then they'll find out about you."

"No, they won't. It so happens you're all wrong, Arbin.
The reason the Institute wants volunteers is that the machine
is still experimental. It's probably killed a few people, so
I'm sure they won't ask questions. And if the stranger dies,
he'll probably be no worse off than he is now." [P. 25]

For one thing, there is no way this kind of information is going
to get printed in a newspaper. It's too much like running an ad,
"Wanted: Volunteers for high-risk, illegal experiment. No questions asked." It is an extremely transparent device for getting
Schwartz treated with the "instrument." (It is called a Synapsifier
and it was invented by Dr. Shekt.) For another thing, as we learn
eventually, Dr. Shekt has absolutely no need for volunteers as he
has already been treating successfully selected Earth scientists
whose increased mental abilities have been put to use developing the strain of virus and the hardware necessary for Earth's
attack on the Empire. Note, too, that no one gives any thought to
asking Schwartz about it. Finally, no motive is ever given for
Shekt's treatment of Schwartz. It is incomprehensible why a man
under close scrutiny by the plotters because they feared he might
give them away by some rash action would practically on impulse
treat the unknown Schwartz. He does it because if he didn't there
would be no story. Schwartz's heightened mental abilities are
crucial to the end of the story. With them, he, Arvardan, Pola,
and Dr. Shekt are able to escape imprisonment so they can have
their useless meeting with the Procurator, and with them he can
manipulate a pilot into bombing that key building near St. Louis.
The whole business of getting Schwartz synapsified is never made
plausible.

One of the more interesting things in all three novels in *Triangle* is that Asimov has included in each of them at least one
character whose job it is to second-guess Asimov's own plotting.

We must always remember that stories are artifacts, and that just because A happens on page 75 doesn't mean that B couldn't have happened if the author had so decided. Asimov uses Balkis, the Secretary to the High Minister on Earth and the villain in the story (i.e., the leader of the plot against the Empire) to construct alternate story lines to the one Asimov has decided on. In so doing, Balkis looks at Asimov's plot and criticizes it.

For example, he, too, is bothered by Schwartz's synapsification and Shekt's motivation for performing it: "It is not *what* Shekt has done, but *why* he has done so. Note that there exists a coincidence about the matter, one of a considerable series of subsequent coincidences. The Procurator of Earth had visited Shekt that same day" (p. 103). Balkis attempts to explain both Shekt's reason for using the Synapsifier on Schwartz and the coincidence of the Procurator's visit that same day by conjuring up an Imperial counterplot with Schwartz an Imperial agent treated by Shekt at the command of the Procurator. This is not the plot Asimov has decided to use, but it does explain two difficulties with Asimov's plot that he himself leaves unexplained. As *Pebble* stands, no reason is given for Schwartz's treatment, and the coincidence of the Procurator's visit the same day remains a coincidence. Balkis's version is a better one—in the sense of having fewer loose ends—than Asimov's.

Balkis continues by explaining another coincidence. In a panic, Schwartz had briefly fled Shekt's laboratory. Pola had gone after him and had by chance met Bel Arvardan for the first time. He then helped her locate Schwartz. Balkis explains:

> "I think that Schwartz is the . . . agent on Earth, that Shekt is the contact man with the . . . traitors among us, and that Arvardan is the contact man with the Empire. Observe the skill with which the meeting between Schwartz and Arvardan was arranged. Schwartz is allowed to escape, and after an appropriate interval his nurse—Shekt's daughter by a not-too-surprising additional coincidence—is out after him. . . .
>
> "Follow it closely now. Schwartz and Arvardan meet first in a Foodomat. They are, apparently, unaware of each other's existence. It is a preliminary meeting, designed,

simply, to indicate that all has gone well so far and that the
next step may be taken. . . .

"Then Schwartz leaves; a few minutes later Arvardan
leaves and the Shekt girl meets him. It is stop-watch timing.
Together, . . . they head for the Dunham department store,
and now all three are together. Where else but a department
store? It is an ideal meeting place. It has a secrecy no cave
in the mountains could duplicate. Too open to be suspected.
Too crowded to be stalked." [Pp. 106–7]

The events have a meaning in Balkis's version. In Asimov all
of the above *is* simply coincidence arranged by the storyteller so
that Arvardan and Pola can meet for the first time under dramatic circumstances and Arvardan can begin to mix with the
other characters in the story. Again, Balkis, in analyzing Asimov's
story line, has found a sore spot.

If we watch carefully the lines of thought of characters like
Balkis, we can participate in Asimov's own thought processes as
he constructs a plot. Dominant is the necessity to tie things together and render plausible the plot-required activity. And like
any one of us worrying an aching tooth with our tongues, Asimov
worries at plot weaknesses with his speculating characters. He—
and therefore they—must try to find ways to explain seemingly
implausible or merely coincidental events. I take constructions
like Balkis's to be Asimov's "second thoughts," so to speak, on
plotting a story, and I think that often—as in the present case—
these "second thoughts" result in more tightly woven stories:
Balkis's version of the events in *Pebble in the Sky* is more inherently self-sufficient and self-explanatory than Asimov's. If it
weren't for the fact that *Pebble* is already a revision and expansion of the earlier "Grow Old with Me," I would take this as a
further example of how Asimov's fiction could more often use
rethinking and rewriting. As James Gunn likes to remark, "Stories
are not written. They are rewritten."

One further observation along these lines. Personally, I have
never met a Balkis-like character in my whole life, that is, a person who, on the basis of a few bits of flimsy information, constructs elaborate spider webs of explanation. My experience
suggests that such characters are purely fictional constructs, with

no counterparts in real life. Or, to put it more exactly, with only one counterpart in real life: the creative writer. It is the creative writer who takes something as ephemeral as the expression on a passerby's face and constructs an elaborate explanation of it, an elaborate explanation called a short story or a novel. Just as the creative writer looks at the people and events around him and tries to make some sense out of them in his fiction, so characters like Balkis look at the people and events around them and try to arrange them into a reasonable pattern. Balkis is a surrogate of Isaac Asimov. And Asimov loves to put such characters in his stories, especially in his novels. They give him a chance to discuss and rework his own plots, and they furnish the reader with possible explanations of events. We will encounter this type of character again in our perambulations through Asimov's works.

I think that the presence of a plotting character in *Pebble in the Sky*—and, yes, I meant "plotting" as a pun—makes it a more interesting novel. It is one of the strong points in it. You might remember that I was lukewarm on the splitting of the central character into two characters, Schwartz and Arvardan. Most of the rest of what I have said has been negative. I consider the Sixty, the time-travel device by which Schwartz was brought into the future, the unexplained synapsification of Schwartz by Shekt, and the germ warfare plot against the Empire to be major flaws in the novel. All of these things have to do with story construction, with craftsmanship.

Yet in a sense they are minor points. The novel is not finally a cautionary tale about how overpopulation can lead to the necessity for euthanasia, nor is it a cautionary tale about the horrors to follow an atomic war, nor is it about germ warfare, or time travel, or technological enhancement of human intelligence. All these things are furniture, trappings in a story about something else. The job of an automobile is to get you from one place to another. One tire may be dangerously worn, the engine may not be exactly in tune, the windshield wipers may need replacing because they smear instead of wipe dry, and the radio may not work, but if it gets you from one place to another, it has fulfilled the function for which it was made. In criticizing *Pebble in the Sky* so far, I have been speaking about tires and windshield wipers.

Pebble in the Sky is a successful novel because its message, its theme, comes through loud and clear and convincingly. A black student of mine, a confirmed Asimov fan, once told me that he had read *Pebble* five times so far, would continue to read it now and again as the mood struck him, and considered it Asimov's best novel. The novel clearly spoke to him, said things that were important to him, that moved him. Even though the people of the Earth and the people of the Empire are theoretically of the same race, having had common origins in the far-distant past, still the theme of the novel is racial prejudice.

The Emperor's representative on Earth, the Procurator, views the planet this way: "It is more or less a pigpen of a world, or a horrible hole of a world, or a cesspool of a world, or almost any other particularly derogative adjective you care to use" (p. 31). The prejudice is externalized, made physical and tangible, in the elaborate self-imposed quarantine by the citizens of the Empire while on Earth. "The garrison was a prison. There were the radiation-proof barracks, and the filtered atmosphere, free of radioactive dust. There was the lead-impregnated clothing, cold and heavy, which could not be removed without grave risk" (p. 91). A citizen of the Empire who goes forth upon the Earth must also dose himself with a protective drug, metaboline, which the Procurator calls "a true symbol" of the difference between Earthmen and Empire-men: "its function is to heighten all metabolic processes while I sit here immersed in the radioactive cloud that surrounds me and which you [Earthmen] are not even aware of" (p. 42). The people of Earth are assumed to be the carriers of certain diseases to which they are immune but which would kill any outsider. The great fear among outsiders is of "Radiation Fever" or "Common Fever," so called because it was supposed to be caught by and from people who had been in or near the huge zones of radioactivity, the forbidden areas. Besides, Earth was the only radioactive inhabited world in the Galaxy. In this variety of physical, semisymbolic ways, the Earth and the Empire are separated from one another.

These barriers made the normal mixture of Earthmen and Outsiders impossible. And yet the barriers existed almost solely in the minds of the Outsiders. The background radiation on Earth outside the forbidden areas was only slightly higher than on many other planets in the Galaxy, certainly not high enough to require lead-impregnated clothing, elaborate air-conditioning systems, and isolation. Furthermore, Earthmen did not carry diseases fatal to Outsiders. The reasons for the separation between the two were mental, not physical. In reaction, Earthmen had come to hate and distrust Outsiders as much as Outsiders did Earthmen. Two groups who hate, fear, and distrust one another for reasons that have no basis in fact: that's the situation.

Asimov dramatizes this situation in a tried-and-true manner. Bel Arvardan comes to Earth from the Sirian Sector, where Earthmen are hated the most. As a scientist he knows no good reason exists for the wearing of protective clothing and the taking of metaboline, so he rejects both and mingles openly with Earthmen. Then he meets an Earthgirl, Pola Shekt, and falls in love with her. Gradually he sheds the last vestiges of his own Sirian-induced prejudices, until by the end he can marry Pola and become a naturalized Earthman. *Pebble in the Sky* is a love story which cuts across racial prejudices to show that people are people. And on the whole the developing relationship between Arvardan and Pola is very well handled.

I have already analyzed the story from the action-adventure point of view: threat to Empire staved off by Earthman from twentieth century (with Arvardan dominating most of the middle of the story as apparent hero). Analyzed as a love story across racial barriers, it becomes Bel Arvardan's story: man overcomes his prejudice to win girl he loves. The action-adventure story was not particularly well handled, as I have tried to demonstrate. But the prejudice versus love story is.

In this context Arvardan becomes one of Asimov's best-drawn characters. One rather lengthy example will have to suffice. Before ever meeting Pola, Arvardan takes an airplane ride on which all his fellow passengers are Earthmen who initially don't know that he is an Outsider. Asimov's portrayal of Arvardan's thinking is marvelous. It contains all the liberal clichés of the basically prejudiced person.

Arvardan was from the Sirian Sector, notoriously the sector above all others in the Galaxy where anti-Terrestrian prejudice was strong. Yet he always liked to think he had not succumbed to that prejudice himself. As a scientist, as an archeologist, he couldn't afford to. Of course he had grown into the habit of thinking of Earthmen in certain set caricature types, and even now the word "Earthman" seemed an ugly one to him. But he wasn't really prejudiced.

At least he didn't think so. For instance, if an Earthman had ever wished to join an expedition of his or work for him in any capacity—and had the training and the ability—he would be accepted. If there were an opening for him, that was. And if the other members of the expedition didn't mind too much. That was the rub. Usually the fellow workers objected, and then what could you do?

He pondered the matter. Now certainly he would have no objection to eating with an Earthman, or even bunking with one in case of need—assuming the Earthman were reasonably clean, and healthy. In fact, he would in all ways treat him as he would anyone else, he thought. Yet there was no denying that he would always be conscious of the fact that an Earthman was an Earthman. He couldn't help that. That was the result of a childhood immersed in an atmosphere of bigotry so complete that it was almost invisible, so entire that you accepted its axioms as second nature. Then you left it and saw it for what it was when you looked back.

But here was his chance to test himself. He was in a plane with only Earthmen about him, and he felt perfectly natural, almost. Well, just a little self-conscious.

Arvardan looked about at the undistinguished and normal faces of his fellow passengers. They were supposed to be different, these Earthmen, but could he have told these from ordinary men if he had met them casually in a crowd? He didn't think so. The women weren't bad-looking. . . . His brows knit. Of course even tolerance must draw the line somewhere. Intermarriage, for instance, was quite unthinkable. [Pp. 70–71]

In a very Chaucerian way Asimov beautifully lets Arvardan condemn himself. No authorial intrusions are necessary.

Immediately thereafter, in conversation, Arvardan admits that he is an Outsider. Here is what happened and his reaction:

The man who had shared his seat rose stiffly and crowded into another, where the pair of occupants squeezed closely together to make room for him. Faces turned away. . . . For a moment Arvardan burned with indignation. Earthmen to treat *him* so. *Earthmen!* He had held out the hand of friendship to them. He, a Sirian, had condescended to treat with them and they had rebuffed him. [Pp. 95–96]

That "condescended" is exactly right, and it speaks volumes. The scene is nailed shut when an Earth agent on the plane makes a notation about Arvardan which includes the remark "anti-Terrestrial attitude very marked."

Asimov has taken the problem of racial prejudice out of our everyday, twentieth-century lives, where it is so mixed up with our own feelings and thoughts, and he has distanced it by garbing it in science fiction images. We can see, understand, and evaluate racial prejudice objectively in this novel, and hopefully we will return from it to our own world better equipped to cope with it in ourselves.

I have one final and admittedly personal remark to make about one of the very minor themes in the novel. When I finished reading the three novels in *Triangle,* all of which made use to one degree or another of a radioactive Earth existing over hundreds of thousands of years—a radioactivity caused by an atomic war in our own immediate future—I reread the beginning of *Pebble in the Sky* and was absolutely chilled by a passage that *now* had infinitely more significance:

In another part of Chicago stood the Institute for Nuclear Research, in which men may have had theories upon the essential worth of human nature but were half ashamed of them, since no quantitative instrument had yet been designed to measure it. When they thought about it, it was often enough to wish that some stroke from heaven would prevent human nature (and damned human ingenuity) from turning every innocent and interesting discovery into a deadly weapon. Yet, in a pinch, the same man who could not find it in his conscience to curb his curiosity into the nuclear studies that might someday kill half of Earth would risk his life to save that of a . . . fellow man. [P. 10]

For three novels, that "might someday" had been "did one day." But it hasn't yet, people, and how are we going to prevent it? Ah well, such are the problems one encounters when reading escape literature.

The Stars Like Dust (1951)

The setting of *The Stars Like Dust* is difficult to date, but it certainly is much, much earlier than that of *Pebble in the Sky*. Where in *Pebble* it had taken man hundreds of thousands of years to spread onto the Galaxy's 200 million habitable worlds, in *Stars* he has barely begun to settle the first few thousand of an estimated 4 million. The dates are not given in terms of Galactic Era (G.E.), and a Galactic Empire seated at Trantor is never mentioned. The planet Tyrann was the 1,099th settled by man. Seven hundred years later it began to spread its control militarily, and in ten years it had conquered fifty planets before its expansion was halted by the planet Lingane. Tyrann's wars of expansion are fifty years in the background of the story, and its encounter with Lingane thirty years. The Earth is the same radioactive Earth we have seen in *Pebble*, but here everyone knows that Earth was the original home planet of humanity. Clearly, *The Stars Like Dust* is set hundreds of thousands of years earlier than *Pebble in the Sky*. Small stellar kingdoms are jostling one another in the first attempts to consolidate into larger political units. The largest such unit of all, the Galactic Empire, is not yet even thought of.

Early in the novel we are given the following description of the night side of Earth as seen from a departing spaceship:

Slowly the shadow of night encroached upon the globe and the huge World-Island of Eurasia-Africa majestically took the stage, north side "down." Its diseased, unliving soil hid its horror under a night-induced play of jewels. The radioactivity of the soil was a vast sea of iridescent blue, sparkling in strange festoons that spelled out the manner in which the nuclear bombs had once landed, a full generation before the force-field defense against nuclear explosions had been developed so that no other world could commit suicide in just that fashion again. [Pp. 32–33]

Besides giving us another view of what the future might hold in store for us if we don't work hard enough at avoiding it, this brings us once again face to face with the paradox of an Earth that had committed suicide being the origin of a Galactic civilization. Perhaps one day Asimov will chronicle for us the story of the colonization of Earth's first star systems. (*The Caves of Steel* and *The Naked Sun* do not do this, because in them the first star systems are settled from a nonradioactive Earth, one in which we have successfully avoided the nuclear horrors assumed in the novels in *Triangle*.)

No Joseph Schwartz figure is in *The Stars Like Dust*, but otherwise the novel contains strong reminiscences of both *Pebble in the Sky* and the Foundation Series. The Foundation Series eventually became a quest for the Second Foundation, with the Second Foundation successfully hiding its identity by tricking the First Foundation into thinking it had destroyed the Second. Similarly, *The Stars Like Dust* eventually becomes a quest for a strange "Rebellion World." A ship piloted by one of the more important characters had been struck by a meteor and knocked off course. Its automatic pilot had continued the preprogrammed flight, and it had appeared at a world that was preparing to overthrow the Tyranni (thus the name "Rebellion World"). The hero of the story, Biron Farrill, must find that world so he can help fight the Tyranni, who have killed his father and seized his property. Commissioner Simok Aratap of Tyrann must locate the Rebellion World in order to protect his government. And the Rebellion World itself must remain hidden until its plans have had time to ripen. So the narrative pattern is the familiar one we saw in "The Mule," "Search by the Mule," and "Search by the Foundation": two groups seeking to find a third, with one of the two groups (the Mule; Aratap) following another (Ebling Mis; Biron Farrill) while the third seeks to remain hidden (the Second Foundation; the Rebellion World). Both Ebling Mis and Biron Farrill find what they are looking for; neither the Mule nor

Aratap succeeds in his quest; and both the Second Foundation and the Rebellion World remain hidden.

The antiviolence theme in the Foundation Series was very strong and may be exemplified by Salvor Hardin's saying, "Violence is the last refuge of the incompetent." The series centered on politics and intrigue rather than bloodshed and violence. Just so with *The Stars Like Dust*. The violent times were fifty years in the past, the rebellion still in the indefinite future. Aratap can contemplate, "Life was simpler in his father's time. To smash a planet had a cruel grandeur about it; while this careful maneuvering of an ignorant young man was simply cruel" (p. 50). Careful maneuvering has been substituted for planet-smashing. The action-adventure space opera has again been relegated to the background.

The Stars Like Dust was written immediately after *Pebble in the Sky*, so some parallels between the two are not surprising. That both make use of the radioactive Earth has already been mentioned. More strikingly, Bel Arvardan and Biron Farrill are both aristocratic outcasts, Arvardan outcast because of his unorthodox theories concerning the origin of the human race, Farrill because of his father's execution and the subsequent seizure of his estates. Most striking of all, Arvardan goes to Earth in an attempt to get proof for his theories and there meets and falls in love with Pola Shekt, daughter of a scientist important in the story, while Farrill goes to Rhodia in an attempt to stay alive and there meets and falls in love with Artemisia, daughter of Hinrik, Director of Rhodia, a politician important to the story. Clearly, both Dr. Shekt and Director Hinrik have beautiful and lovable daughters because they are convenient in the plot. They make for economical storytelling.

The similarity I am most interested in, however, is the one I want to spend some time on. In *Pebble in the Sky* Balkis was the character who constructed alternate plot lines to the one Asimov decided to use, and Balkis in the story line was an out-and-out villain. In *The Stars Like Dust* Simok Aratap does the story criticism, and he is an opposing force rather than a villain. As has been mentioned, had he lived two generations earlier, he could have participated in the wars of the expansion of Tyrann's empire. Now, however, "the most dangerous Tyrannian of them all" has been forced by history to play the role of plotter and counter-plotter. He is a manipulator of individual men.

But he is a sympathetic human being. When Farrill is first brought before him, "Aratap was sorry for him. He was obviously frightened" (p. 45). When he is in the presence of the weak-minded and frightened Hinrik, "Aratap felt a twinge of compassion" (p. 92). He also has an artistic bent. After Farrill has been taken away, he speculates to a scornful aide about the use of a photo-cube as a new art form (p. 49). Elsewhere we are told that "Aratap liked the night air of a planet full of green and growing things. Tyrann was more beautiful in its way, but it was a terrible beauty of rocks and mountains. It was dry, dry!" (p. 94). Asimov occasionally speaks of Aratap in a surprising way. For example, after one of Aratap's captains has spoken "abruptly," Aratap interposes "gently" (p. 93). I submit that empathy for other human beings (e.g., Farrill and Hinrik), an interest in art (the photo-cube) and nature (the landscapes of Rhodia and Tyrann), and gentleness are not the traits of an evil villain. Asimov has made a human being of Aratap.

Besides, Asimov also gives to Aratap one of the pre-eminent traits of an Asimovian hero: the ability to react calmly and rationally rather than emotionally. "He was completely self-possessed" and confident (p. 45). in trying to analyze a certain turn of events, he remarks, "Let us take that into account objectively, without growing angry about it" (p. 95). And his building of detailed explanations for events is a rational response to those events.

I think Asimov sees the kinship between himself and Aratap, that he identifies with Aratap. Substitute "Asimov" for "Aratap" in the following statement: "Aratap had a neat and tidy mind which could not bear the thought of individual facts loosely clumped together with no decent arrangement" (p. 91). Surely this applies to Asimov the science writer, Asimov the science fiction writer, Asimov the scientist.

For our purposes, the greatest similarity is that both of them like to organize the experiences and actions of human beings into unified, consistent stories. Both of them show the instinct to "plot," in the storyteller's sense of the word. "There was no pattern!" Aratap complains to himself at one point. "Events lacked a design" (p. 91). Later, things seem to snap into place for him. "Aratap was delighted. . . . It formed a pattern now, after all. A better pattern than he could have anticipated" (p. 93). According to that pattern, Farrill came to Rhodia to contact Artemisia and her uncle, Gillbret, and then to escape in a Tyrannian spaceship. All this makes a nice alternate story to Asimov's, and obviously one Asimov considered, either before actually writing *The Stars Like Dust* or at least *now*, while writing it. In Asimov's story line, Farrill was tricked into coming to Rhodia, he fell in with Artemisia and Gillbret by accident, and they escaped in the Tyrannian ship because it was there. Things that Aratap sees as tightly plotted happen in Asimov fortuitously. Again, I think such of Asimov's characters as Balkis and Aratap are giving us more thoughtful and better developed plots than Asimov is. Or, to put it differently, Balkis and Aratap give us Asimov's further thinking in their respective novels—flaws he sees in them, tighter plotting he could have used. Asimov is more slapdash and makeshift in his plots than these characters who give us Asimov's second and third thoughts.

Theoretically, Farrill is the central character of the novel. We spend most of the time with him. Deprived of his land and running for his life at the start, he gets his land, the girl, and a bright future. The male Cinderella has won through again. But he never comes alive as a center of interest. We don't care about him. At the beginning, he is the passive dupe of others, reacting instead of acting. In the middle, he treats Artemisia shamefully for reasons that we are not given until too late to change our opinion of him. At the end, his stalwartness and intelligence are simply demonstrated too late. Besides, Simok Aratap has by then seized control of the novel. Aratap is the memorable character in *The Stars Like Dust.*

The Stars Like Dust is much better constructed than *Pebble in the Sky.* Aratap is a much more interesting character than Balkis. The romance between Farrill and Artemisia is not so well handled as that between Arvardan and Pola, but that is at least partially because Arvardan is a better drawn character than the wishy-washy Farrill.

The theme of the absurdity of racial prejudice was clearly demonstrated in almost every page and in almost every scene of

Pebble in the Sky. It was—and is—an important theme and makes
the book worth reading despite its many flaws in construction.
The main theme of *The Stars Like Dust* is not so pervasive, the
melodrama often displacing it for chapter after chapter. But it
is still there, and it is important. Early in the novel, Gillbret questions Farrill's motivation in hating the Tyranni:

> "In other words, you decided they were strangers and out-
> landers only after they executed your father, which, after
> all, was their simple right. . . . Your father was a Rancher.
> What rights did his herdsmen have? If one of them had
> stolen cattle for his own use or to sell to others, what would
> have been his punishment? Imprisonment as a thief. If he
> had plotted the death of your father, for whatever reason,
> for perhaps a worthy reason in his own eyes, what would
> have been the result? Execution, undoubtedly. And what
> right has your father to make laws and visit punishment upon
> his fellow human beings? He was *their* Tyranni.
>
> "Your father, in his own eyes and in mine, was a patriot.
> But what of that? To the Tyranni, he was a traitor, and they
> removed him. Can you ignore the necessity of self-defense?
>
> "So find a better reason to hate the Tyranni. Don't think
> it is enough to replace one set of rulers by another; that the
> simple change brings freedom." [P. 70]

The point is perhaps best made by Hinrik at the very end of
the novel. Without a certain document that has been lurking
in the background since the novel's first scenes, Hinrik says, "we
would only have exchanged one feudal despotism for another"
(p. 217). And occasionally characters suggest that it's better to
be on the winning side than the losing one, since someone must
rule.

What the novel eventually suggests is that there is an alternative to the traditional system that distinguishes between the ruler
and the ruled, between the government and its people, between
the powerful and the powerless. The alternative is to let the governed govern. The document whose existence and content has
been mentioned off and on throughout the novel—and which for
rhetorical purposes turns out to be the original real document
and not one of its hundreds of thousands of duplicates—is the

Constitution of the United States of America. This may seem provincial of Asimov, but actually the historical context that generated the Constitution and the historical context that Asimov creates in *The Stars Like Dust* are very similar to one another. In both, the Constitution is presented as an alternative to the rule of the many by an aristocratic and powerful few. The theme of *The Stars Like Dust* is the nature of leadership and an expression of Asimov's belief that people can govern themselves.

It would seem, by the way, that in Asimov's future history all of this came to nothing. The Emperor of Trantor thousands of years later does not seem to be guided by the Constitution of the United States. He is, in fact, another feudal monarch. This is not to be taken as pessimism on Asimov's part, as a demonstration that over the long haul the Constitution won't work. Rather, it indicates that Asimov is writing a series of disconnected—or only roughly connected—stories and novels. Each one is largely a unit in itself. *The Stars Like Dust* is a novel in which the Constitution was important; the Foundation Series is a collection in which it wasn't. That's all.

The Currents of Space (1952)

In *The Currents of Space* Asimov raises as minor topics the two themes that had dominated *Pebble in the Sky* and *The Stars Like Dust*. A relatively minor character is from the planet Libair and therefore has skin of a deep, rich brown. "Libairian myths . . . spoke of times of war between men of different pigmentation, and the founding of Libair itself was held due to a party of browns fleeing from a defeat in battle" (p. 59). This demonstrates again the insanity of racial war, and some feel it is in our immediate future now. The character also recalls chancing on a world where the language was so old it might even be a form of the long-lost English, and he notes, "They had a special word for a man with dark skin. Now why should there be a special word for a man with dark skin? There was no special word for a man with blue eyes, or large ears, or curly hair." This is a patently superficial observation. There is a word for a man with yellow hair—a blond—and a woman with dark hair—a brunette. And there are words to distinguish one racial group from another: Caucasian and Asian and Negro. It would be surprising if, in Asimov's created future, "Libairian" meant something strictly geographical and did not call to mind a brown-skinned Libairian. Merely having a name for a dark-skinned man is not evil. But the import of Asimov's remark is to remind us of the irrationality of racism; it is clearly a concern of his, and it was extremely important in *Pebble in the Sky*. Here it is a one-page, superficial discussion.

The setting of *The Currents of Space* can be dated as well after that of *The Stars Like Dust* and well before that of *Pebble in the Sky*. In the last five hundred years Trantor had become a political power but not yet a Galactic Empire. "Trantor . . . had swollen in the last few centuries until half the inhabited worlds of the Galaxy were part of it" (p. 70). The story is laid on Florina, a planet seeking to free itself from the control of Sark. One group wants to ally Florina with Trantor, and the response is "would not Trantor simply replace Sark as a still larger and more tyrannical master? . . . Better the master they knew than the master they knew not" (p. 70). This was exactly the problem in *The Stars Like Dust*, and there it was solved by the Constitution. Here it is raised and then allowed to trickle away.

The central character in *The Currents of Space* is Rik, an Earthman whose memory has been destroyed, though bits and pieces of the past occasionally float back to him. He has the key piece of information in the story, that Florina's sun is about to go nova, but he doesn't know he has it. Basically, then, the story revolves around Rik's two problems: the gradual reassembling of his memory and personality, and the saving of the population of Florina. He is helped by Lona, the peasant girl assigned to care for him, and by the Townman, Myrlyn Terens, a Florinian educated on Sark for the civil service.

The story is an involved one, full of intrigue and suspense and violence. That it does not come off is not due to plotting problems such as mar *Pebble in the Sky*, though there are some such problems. For example, when Rik is first found, memoryless, naked, and gibbering, the Patrollers incredibly decide, "It isn't even worth making a record of. It has nothing to do with us. Get rid of it somehow" (p. 30), and that's when the Townman turns it (Rik) over to Valone. Later, Rik and Valone manage to stow away on a spaceship leaving Florina—and guess what? The ship just hap-

pens to be the one carrying the daughter of the Squire of Fife
back to Sark, and the Squire of Fife is the Balkis-Aratap figure
in *The Currents of Space,* the leader of the opposition who is
given to constructing alternate plots and counterplots. It is the
sort of wild, improbable coincidence one only accepts for the
sake of the story. It couldn't happen, but it makes the story
tighter.

Nor is the major problem with *The Currents of Space* to be
found in its style, though flatness of style is a difficulty in all three
of these works he wrote after abandoning the light, varied style
of the Foundation Series. One never smiles while reading these
novels. Everything is deadly serious. No one seems to delight in
anything (unless it's Aratap in building his elaborate patterns),
and that applies even to the narrative voice. The stories almost
seem to have been written as an unpleasant task, self-imposed because he had nothing better to do or because it was expected of
him. If a remark like this can ever make sense, let me say the
three novels in *Triangle* seem to lack authorial enthusiasm. They
were written with Asimov's left hand while his interest was directed elsewhere in his life, teaching, children, nonfiction, whatever.

The major problem in *The Currents of Space* lies in its narrative technique. For all intents and purposes, the novel has no
"now." It is a constant series of flashbacks and overlappings of
varying lengths. Too much of the reader's time is spent catching
up with a present which too often is itself several hours behind
the present of the last chapter.

Flashbacks are certainly appropriate and useful, especially
early in a novel when the pieces are being set on the board in the
first place and anywhere during the novel when new pieces (or
characters or settings) must be added. Asimov uses it early in
The Stars Like Dust (pp. 33–35) when the present is Farrill's
open flight away from Earth and the past is an account (in past
perfect tense) of his leaving the university he had been attend-
ing. Judiciously used, the flashback is a useful tool.

But it is not judiciously used in *The Currents of Space.* The
difficulties begin in the first chapter, but let's look farther into
the novel where the necessity for flashbacks might seem less.
Chapter 5, "The Scientist," is about Dr. Selin Junz, the Libair-

ian referred to earlier. The content of the present of the chapter
—its *now*—is an appointment Junz is keeping with a minor Sarkite clerk. It begins with a reference to his having been impatient
about something for a year. Then there is a flashback to a conversation between Junz and Abel, the Trantorian ambassador,
on the subject of the personnel in the Sarkite civil service. Back
to "now": he is transferred from one waiting room to another.
Then we get a page of his reflections on racial prejudice, admittedly not flashback but not moving the story forward, either. He
begins his conversation with the clerk, seeking information about
a missing member of the Interstellar Spatio-analytic Bureau.
Then we are given a flashback to "eleven months and thirteen
days ago," when Junz had gotten involved in the first place. The
lengthy flashback concluded, the conversation with the Clerk ends.
Almost nothing has happened in the "now" of the chapter.

The next chapter, "The Ambassador," consists of two different "nows," each of which is introduced with the following sentences: "It was ten hours before Junz had his interview with the
Clerk that Terens left Khorov's bakery" (overlapping the previous
chapter, right?), and "It was ten hours after Junz had had his
interview with the Clerk that he met Ludigan Abel again." So
the *now* of Chapter 5, with its bundle of flashbacks, really belongs
in the middle of Chapter 6; the first half of Chapter 6 intersperses
a *now* of Terens slinking through the city with vivid recollections
of his youth and of his reasons for becoming a Townman; the
second half concentrates primarily on the *now* conversation between Junz and Abel, even though it does include a one-page
digression on the history and growth of the Trantorian Empire.

Perhaps the nadir in Asimov's use of this technique is reached
at the beginning of Chapter 7, where Rik, in an unspecified *now*,
is remembering seeing a man killed, and in the midst of *that*
memory flashes back to his awakening that morning. Here we
have a flashback within a flashback within an unspecified now.
This is all very confusing.

One or two extenuating arguments might be offered here. One
might argue that the story is a complex one and the cast of characters unusually large, and that therefore the constant flashbacking was necessary. If this is true, then the novel demonstrates
that Asimov cannot handle a complex plot involving a large cast

of characters. *Pebble in the Sky* was just such a novel, however, and he did not misuse the flashback technique in it. No, it was not the intractability of the material, but the conscious decision to tell the story the wrong way that ruined the novel.

Another—and, I think, subtler—argument would be that Asimov decided to use this muddled patterning because it best represented externally the state of Rik's mind. Rik's problem is to discover the past and integrate it with the present. And that is precisely the problem I am complaining Asimov did not solve in telling this story. By this argument, the form of the novel would have been determined by the confusion in Rik's mind. My worry is that I see art as a process of clarification, and it seems strange to me that anyone would argue in favor of confusion as a principle of organization and clarification.

I think *Pebble in the Sky* lets us see clearly the absurdity and irrationality of racial prejudice, and therefore it transcends its many and obvious structural flaws. I think *The Stars Like Dust* suffers from having a too-passive hero, but it is nicely plotted and contains Simok Aratap, the best single character in *Triangle*. And I think *The Currents of Space*, despite the nice astronomical relationship between the radiations of the near-nova sun and the widely used fiber kyrt, fails badly because of its too-widespread misuse of the narrative technique of flashback. Anyone can read and enjoy *Pebble in the Sky* and *The Stars Like Dust*, but only a died-in-the-kyrt Asimov fan could ride out *The Currents of Space*.

The End of Eternity (1955)

It is not immediately apparent while reading the novel, but *The End of Eternity* is set in the same universe as *Triangle*. More accurately: By the time the sequence of events in *The End of Eternity* has run its course, the universe in which we live, and in which Asimov projects his future Empire, has been brought about. Let me explain. The novel ends in 1932 with Nöys Lambert, the female lead, telling Andrew Harlan, the male lead, that she is going to write a letter to a scientist in Italy which will eventually cause the first nuclear explosion to be set off in 1945 instead of in the thirtieth century. As a result of tinkering with the normal course of events—what the novel refers to as the "Basic

State"—the probability develops "that Earth will end with a largely radioactive crust" (p. 190). This is clearly a reference to the radioactive Earth of *Triangle*.

The "Eternity" of the title is an organization that exists outside of and parallel to human history from the 27th to the 70,000th century. It has taken upon itself the smoothing out of history, preserving the greatest good for the greatest number. It looks to the Foundation Series in several important ways. Just as Hari Seldon and his Foundation sought to manipulate history so that 29,000 years of human suffering could be avoided, so Eternity seeks to manipulate history so that decades and centuries of human suffering may be changed into something safer. Both Eternity and the Foundations make heavy use of mathematics in their analyses of human history. In the Foundation Series, however, the mathematics was used only to describe large and inevitable movements in history, whereas in *The End of Eternity* the effects of minute historical changes on individuals can be computed using the technique of "life-plotting."

Furthermore, there is a direct causal relationship between the existence of Eternity and the nonexistence of the Galactic Empire, and vice versa. "The mere existence of Eternity at once wiped out the Galactic Empire. To restore it, Eternity must be done away with" (pp. 187–88). At the end of the novel Harlan makes a decision that causes the end of Eternity (thus the title) and therefore also causes/allows the rise of the humans-only Galactic Empire.

The relationship between Eternity and Empire is as follows. By making things safe for humanity, Eternity had delayed the development of an interstellar, hyperspace drive by more than 120,000 centuries. When man finally got out among the stars, they were all occupied already. Alien intelligences had spread throughout the Galaxy before man. As a result, man was confined to Earth and eventually became extinct. One result of Harlan's destroying Eternity is that man leaves home to travel to the stars much sooner. In fact, some further tinkering sees to it that man gets to the stars first, not last. Therefore, when the aliens come out, we are there. They must back down, and a humans-only Galactic Empire results.

So *The End of Eternity* establishes a time-line in which the first atomic bomb is exploded in 1945, in which the Earth will probably become a largely radioactive planet, in which man develops an interstellar drive first among intelligences in the Galaxy, and in which a humans-only Galactic Empire is established. This is clearly the universe of *Triangle* and the Foundation Series.

At least one of the assumptions behind all this needs some further discussion. Asimov seems to assume that all the intelligences in the Galaxy will develop an interstellar drive within roughly the same period of time. When Earth-plus-Eternity gets an interstellar drive, the aliens have already settled the Galaxy. When Earth-minus-Eternity gets its drive earlier, man has the Galaxy to himself. The assumption that all galactic civilizations will come to fruition and venture out into interstellar space at roughly the same time is surely a faulty one. Just as young, middle-aged, and old stars exist, so young, middle-aged, and old civilizations must exist simultaneously on the various planets of those stars. Merely getting us started a few centuries earlier or 100,000 centuries later would not—considering the astronomical times involved—prove that great an advantage or disadvantage.

Besides, it strikes me that there is a certain provincialism in assuming that the eventual establishment of a humans-only Galaxy is grounds for a happy ending to a novel. Don't the aliens who are being displaced and constricted—and the generations of human beings for whom their present has been changed or taken away—have any rights in the matter? Isn't there something at least vaguely unsatisfactory about an ending that makes the Galaxy safe for humanity at the expense of unknown numbers of future men and all aliens?

The End of Eternity is extremely well plotted. Everything is thought out in detail and fits together smoothly. The plot has none of those unexplained actions and improbable coincidences that so mar *Pebble in the Sky*. We see here once again the Asimov who had so carefully preplanned his first stories, "Marooned Off Vesta" and "The Callistan Menace." Asimov deserves nothing but the highest praise in this connection. Anyone wishing to see a sustained feat of truly creative imagination should examine carefully the background and story line of *The End of Eternity*. From this point of view—from the point of view of a sustained *vision*—it is an altogether dazzling and extraordinary performance.

But—and in criticism, there's always a "but," isn't there?—the novel fails badly in two areas. The first is characterization; the second is the sequence in which Asimov chose to present to us that remarkable world and story line. Damon Knight puts us firmly on the track of this second problem: "The background is extremely complex, involving a race of Eternals with a self-appointed mission to doctor reality all up and down the time-line—with a technology, mores, anxieties, a world-view and a terminology to fit—none of which the reader has a fair chance to absorb before he is flung into the story proper" (*In Search of Wonder*, p. 94). In other words, even though it has long been standard practice to begin a work of fiction in the middle of the action with some conflict already going on, the complexity of Asimov's vision in this particular novel is so great that the standard and usual procedure obscures rather than clarifies. Asimov chose the wrong place to begin. Exposition was needed *before* the onset of the conflict rather than piecemeal and confusingly *during* the conflict.

The first scene in the novel lasts from the beginning of Chapter 1 on page 11 through to the middle of Chapter 10 on page 106. In it Harlan goes to the 2,456th century to initiate a reality change requested by an Eternity sociologist there named Vay. In preparing his recommendations, Vay had missed something and therefore deserved to be reported and demoted. But Harlan uses that mistake to blackmail Vay into having a life-plot prepared for Nöys Lambert, a resident of the 482d century. Having fallen in love with her, he wants to know what will happen to her when a scheduled reality change is performed on her century.

This scene's place in the chronological development of the story line is indicated on page 106 with the sentence "He traveled to the 2456th and bludgeoned Sociologist Vay to his own exact will." But Asimov has chosen to start the novel with this scene, out of its chronological place. It lasts from page 11 to page 106 because it is interrupted and strung out by long passages of exposition. Taking that scene as the "now" of the story and the long passages of exposition as the past leading up to the "now," here is how the first half of the novel is constructed: pp. 11–22, now;

pp. 22–62, the past; pp. 62–68, now; pp. 68–71, the past; pp. 71–73, now; pp. 73–106, the past. The rest of the novel, pp. 106–191, runs smoothly and regularly in the present with a few minor and irrelevant exceptions.

My argument is that in the first half of *The End of Eternity*, as in all of *The Currents of Space*, Asimov has needlessly confused and obscured the time-line of his story. This is bad enough in *The Currents of Space*, which after all starts at a certain time and moves steadily forward in time to its conclusion. It is worse in *The End of Eternity* because it is a time-travel novel. Its male lead is born in the 95th, educated in the 482d, works in the 575th, runs all up and down the centuries during the course of the novel, and eventually lives out his life in the 20th. His female lead is born in the 111,394th, works in the 482d, and joins the male lead in the 20th. Of a subsidiary character we are told, "He was born in the 78th, spent some time in Eternity (in the 575th), and died in the 24th" (p. 123). There is enough nonchronology in the plot itself. To tell the story nonchronologically is mere obfuscation. And to break that initial out-of-chronological-order scene into four parts and stretch it over nearly a hundred pages is simply bad storytelling. There is enough complexity in the background and the plot. What is needed is straightforward clarity in the storytelling itself, not more complexity.

Perhaps it is enough to say that for a short period in his novel-writing career—in the beginning of *The Stars Like Dust*, all of *The Currents of Space*, and the first half of *The End of Eternity* —Asimov got mired down in mishandling the flashback technique. Since this does seem to have become a major problem for him, it is something we ought to watch out for in his work from here on. (As we will see, the first section of *The Gods Themselves* [1972] is very interesting in this regard.)

The second major problem area in *The End of Eternity* is characterization, and I want to concentrate here on one character, Andrew Harlan. One technique often used for authenticating a character, for convincing the reader that a given character is an actual person, is physical description. This may be merely a personal reaction on my own part as reader, but I never remember the hook of a character's nose, the slant of his eyes, or even the color of his hair. Still, if I am told these things, I believe that the person described is a physical object, that he is real in that sense, and I accept his reality and forget his features. Asimov does make a halfhearted attempt to authenticate Harlan in this manner. He has Harlan describe his own reflection in a tabletop (p. 15). He looks older than thirty-two, and he has a long face and dark eyes and eyebrows. That's it, and it's not enough. He can cause a reflection, but he never becomes a physical object.

Still, convincing a reader of a character's physical reality is only one way of authenticating a character, and it is surely not necessary that it be done with all fictional characters. Very often the writers of popular fiction will deliberately avoid giving physical details, especially about their narrative-point-of-view characters (which is what Harlan is in the novel). In this way, no physical details stand between the reader and his placing himself in the hero's person. He does not have to imagine himself medium-sized, overweight, dark, bespectacled, and walking with a limp down a dark alley. He need only imagine himself—whatever his physical features—walking down a dark alley. The trick is to give enough physical features to convince the reader that the character is a "real" physical object, a separate human being in at least that sense.

The major problem with Harlan, however, is that he spends the story reacting rather than acting. As he himself finally comes to put it, "But to be *fooled* into it, to be *tricked* into it, by people handling and manipulating my emotions—. . . . I've got to undo what I was marionetted into doing" (pp. 179–80). Eternity was founded according to a specific series of events described in "the Mallansohn memoir," written by a time-traveler sent into the past by Eternity. Mallansohn knew that the director of the project was Twissell, and therefore Twissell was made director when the project was established. Knowing the effect, the cause was supplied. More importantly for our purposes, Mallansohn knew that Harlan, a trusted subordinate of Twissell's, had taught him primitive history and had handled the control room the day Mallansohn was returned to the 24th century to start Eternity. And *therefore*—not because he earned it by being good at his job or knowing primitive history well, but because the Mallansohn memoir so described it—Harlan was made Twissell's assistant, was made Mallansohn's instructor in primitive history, and was put in the control room. He was not struggling and achieving. He was being manipulated by others to fulfill a pattern.

He is even used by Nöys Lambert, that lovely creature from more than a hundred thousand years in the future. She and her unnamed, unshown co-conspirators want to end Eternity, so she seduces Harlan in the 482d, and in the process, through a drugged drink and hypnosis, she induces in him an awareness of how Eternity was working to found itself centuries earlier than it would have naturally evolved and of his own role in the plan. This awareness gives him the power to destroy Eternity—by refusing to follow the role he had to have followed if it were to be established—and his love for Nöys gives him the motivation.

My point at this moment is that it's not enough to say that yes, the Mallansohn memoir got him his job with Twissell, but he was also a good worker, or that yes, Nöys permitted him to love her as a part of her plan to end Eternity, but she also loved him. Harlan's role in the novel—his preplanned-by-Asimov role—is too passive for him to be a completely satisfactory central character.

This brings me to another point about Harlan's characterlessness. Asimov is rather proud of the purity of his fiction so far as sex scenes are concerned. In a letter to Richard E. Geis's *The Alien Critic,* Number 6, Asimov writes,

> on pages 54–55 I came across John Boardman's letter in which he says (In TAC #5) "Personally, I can't think of an Asimov book where the addition of sexual scenes would help the plot any."
>
> So help me Hari Seldon, I never really thought I'd hear anyone say something as simply factual as that.
>
> It is nice that someone sees that I omit sex not because I am a prude but because the kind of stories I write don't require it. To insert sex when the story does not require it does not help the story. [P. 38]

I would like to disagree with both Boardman and Asimov by instancing *The End of Eternity* as an Asimov book where the addition of sexual scenes would indeed help the characterization in the book, and therefore the book and its plot.

Harlan is a Technician in Eternity. As such, it is his responsibility to initiate reality changes, and these changes affect the lives of millions of people. To be able to do this, he must turn off his emotions. He is continually described as expressionless and emotionless. When an enemy of his is pressing home the point that Nöys had sexual relations with him not because she found him attractive, but for her own ulterior reasons, that enemy says truthfully, "Look, Harlan, you're a coldfish product of Eternity. . . . You consider [women] sinful. The attitude shows all over you, and to any woman you'd have all the sex appeal of a month-dead mackerel" (p. 79).

This is the Harlan in whose company we spend the novel, and something is needed to balance this coldfish side of him. Is it plausible that such a month-dead mackerel would (a) destroy Eternity for love of a woman and (b) attract Nöys to live out life with him in the 20th? The plot calls for these things to happen, yet they do not flow naturally from the incomplete Harlan we are allowed to see. The first sexual encounter between Nöys and Harlan—and the only such encounter really mentioned at all—is described this way: "It all happened dreamily, as though it were happening to someone else. It wasn't nearly as repulsive as he had always imagined it must be. It came as a shock to him, a revelation, that it wasn't repulsive at all" (pp. 60–61). And that's it, and it's not enough to properly motivate and explain Harlan's decisions and actions in the story. To restate one of Asimov's remarks in its positive form: "To insert sex when the story does . . . require it does . . . help the story." It would have helped *The End of Eternity*.

It is instructive that Asimov believes that *The End of Eternity* is "explicitly sexual"—or, at least, that it contains one such character. Here is that remark in its context:

> *The End of Eternity* was written in a deliberate attempt to be different. I made up my mind to insert more emotion and a heroine who was as explicitly sexual as I could manage. —I did the precise same when I wrote *The Naked Sun* and *The Gods Themselves*. A couple of points about *The End of Eternity* before you ask. The name "Andrew Harlan" was not written with [Harlan] Ellison in mind. At the time I wrote the book I barely knew Ellison if at all. *The End of*

Eternity was the only novel I wrote after *Pebble in the Sky* that was not serialized in the magazines. The reason (at least the one given me) was that it did not break naturally into parts. That may even be so. Despite the lack of serialization, it did not do noticeably worse in book form than my other novels—or better. [Personal letter, November 15, 1973]

Asimov is willing to talk about (but not show) societies with different and more relaxed sexual codes. For example, at one point Nöys remarks that one of the reasons she went to bed with Harlan was that she felt sorry for him. When he asks, "What were you sorry about?" she replies, "That you should have such trouble about wanting me. It's such a simple thing. You just ask a girl. It's so easy to be friendly. Why suffer?" And a moment later she continues with, "The girl has to be willing, of course. Mostly she is, if she's not otherwise engaged. Why not? It's simple enough" (p. 87). But talking like this in a theoretical fashion at a distance is different from living in such a society with such sexual attitudes even vicariously in a work of fiction.

In any event, the characterization of Andrew Harlan is unconvincing because he is not given a solid body, because his role is too passive and too much manipulated by the necessities of Asimov's—and Mallansohn's and Nöys's—plot, and because Harlan is not given a passionate enough nature to make his destroying Eternity and winning Nöys believable.

Finally, I did want to point out that one of the more appealing things about *The End of Eternity* is that it can be read as an analogue to a variety of present-day situations, and as a result it distances those things and permits us to see and evaluate them, as it were, abstracted from our everyday lives. What *is* Eternity? For one thing, it is the artist standing outside of the events of everyday life, observing them, sorting through them, rearranging and re-emphasizing them, to tell a different story than mere history, a more significant and insight-bearing story. What is a novel but a carefully considered and built reality change?

Perhaps more importantly, Eternity is the paternalistic state, working to make its citizens comfortable and secure. "Any system, like Eternity, which allows men to choose their own future, will end by choosing safety and mediocrity" (p. 187). The individual wants to face his own problems, solve them himself, not simply turn them over to higher authorities. Eternity was destroyed so that the individual could be free.

> Man would not be a world but a million worlds, a billion worlds. We would have the infinite in our grasp. Each world would have its own stretch of the Centuries, each its own values, a chance to seek happiness after ways of its own in an environment of its own. There are many happinesses, many goods, infinite variety. . . . *That* is the Basic State of mankind. [P. 187]

And that is also the basic theme of one of Asimov's most brilliantly conceived novels, *The End of Eternity*.

CHAPTER SIX

Asimov's Novels II

The Lucky Starr Juveniles (1952–58)

Writing under the pseudonym Paul French, Asimov produced during the seven years 1952 through 1958 six juvenile novels featuring David "Lucky" Starr and his pint-sized companion John "Bigman" Jones. In *Opus 100* Asimov gives the following account of the genesis of the Lucky Starr series and of his reasons for and choice of a pseudonym:

> It was Walter I. Bradbury of Doubleday who first suggested the idea that I write them. The intention was that of supplying a serial hero for television, so that both the publishers and I, myself, could make an honest dollar.
>
> But I hesitated. I don't object to money, in principle, but I have a set of hang-ups about what I'm willing to do in exchange. I said, "But the television people may ruin the stories and then I would be ashamed to have my name identified with them."
>
> So Brad said, "Use a pseudonym."
>
> And I did. I chose Paul French and wrote all my Lucky Starr books under that name.
>
> As it turned out, television turned out to be utterly uninterested in the Lucky Starr stories and the precaution was unnecessary. . . .
>
> I have been asked a thousand times, by the way, why I picked that particular pseudonym. . . . At the time . . . I heard that the suspense writer, Cornell Woolrich, deliberately chose a nationality as his—William Irish. So I chose Paul French. [P. 22]

The series is set "ten thousand years after the pyramids were built and five thousand years after the first atom bomb had exploded" (*Ranger*, pp. 9–10). The physical location of each of the stories is somewhere inside the solar system, depending on which novel one is reading, though we are to assume a Galactic civilization of uncertain extent "out there." For example, in the fourth novel, *Lucky Starr and the Big Sun of Mercury*, we find a reference to "this age of Galactic civilization, with humanity spread through all the planets of all the stars in the Milky Way" (p. 21). Despite a certain discrepancy in the timing, then—the Galactic Empire of *Pebble in the Sky* and the Foundation Series is hundreds of thousands of years in the future, that of the Lucky Starr series only five thousand—the Galactic setting of all these stories seems to be the same, until, that is, the last few stories of the Lucky Starr series. In them, the Galactic Empire seems to fade and to be replaced by a much smaller colonized volume. For example, in the last novel in the series, *Lucky Starr and the Rings of Saturn*, an interstellar conference is held at which a vote is taken: four planetary systems vote one way and over fifty the other. It is Earth versus the Outer Worlds, and no indication is given that human civilization is Galactic in extent.

To put all this in a slightly different way: As Asimov worked on the Lucky Starr series over a period of seven years, its background unobtrusively shifted from that of the Galactic Empire of *Triangle* and the Foundation Series to that of the Earth versus the Outer Worlds of *The Caves of Steel* and *The Naked Sun*, which novels were being conceived and written during this same period. Asimov started writing the series against a background he had previously worked out for earlier stories and novels, and he ended the series against a background he was developing for two novels he was working on at the same time.

This shift in background is not the only development that took place as the Lucky Starr series unfolded. In the first novel, *David Starr: Space Ranger*, Lucky stumbles across a lost race of disembodied Martians who give him "a strip of gauze" (p. 99) to wrap around his head. Basically, it is "a personal force-shield" (p. 98) which renders him invulnerable to attack and which has certain awe-inspiring side effects like making him appear to others like a shimmering ghost and like giving his voice a deep resonance. Without his mask he is David Starr, ordinary (though extremely intelligent) human being; with it he becomes the mysterious and invulnerable "Space Ranger," righter of wrongs, enemy of evil, and distributor of justice. The parallel with a certain Masked Rider of the Plains is clear. Wisely, Asimov drops this whole incredibly childish business by the third novel in the series, and Lucky Starr settles down to become a human being who solves crimes with rational thought and action rather than a nearly supernatural being who goes around scaring clues and confessions out of people. This change from Lucky Starr, Space Ranger, to Lucky Starr, scientific detective, is a second major development in the series.

The first novel was set on Mars, and in it Lucky acquired a friend named John "Bigman" Jones. Bigman is 5'2" tall (or short) and feisty. He is unbelievably sensitive about his height or lack thereof, and he is incredibly willing to assault physically anyone who makes any chance remark that violates that sensitivity. He is an extreme and melodramatic character, and wherever he goes, exclamation marks trail along. I am aware that Sherlock Holmes had his Dr. Watson and that Gene Autry had his Smiley Burnett. But Bigman is so overdone that it leaves the unfortunate impression that Asimov is writing down to his young audience. As the series develops, Bigman's character is somewhat tempered (if I may be excused a pun), and the series improves as a result.

It is worth noticing that an overreacting Bigman fits into the pattern of many other Asimov stories. In "Marooned Off Vesta" Warren Moore's calm collection of data and his cool reasoning and acting on the basis of that data were counterpointed by Mark Brandon's wildly emotional reaction to crises. The Robot Stories played Gregory Powell's reason against Mike Donovan's emotions. In *Lucky Starr and the Moons of Jupiter* an experimental spaceship is sabotaged so that it is falling directly onto Jupiter. One character's evaluation is "We're all dead men!" But Lucky, "in sharp, incisive tones," says, "No man is dead while he has a mind capable of thought" (p. 118). It is not Bigman's emotionalism in itself that is objectionable: that fits into the pattern of reason versus emotion that Asimov uses so well. It is the pugnacious extremes to which Asimov has Bigman go. In the best Lucky Starr stories Asimov does not have Bigman overdo it.

Getting rid of Lucky's "Space Ranger" role and calming down Bigman's anger contribute to another major change in the series, this one a change in tone. From melodramatic, overemotional, over-exclamation-pointed silliness, the stories evolve into excellent science fiction detective stories. From the childish action-adventure of *Lucky Starr and the Pirates of the Asteroids* they develop into the tense intellectual puzzles of the two best novels in the series, *Lucky Starr and the Big Sun of Mercury* and *Lucky Starr and the Moons of Jupiter*.

In summary, four major changes took place in the seven years of the series: (1) the background shifted from the Galactic Empire of the Foundation Series to the relatively newly colonized Outer Worlds of *The Caves of Steel*, (2) Lucky Starr stopped being a masked Space Ranger and became a scientific detective, (3) Bigman Jones got better control of his temper, and (4) the stories became less melodramatic and more intellectual, less action-adventure and more detective, less extreme and more realistic.

The Lucky Starr series shows us techniques and habits that we have already noted in other of Asimov's works. For example, we saw in the Foundation Series that Asimov liked to hide his characters' planning and actions so he could spring them on us at the end. The whole of *Lucky Starr and the Rings of Saturn* is ruined (for me at least) because Lucky has a plan from the very beginning, because some selected characters in the story are allowed to share in it and its execution, but it is so well hidden from us the readers that we don't even know it's there. As a result, Lucky is allowed to appear too passive and the novel too structureless—until the end, and by then it's too late.

In *Lucky Starr and the Big Sun of Mercury* Bigman interprets one of Lucky's silences as follows: "He knew what that silence meant. Lucky had thoughts which later he would claim had been too vague to talk about" (p. 59). Lucky is not made to speak these thoughts aloud to Bigman so we can overhear them, nor are we allowed inside Lucky's head to share them. Instead, we get mysterious remarks like "Lucky nodded thoughtfully. It all fit well," and "It was as he thought" (p. 93). We are not told what fit well or what was as he thought. The disease even spreads to Bigman: "And because Bigman had to make arrangements about the gravity, he explained some of his plan" to one of the other characters (p. 106). But the scene ends without our hearing that explanation, so we don't know what that plan is. Asimov loves to look up from the pot on the stove and mutter promisingly, "Oh what I've got cooking for you! Are you going to like this!" without telling us either the ingredients or the dish.

Another connection with Asimov's other works is that the Lucky Starr series includes two mystery stories based on the Three Laws of Robotics. In this way both *Big Sun of Mercury* (which is very reminiscent of "Runaround") and *Moons of Jupiter* are obviously related to the Robot Stories. The discipline involved in constructing mysteries around the Three Laws may contribute to the extraordinary success of these two novels. I do not find the mystery stories themselves in these two novels in any way inferior to those in the more famous (and perhaps more respectable because not labeled *juveniles*) *The Caves of Steel* and *The Naked Sun*. I would hope that no one deprives himself of the pleasure of reading these two novels simply because they feature Lucky Starr and Bigman Jones instead of Lije Baley and Daneel Olivaw.

One of the strongest points of any Asimov story or novel is the detailed way Asimov works out his settings and the care with which he presents those settings to us. Each novel in the Lucky Starr series is set in a different part of the solar system. Each of these locales has its own well-researched environment and its own human organization specifically tailored to fit that environment. Mercury had been a mining center and is now the location of an experimental station using the huge energies of the sun to do research into the driving of energy through hyperspace to specific destinations. Venus has gigantic, domed, underwater cities specializing in yeast products—i.e., food—for the rest of the solar system. Mars has huge farming combines. Jupiter's moons are a base for research into a new kind of space drive. And Saturn's moons are in the process of being colonized for the first time. Each of these environments has attracted people for different reasons, and as a result, different kinds of human organizations have been set up. Asimov has thought out these new organizations in some detail, giving them sights, technologies, social patterns, and habits of mind of their own. Each novel becomes a little experiment in the relationship between man and environment, and Asimov sets up and performs each experiment with meticulous control of detail.

In one way his insistence on being scientifically accurate has gotten him into what he believes to be trouble. Since the novels were written in the fifties, they make use of the scientific knowledge of the fifties. His Mercury keeps one face to the sun, whereas we now know Mercury rotates. His Venus is a water-world, whereas we now know that Venus has no water. His Mars has a breathable atmosphere, whereas we now know that the atmosphere of Mars is too thin to support human life. What was the best science could offer in the fifties is not the best it can offer in the seventies. As a result, Asimov is concerned that his Lucky Starr series is popularizing scientific inaccuracies, especially among the young. (This concern ties in with his belief that science fiction is a good way to learn science and to become interested in science. See, for example, the collection of stories he edited called *Where Do We Go from Here?*) He also fears that these new scientific discoveries have ruined the series. While the first fear, that of misleading his readers, is certainly valid, just as certainly the second, that of advances in science ruining works of fiction, is not. A work of fiction stands or falls on its internal consistency. A novel is ruined not when its givens turn out to be wrong, but when its givens are mishandled. Asimov does not mishandle his givens, and therefore this bit of Asimovian self-criticism seems to me to be beside the point.

One unusual thing about the Lucky Starr stories is that Asimov does admit aliens into them. It was ancient and disembodied Martian intelligences who gave Lucky that strip of gauze in *David Starr: Space Ranger*. Asimov conjures up some rather awe-inspiring creatures with which to populate the oceans of Venus. There are sea ribbons "of different lengths, varying from tiny threads two inches long to broad and sinuous belts that stretched a yard or more from end to end. They were all thin, thin as a sheet of paper. They moved by rippling their bodies into a series of waves that rippled down their full length. And each one fluoresced, each one sparkled with colored light" (p. 24). At one point Lucky and Bigman are trapped in the ocean under "a two-mile-wide inverted bowl of rubbery flesh" weighing 200 million tons. And the story hinges on the telepathic V-frogs that live by the hundreds of thousands in the tangled seaweed atop the ocean and that raise and lower themselves by unfolding long legs like carpenter's rules. *Big Sun of Mercury* features a creature made of rock that lives in abandoned mine shafts and absorbs heat from any source, including space-suited humans it wraps its tentacles around.

These aliens supply some of science fiction's fabled sense of wonder to the series, but what awes us most often is effects that grow out of the scientific background of the stories. Jules Verne's *Twenty Thousand Leagues Under the Sea* is carried along by an interest in the submarine and in what the submarine enables its occupants to see. It is a series of wonders with little or no story line. Asimov's Lucky Starr stories are first and foremost *stories*. Yet more than once—and with telling effect—the story is set aside so its characters and its readers can simply stand in awe before some natural wonder that space flight has made available. One extended example from many will have to suffice. In *Big Sun of Mercury* the plot requires Lucky to walk from point A to point B on that planet's surface. Here is what happens:

> The ground was sloping upward and he had adjusted his stride to suit it automatically. So preoccupied was he with his thoughts that the sight that caught his eyes as he topped that rise found him unprepared and struck him with amazement.
>
> The extreme upper edge of the Sun was above the broken horizon, yet not the Sun itself. Only the prominences that edged the Sun showed, a small segment of them.
>
> The prominences were brilliant red in color, and one, in the very center of those visible, was made up of blazing streamers moving upward and outward with inching slowness.
>
> Sharp and bright against the rock of Mercury, undimmed by atmosphere, unhazed by dust, it was a sight of incredible beauty. The tongues of flame seemed to be growing out of Mercury's dark crust as though the planet's horizon were on fire or a volcano of more than giant size had suddenly erupted and been trapped in mid-blaze.

Yet those prominences were incomparably more than anything that could have appeared on Mercury. The one he watched, Lucky knew, was large enough to swallow a hundred Earths whole, or five thousand Mercuries. And there it burned in atomic fire, lighting up Lucky and all his surroundings.

He turned off his suit-light to see.

Those surfaces of the rocks that faced directly toward the prominences were awash with ruddy light, all other surfaces were black as coal. It was as though someone had painted a bottomless pit with streaks of red. . . .

The shadow of Lucky's hand on his chest made a patch of black. The ground ahead was more treacherous, since the patches of light that caught every fragment of unevenness fooled the eye into a false estimate of the nature of the surface.

Lucky turned on his suit-light once again and moved forward toward the prominences along the curve of Mercury. [Pp. 84–85]

Strictly speaking, this sort of thing impedes the forward movement of the story. But who cares? Isn't standing on Mercury and seeing this as exciting as finding out whodunnit? That sense of wonder stimulated in those who first saw the land of Genghis Khan and Prester John and Niagara Falls and the Grand Canyon can still be stimulated in us today by that fantastic photograph of the Earth hanging over the barren lunar horizon, by the interplanetary scenes in 2001: A Space Odyssey, by the astronomical art of a Chesley Bonestell, and by the imaginative visualization of such scenes as Asimov has described above. In science fiction the sense of wonder is often sight.

Most of us like to read series in their proper sequence. This means that the first Lucky Starr stories one is likely to read are the first two in the series. After reading them, one probably is tempted to put the whole thing aside as an aberration on Asimov's part. Even Homer nods, etc. But two thirds of the way through *Oceans of Venus,* the third in the series, something happens. One becomes aware that this rather silly kid's story has somehow become an absorbing mystery story. *Big Sun of Mercury* and *Moons of Jupiter* are first-rate science fiction mystery stories that anyone—science fiction fan or mystery fan—can enjoy reading.

The Caves of Steel (1954)

The Caves of Steel is Asimov's favorite from among his own novels. It was written at the request of Horace L. Gold, then editor of the newly established *Galaxy Science Fiction* magazine, and Asimov wrote it only after some serious hesitation. He had come to think of his Robot Stories as short stories, and he doubted that one could be sustained to novel length. Besides, he had absorbed the rather hazy critical idea that one could not combine science fiction and mystery and still play fair with the reader. One could too easily conjure up a semiplausible technological gimmick with which to solve the crime. Still, Gold set him the challenge, and Asimov responded with *The Caves of Steel*.

In its simplest terms, Asimov solved the problem of how to combine science fiction and mystery story by having the science fiction supply the setting and the mystery supply the plot. This is a very simple, straightforward, and even obvious solution—after the fact. Note, for example, that the easily conjured-up gimmick mentioned above would fit into the novel as a part of the plot (rather than as a part of the setting), that is, as the device by which the difficulties of the plot were resolved. By relegating the science fiction elements to the setting, Asimov has removed the calibrated magic wand from his hero's hand and made his story line legitimate.

In fact, as Larry Niven, Roger Zelazny, and Suzette Haden Elgin (among others) have been demonstrating, the intellectual puzzle of a mystery story supplies a perfect excuse for a central character's exploring the ins and outs of an alternate world and/ or society. Put slightly differently, a mystery story plot can be an excellent expository device in a science fiction novel. In *The Caves of Steel*, for example, forty-two-year-old Elijah Baley, the detective, spends most of his time out of his office in the City following up leads and clues, first in one location, then another. In this way the mystery story is being forwarded while we are being taken on a tour of the City. Rather than give us a static explanation—a sort of futurologist's essay—on how a future city might function, Asimov uses the mystery story as his structural device in helping us imaginatively live in that City. We eat in a community kitchen, freshen up in a community bathroom, ride the moving strips which furnish the City's transportation, visit the huge yeast vats where the food is cultivated. The mystery story allows us to experience the City.

I have talked with science fiction fans who objected to the mystery story on the grounds that it got in the way of their understanding and appreciation of Asimov's imaginative feat in creating the City in all its details, and I have talked with mystery story fans who objected to the science fiction setting on the grounds that its development required long passages of exposition which slowed down the working out of the mystery. Personally, I feel that Asimov's solution to the problem of joining the two genres—putting the science fiction in the setting and the mystery in the plot—is entirely satisfactory. The necessary science fiction exposition is worked into the action of the story line so well that almost never am I personally aware of a slowdown in the story.

What makes the performance even more impressive is that the two elements of science fiction and mystery story clearly depend upon one another. One cannot argue that Asimov has achieved novel length simply by stuffing together two novelettes. Take away the mystery and there is no science fiction *story* left; take away the science fiction setting as given and this particular mystery story cannot happen. *The Caves of Steel* cannot work in any other setting because the mystery story depends upon the psychology of the characters, and that psychology in turn depends on the environment in which the characters live. The science fiction setting causes the characters to think and behave in ways that make the mystery story possible.

As one major example of this, consider that the people of the City have lived in their caves of steel for so long that they are psychologically unable to go out of doors, into the atmosphere, under the sun and stars. The murder scene could have been reached by anyone in the City had he simply left the City by one of its twenty or more unguarded exits and then walked across country. But since City-dwellers are psychologically unable to do this, the conclusion must be that it was not done. The City has conditioned its people so that this action is impossible. The science fiction setting establishes the ground rules by which the mystery must be played.

Asimov tells us in the novel that its events take place 3,300 years after people started living where New York City is. If one ignores Indian settlements, this would date the story at about A.D. 5000. From one point of view this is clearly too far in the future. The City seems not that different from the ones in which we now live. It certainly is not 3,000 years different from today. New York is imagined to have 20 million people living on two thousand square miles. Economically, it is self-sufficient. The great majority of the food is cultivated in the great yeast vats. As with Trantor in the Foundation Series, people are not much interested in the out-of-doors, and they are frightened by it when exposed to it. In a time when sections of cities are being converted into gigantic, air-conditioned, enclosed shopping centers, when these shopping centers and apartment buildings are connected by underground walkways, when gargantuan apartment complexes containing grocery stores, barbershops, theaters, etc., are lessening the need and urge to go outside, it is difficult to believe that we need those extra three thousand years to get to the caves of steel. They're here already.

But the novel also assumes a certain amount of interstellar travel and colonization. There are some fifty Outer Worlds which had to have been discovered, explored, and colonized, and cultural patterns different from those on Earth had to have time to develop and stabilize. It was surely this consideration that forced Asimov to set the story so far in the future.

Once again, I think, as in *Pebble in the Sky*, Asimov is trying to put two different futures together in the same novel, with some difficulty. In *Pebble* it was the post-atomic-war cautionary tale welded to the Galactic Empire. Here it is the immediate overpopulated future put in with the much more distant in time fifty colonized Outer Worlds. In *The Caves of Steel* Asimov brings it off well enough that I for one don't feel it to be the major flaw it was in *Pebble*. Perhaps I could put it another way: Logically, the overpopulated City can be forced into the same future with the Outer Worlds, but emotionally the one is almost here, the other is far away. The two world views are emotionally incongruent.

One other thing must be noted about the setting of *The Caves of Steel,* especially because of the view it gives us of much of Asimov's total output. The Earth of *The Caves of Steel* and of its companion novel *The Naked Sun* is not the radioactive Earth of *Triangle.* If *Caves* is a cautionary tale, it cautions against overpopulation rather than atomic war—and these two alternate futures are surely mutually contradictory. This seems to mean that Asimov has not one but two future histories going. The Robot Stories and the Robot Novels (*Caves* and *Sun*) assume a future in which mankind "solves" its overpopulation problems by developing the great Cities. *Triangle* assumes a future in which the population is kept down by the Sixty. Asimov's future histories diverge according to whether they assume the Cities or the atomic war. (I might remind the reader that the early Lucky Starr stories seem to take place against a Galactic Empire setting, while the later Lucky Starr stories seem to shift to a background of fifty Outer Worlds. Thus the Lucky Starr series may be viewed as an attempt to bridge the gap between Asimov's future histories.)

That *The Caves of Steel* is an extension of the Robot Stories is clear. The secondary hero, Lije Baley's partner, R. Daneel Olivaw, is a robot. He and the other robots in the story are programmed according to the Three Laws of Robotics. Baley first suspects that Daneel is a human being and not a robot; later he thinks that Daneel has been constructed without the First Law. In *I, Robot* and in *The Caves of Steel* robots are feared and rejected on Earth while developed and used in space, so both works make use of the same attitudes toward robots.

Besides being related to the Robot Stories, *The Caves of Steel* also shows close connections to both *Triangle* and the Foundation Series. In *Triangle,* for example, we encountered characters (Balkis, Aratap, the Squire of Fife) whose function it was to suggest alternate explanations for the events of the novels, explanations that occasionally were more consistent than those Asimov himself eventually used. Here, largely I suspect because of the mystery story element, the Balkis-type character is merged with the central character, Lije Baley. In the course of the novel Baley is constantly trying to fit events into a pattern. In fact, he develops three separate explanations—solutions—of the murder. Any of the three would do, really. Were Asimov writing a novelette, the first solution could have been correct: Daneel is a human being, not a robot; the "corpse" was a robot; and the murder was faked for political reasons. If he were writing a novella, the second explanation would do: Daneel was constructed without the First Law, and therefore he was the murderer. But Asimov was writing a novel. He got novel length by working in the details of the science fiction setting and by having Baley construct two very good but wrong solutions, and one very good and right one. *Caves* differs from *Triangle* in this respect, first, by combining the Balkis-character with the lead character, and second, by having Asimov's correct solution every bit as good as Baley's two incorrect ones.

Caves also uses a technique found most obviously in *Pebble*. In *Pebble* a definite time was established for when the rockets carrying the disease germs would be sent out, and the protagonists had to beat that time limit. In *Caves* the Spacers decided to drop the case on a certain day, and Baley must solve it by midnight of that day. This establishing of a time limit is a useful device for intensifying the drama.

Asimov also reuses techniques he had used in the Foundation Series. He conceals from his readers exactly the same things about Baley as he earlier had concealed about Salvor Hardin and Hober Mallow: their intentions, their plans for solving the problems facing them, the reasons for certain things that they do. When a pattern finally takes shape in Baley's mind, we are never allowed inside to find out what he's thinking. (Bigman Jones complained of this same habit in Lucky Starr.) For example, as the first climactic scene is building (there is, of course, one climactic scene per solution), Asimov says of Baley, "he was almost mad with desire to go through with his exact plan" (p. 232), but he does not tell us what that plan is. As the second climax develops, Baley makes a call to Washington and arranges for someone to come to New York. We are not told whom Baley called, why he wants him in New York, or what's going on. We are simply asked to wait patiently for it all to come out in the end. To the extent that Asimov does this sort of thing, while he may be building suspense and preparing for the proper dramatic moment of revelation, he is also depriving us of the opportunity to participate with the central character in his attempts to resolve his problems. Whatever one's attitude toward it, it is clearly a technique that Asimov uses over and over, from "Marooned Off Vesta" on.

Another strategy used by Asimov here in *Caves* as well as in the Foundation Series and elsewhere is that of giving a conjectural solution or two before giving the actual solution. If *Caves* is a "whodunnit?" the Foundation Series eventually became a "whereizit?" The Second Foundation was located by both Ebling Mis and Bail Channis. (The reader, of course, is not told.) Where is it? The parallels in story construction among "Search by the Mule," "Search by the Foundation," and *The Stars Like Dust* (with its hidden Rebellion World) have already been discussed (see pp. 132–33). Here, I am simply trying to show that *The Caves of Steel*, with its two false solutions followed by its correct one, also fits the pattern. Of course, this may just as well—or just as equally—be due to *Caves'* being a mystery story, in which false solutions are mandatory, as much as to Asimov's demonstrable delight in alternate explanations. Surely, in the science fiction mystery story Asimov has found the ideal form because it permits him to do all those things he wants to do anyway.

Anyone really seeking them could find "flaws" in the novel. There is in *Caves* the smallest hint of the misuse of flashback that made *The Currents of Space* such a muddle, and that small hint comes in the flashbacks devoted to Baley's relationship with his wife. The lengthy explanation of "Jessie" versus "Jezebel" seems unjustified by the little return in characterization that Asimov gets from it. One has the feeling that Asimov's interest in the Bible and in the history of words and proper names simply got the better of him here. (See especially pp. 198–200.) But it's just an irrelevant flashback to a discussion of the name Jezebel, and not all that crucial to the novel.

In a different sort of way—and still a minor criticism—*The Caves of Steel* tends to date itself in that curious way much science fiction does: when the future is simply the present in new clothes, sometimes the present is still detectable. Then, years later, that "present" becomes the past and the story is dated. I remember that in the forties and fifties the popular magazines and Sunday supplements, extrapolating from huge conveyer belts used to carry coal, occasionally ran articles about conveyer belt transportation systems for our cities. Heinlein's "The Roads Must Roll" grew out of this idea. So do the "strips" in Asimov's *The Caves of Steel*. As a result, the novel is dated as being from the period when that gimmick was popular.

Commissioner Enderby's broken glasses, so important to the story, are another example of this curious way science fiction tends to date itself. True enough, Asimov does point out that contact lenses will be worn by most people and Enderby's glasses are an affectation. But while he "predicts" widespread use of contacts, he does not foresee—or he chooses for the sake of the story line to ignore—glasses made of unbreakable glass. Does anyone endanger his vision by wearing breakable glasses anymore? Would glasses of the year 5000 be breakable? The major clue in the story is a mid-twentieth-century clue, not a clue of the future.

Asimov's attempt to play completely fair with the reader is frayed just a bit at the edges. Daneel is given the ability to psychoprobe. This means he can read a person's character enough to know what his basic motivations are, and thus he can tell what a person is psychologically capable and incapable of doing. I'm not sure to what extent such a technological gimmick is a valid way of getting inside people and passing characterization on to the reader. (See, for example, Daneel's analysis of Baley's motivation and character, pp. 303–5.) To what extent is this simply an easy substitute for the more difficult task of showing us what people are like through their own thoughts and actions? Is such short-circuiting of the job of characterization playing fair?

Still, what we—and Asimov—normally mean by "playing fair" is as Asimov put it, "not solving the mystery with a pocketfrannistan" (see p. 78). Everything should be there for us to see, too, along with the detective. Yet in the very last chapter, when Baley's case seems for a third time to be dissolving around him, we get this scene:

R. Daneel said, "I am sorry, partner Elijah, though happy for the Commissioner, that your story explains nothing. . . . The Commissioner did not murder."

"Thank you," muttered Enderby. His voice gained strength and confidence. "I don't know what your motives are, Baley, or why you should try to ruin me this way, but I'll get to the bottom—"

"Wait," said Baley. "I'm not through. I've got this."

He slammed the aluminum cube on Enderby's desk, and tried to feel the confidence he hoped he was radiating. For half an hour now, he had been hiding from himself one little fact: that he did *not* know what the picture showed. [Pp. 355–56]

When Baley says, "I'm not through. I've got this"—and he then slaps down that aluminum cube—I'm afraid I get a distinct mental image of him reaching into a big, black top hat and whipping out a rabbit. Admittedly, this "micro-projector," as it is later called, is not exactly a pocket-frannistan. Its existence has been known to Baley and to us since the beginning of the novel. But that Baley, the detective assigned to the case, had never bothered to examine it before is incredible. And that Baley's negligence had concealed the final clue from him—and from us—certainly leads to that old *deus ex machina* feeling.

This is not the only occasion on which we learn that Baley had failed to do the obvious. The novel is half over before Baley is reminded by Daneel that he ought to interview the person who discovered the body in the first place. Pacing is extremely important in a detective story. The problem is not only how to present the clues—all of them; none tucked away until the last scene —but when and in what order. I think Asimov has Baley behave in accordance with the necessities of the plot rather than naturally when he has Baley neglect the discoverer of the body until the middle of the novel and when he has him neglect the photo-cube of the murder scene until the end. The carpentry of the novel is showing a bit too much.

Two other things might also be mentioned as flaws in this novel. First, though Daneel is present most of the time, he doesn't really contribute much. He quells a potential riot in a shoe store and he suggests that Baley question Enderby. Most of the time, however, he is simply someone for Baley to talk to us through. Daneel's uselessness is heightened when we remember the challenge put to Baley by the Commissioner in the beginning: Baley must solve the case before Daneel. Yet Baley is given all the initiative, and Daneel merely tags along. No wonder Baley beat him to the solution. Daneel never tried.

The biggest flaw I can see in the novel is connected to it as detective story (rather than as science fiction). It can be simply stated: There are no suspects. As the detectives, Baley and Daneel are clearly out of consideration, despite Baley's first two solutions. Baley's wife is suspected slightly for a while by the characters in the story, though never by the reader. The only other person in the story is Commissioner Enderby. These are the only suspects available. Oh, there are groups lurking around—the medievalists, the Spacers, and so on—but no individuals. This probably reflects once again Asimov's concern for groups rather than individuals. As he has Daneel express it, "We were never under any delusions as to which was more important, an individual or humanity" (p. 344). In context, it is clear that this statement means that humanity transcends the individual. Asimov wants to show us life in the City. He is not concerned with any particular life. Baley's quirks are those that characterize the City-dweller, not those that characterize Baley. Be all this as it may, a group is not a suspect, and in *The Caves of Steel* there are no suspects. How, then, can we weigh the evidence and decide whodunnit?

It is necessary to continue the line of argument of the preceding paragraph one more step. In the course of the novel Baley does eventually come to stand out as an individual from the group to which he belongs. He shares the quirks of the City-dwellers initially, but he can cure himself of them, with a little help from Daneel and the Spacers. His willingness to consider change made him an ideal subject for a Spacer experiment performed mainly by Daneel, "the experiment of persuading you that colonization was the answer to Earth's problems" (p. 341). Baley's willingness, combined with "a mild drug intended only to make your mind more receptive," leads Daneel and the others to close the case and end the experiment when they become convinced that Baley—and therefore other Earthmen—can accept the idea of colonization. The real goal of the Spacers on Earth was not to solve the murder mystery, but to free Earthmen from their Cities.

Perhaps this is as good a place as any to mention that Daneel's passivity is only apparent. He is not interested in the murder case. Like Lucky Starr in *The Rings of Saturn,* Daneel has his plan (which Asimov does not tell us about), and he only seems passive because his working out of that plan is hidden from us. When we do finally learn what is really going on, it is too late. We have not been permitted to share Daneel's aims, so we do not share a sense of satisfaction at his achieving them. Only in retrospect is Daneel an active character.

As Damon Knight observed in his review of *The Caves of Steel* in *In Search of Wonder,* colonization cannot be the solution to Earth's overpopulation problem, despite everyone's apparent satisfaction with it. It may work aesthetically on paper, but it could never work in practice. Taking Asimov at his word—he has said that the ideal population for the Earth is one billion—Earth would have to develop and build a space fleet capable of transporting seven billion people off planet to the new worlds. (One of the aesthetically attractive features of this solution, it seems to me, is that by breaking humanity's stasis and beginning anew the spread of mankind among the stars, this solution would seem to fit *Caves* into Asimov's whole future history. This is the way we get Galactic Empire from the overpopulated, fearful Earth of *The Caves of Steel.*)

Finally, I'd like to develop a discussion of the theme of the novel. Psychologists are constantly reminding us that man is a product of his heredity and environment. One of the major differences between the Spacers of the Outer Worlds and the City-dwellers of Earth is that the City-dwellers regulate how many children a couple may have and the Spacers regulate the genetic quality of their children. The major problem of Earth is overpopulation, so they would naturally concentrate on quantity. The thin populations on the Outer Worlds enable them to concentrate on quality of both the people and their lives. In this connection the novel raises, only to ignore, a very interesting point. Baley asks a Spacer, "Who's to judge which children should live?" and the reply is "That's rather complicated and not to be answered in a sentence. Someday we may talk it out in detail" (p. 255). The occasion for that discussion never arises.

But if the Earth does not control heredity, it certainly—by constructing and maintaining the Cities—controls environment. In turn, the environment determines the inhabitants. The City-dweller about whom we know the most, Lije Baley, is made comfortable or uncomfortable according to reactions taught him by his City. He is uncomfortable going to the Spacer colony because he must breathe natural rather than artificial air. And for another reason: "the air currents hit amazingly against his face. They were gentle enough, but they were erratic. They bothered him" (p. 233). Once in the colony he "was thankful for the feel of the conditioned air." He is offered some natural food and is unnerved because he has always eaten processed food. "Fruit, now, properly speaking, should come in the form of sauce or preserves. What he was holding now must come straight from the dirt of a planet's soil. He thought: I hope they've washed it at least" (p. 235).

So the City has shaped its dwellers' thinking habits until they are comfortable in it and uncomfortable out of it. But the City's influence has been even more pervasive than that: "The City was the acme of efficiency, but it made demands of its inhabitants. It asked them to live in a tight routine and order their lives under a strict and scientific control" (pp. 187–88). The class structure, for example, is based on C-ratings. Baley is a C-5 at the start of the novel and may be made a C-7 if he successfully handles the case. (In the next novel we learn he was in fact promoted to C-6.) Each C-rating has its privileges: a private shower room, a seat on the transportation system. The ultimate horror is declassification.

The Caves of Steel generally is about man's relationship to his environment. Since in this novel the environment itself is man-made, the question that is raised is Who's in charge here? Has man shaped the Cities in his own best interests, or are the Cities shaping him? Bluntly put, are the Cities a good thing or a bad thing? It probably should be noted that both the Cities and the spaceships which theoretically make colonization possible are the products of technology. The choice is not between technology and a lack thereof, but between two different applications of technology. Asimov is proscience and protechnology.

Early in the story Asimov stops the action for several pages of exposition on the development of the Cities. They are presented as the technological solutions to man's problems with overpopulation. We are told bluntly, "The Cities were good" (p. 182). In *Nightfall and Other Stories* Asimov remarks, "I wrote a novel in 1953 which pictured a world in which everyone lived in underground cities, comfortably enclosed away from the open air. People would say, 'How could you imagine such a nightmarish situation?' And I would answer in astonishment, 'What nightmarish situation?'" (p. 244). Asimov seems, then, to like the City.

Still, as the novel goes along, the City begins to seem less and less satisfactory. Baley and we have listened to such Spacer arguments as "Earthmen are all so coddled, so enwombed in their imprisoning caves of steel, that they are caught forever. . . . Civism is ruining Earth, sir" (p. 254). By the end of the novel, we and Baley see the Cities as prisons rather than solutions, and we are willing to accept colonization as an escape from those prisons, as a way to free man. If colonization cannot work in actual practice, it certainly can work as a thematic solution to the novel's problem: how can man control his environment for his own benefit rather than have it control him?

The whole question of man's relationship to his technological environment is put into the novel in another way: Lije Baley is man and R. Daneel Olivaw is technology. Lije has Daneel forced upon him. He does not like it, but he does the best he can. (Which of us chose freely to live in a world of automobiles, air conditioning, and television?) In casting about for responsibility for the crime, Baley twice accuses Daneel. (Which of us doesn't know that the world would be better off without those unforeseen by-products of technology—air pollution, atomic weapons, enervating television programming, traffic deaths?) Baley does not trust the unemotional, rational Daneel, and we do not trust an impersonal technology.

By the end of the novel, however, Baley has established a working relationship with Daneel. He has even come to like him. They have, if you will, learned to get along. Some may feel that this is an analogue of the relationship established between man and the City at the beginning of the novel. Man has adapted to that environment to such an extent that he is more comfortable in prison than out. But I feel that Baley's relationship with Daneel is an analogue, not of the City-dwellers' subservient relationship with the City, but of man's potentially beneficial relationship with technology. Daneel is a representative not of the City, but of the Spacer hope for freedom for man among the stars.

Several times in the novel the subject of a C/Fe culture arises. Baley asks about it—"What's see fee?"—and Daneel replies, "Just the chemical symbols for the elements carbon and iron, Elijah. Carbon is the basis of human life and iron of robot life. It becomes easy to speak of C/Fe when you wish to express a culture that combines the best of the two on an equal but parallel basis" (p. 213). A C/Fe culture is one in which man and the products of his technology work together. *Pebble in the Sky* was constructed to show the insanity of racial prejudice. *The Caves of Steel* deals with prejudice also: man's prejudice against his own technology.

Once again: Asimov does not have a Frankenstein complex. The products of our intelligence will not turn on us. The City (in which we all, to one extent or another, live today) may be a stultifying dead end. But if we continue to work at it—if we learn to get along with science and technology as Baley learned to get along with Daneel—beyond the City is the Galactic Empire. Man among the stars is surely science fiction's best symbol of the freedom of man.

The Naked Sun (1957)

The Naked Sun reunites Lije Baley and R. Daneel Olivaw, and sends them to solve a murder on the planet Solaria, where robots outnumber people ten thousand to one, where everyone has an estate numbered in the hundreds of square miles, and where people almost never come into the physical presence of other people. Instead, they meet and communicate with one another via devices that set up trimensional images, indistinguishable from physical presence except by different backgrounds and by the instant disappearance of the images once the conversation has ended. A strong distinction is maintained between "viewing" trimensional images and "seeing" in the flesh.

This setting is obviously in strong contrast with that of *The Caves of Steel*. There, Earth had eight billion people grouped in eight hundred Cities averaging ten million each, and robots were opposed because they took jobs from real human beings. Clearly, the Earth of *The Caves of Steel* is not all that different from our own civilization. Just as clearly, little connection exists between our world and Solaria. It is very curious, then, that *The Naked Sun* is a more accessible, more familiar, novel than *The Caves of Steel*.

The reason for this is, it seems to me, that *The Naked Sun* has about it the identical atmosphere of a classical English detective story set in the sparsely populated English countryside. [Robots stand off to the side like servants ready to do the master's bidding.] The murder occurs in a large manor house on a large country estate. The body is discovered by the wife. An expert detective is called in from the big city. He conducts a round of interviews—both viewing and seeing—and collects data and suspects. Eventually everyone is gathered together, and the mystery is unraveled in a great climactic drawing room scene.

The best thing about *The Naked Sun* is the way it develops further certain implications in the Three Laws of Robotics. As usual, the First Law—"A robot may not harm a human being, or, through inaction, allow a human being to come to harm"—is the key one. What the novel effectively does is destroy that First Law by showing that a well-trained roboticist could commit murder by using two or more robots in combination. One robot is given an order, a second is given a second order related to the first, and the two added together result in murder, carried out at the direction of a human being, it is true, but committed by the robots. *The Naked Sun* shows that robots can kill.

A minor character, Dr. Gruer, drinks a glass of water and almost dies because it was poisoned. ("Almost dies" because the poisoner bungled the job by putting in too much poison, which caused Gruer to regurgitate most of the fluid.) Here is Baley's analysis of how the crime was committed:

"Suppose a man says to a robot, 'Place a small quantity of this liquid into a glass of milk. . . . After you have performed this action, forget you have done so.' . . . Now a second robot has poured out the milk in the first place and is unaware that the milk has been tampered with. In all innocence, it offers the milk to a man and the man dies." [P. 502]

Fortunately for the plot, Gruer had the habit of drinking his water at room temperature, so his robots were in the habit of letting a glass of it stand out unattended. One robot poisons the water, another unwittingly serves it. And Baley insists that the First Law should actually be stated, "A robot may do nothing that, *to its knowledge,* will harm a human being; nor, through inaction, *knowingly* allow a human being to come to harm."

There are three murders or attempted murders in the novel. This is the best handled of the three. The weakest is the attempt on Lije Baley himself. While out collecting data, Baley goes to the "farm" where month-old fetuses are brought and where the resulting children are raised past puberty. A child playing with a bow and arrow is given by a robot a poisoned arrow, which the child shoots at Baley, narrowly missing him. Item: No one knew Baley was going to the farm. Who knew to set the trap? Item: Even granting that the villain got the information from the robots, who were everywhere and in constant radio communication with one another, when did he have time to set the trap? Baley is at the farm too short a time to allow one robot to poison the arrow and a second to put it in the boy's quiver.

Asimov does a good job of anticipating and explaining as many other problems with this assassination attempt as he can think of: the boy, used to shooting at robots, had been told Baley was a dirty, disease-ridden Earthman (furnishing motive); the robot who told that to the boy couldn't remember who had told *him* (villain covering tracks); the poisoned arrow had gray feathers instead of black (so the robot could easily pick it out); the boy aimed and shot too quickly for the robot to prevent him from harming a human being (circumventing First Law); etc., etc. Still, the whole business is contrived and unconvincing, and in the climactic scene Asimov wisely doesn't go back over it in detail. He merely has the villain admit, "I arranged the arrow meant for you" (p. 543).

The central murder in the story—the one Baley is called from Earth to solve—is handled better than this attempt on his life but not as well as the attempt to poison Gruer. Rikaine Delmarre's head has been crushed by a blunt instrument which is not found at the scene of the crime. His hysterical wife, who recalls nothing, is present, as is a shorted-out and therefore useless robot. The suspects include: Gladia, the wife; Attlebish, Acting Head of Security on Solaria; Leebig, a roboticist and a close friend of the Delmarres'; Quemot, a sociologist; Klorissa Cantoro, Delmarre's female lab assistant; and Dr. Thool, Gladia's father. Strictly speaking, I suppose, only Gladia, Leebig, Klorissa, and Thool are really suspects, though in mystery stories it is often the least suspected who is guilty. Still, all these people are present for the résumé of the evidence and the pointing of the finger in the grand climactic scene. Suspects and a final gathering—two elements missing from *The Caves of Steel.*

With apologies to anyone who has not yet read *The Naked Sun*—and with the repeated urging to get it and read it, and then see if you agree with my observations—I must discuss that scene. It turns out that Rikaine Delmarre was murdered because he had discovered that his roboticist friend Leebig was working on certain new developments in robot design. One of these developments, a minor one yet the key to what happened to the murder weapon, concerned replaceable and interchangeable limbs for robots. Using such a limb, the murderer could bash in Delmarre's head with the robot's arm, then replace that arm so that no one would notice it. Who on Solaria paid any attention to robots?

More significant were Leebig's experiments with spaceships controlled with positronic brains. Such unmanned ships could be programmed to fight manned ships—and even inhabited worlds—because they would not know those ships to be manned or those worlds to be inhabited. (Remember Baley's rewording of the First Law?) First Law could be circumvented and—shades of *Pebble in the Sky!*—a few men on Solaria could successfully take over Earth and the Outer Worlds. Once more, in good science fiction fashion, a threat to civilization has been met and thwarted.

Yet some nagging doubts linger around that last scene. For example, referring to an earlier conversation, Baley says to Leebig, "You mentioned spaceships with built-in positronic brains" (p. 541). But the statement of Leebig's that Baley evidently has in mind is "Why have a robot manipulate controls when a positronic brain can be built into the controls itself?" (p. 503). Leebig does not mention *spaceship* controls. How does Baley get from Leebig's statement about "controls" to a plot to use positronic brains against the universe?

Leebig's confession presents a second problem. He is illegally coerced into confessing. He cannot psychologically stand the physical presence of another human being. When he learns that Daneel, who has been masquerading as a human being, will enter his room, he will confess anything to keep Daneel out. So he babbles, "Do you want a confession? Delmarre's robot had detachable limbs. Yes. Yes. Yes. I arranged Gruer's poisoning. I arranged the arrow meant for you. I even planned the spaceships as you said. . . . Only keep the man away. Don't let him come. Keep him away!" (p. 543). Note how carefully this frightened man's confession has been worded by Asimov to keep his story line going. Leebig has confessed that the robot had detachable limbs, not that he used one of those limbs to kill Delmarre. And no one notices.

When Daneel appears, Leebig commits suicide, which also protects Asimov's story line. Now there is little chance that anyone will learn that he didn't kill Delmarre after all. Just as the obvious murder weapon was the one at the scene, the robot, so the obvious murderer was also the one at the scene, the wife, Gladia. Baley righteously takes the attitude that she was used by Leebig to kill Delmarre just as methodically and mechanically as he had used the robots in the attempts on Gruer's and Baley's lives, and that therefore she is not morally guilty. Baley next arranges for her to emigrate to Aurora and tells no one on Solaria of her part in the crime. Leebig commits suicide so that Baley can successfully shield Gladia, which means that Leebig's action is as much motivated by the necessities of the plot as it is by his own internal nature. There is nothing inherently wrong with this. It is the way all fiction—and especially great fiction—operates. In this instance, however, I think it's all too obviously pat and mechanical. This is probably because the characters' inner natures are not so well developed that we recognize what they do as inevitable. We feel that what they do, they do because of the plot and not because of themselves. Had Leebig not committed suicide, I could have believed that, too. The various parts of the ending click into place instead of growing quietly and naturally out of what has gone before. The ending is mechanical and constructed rather than organic and inevitable.

Besides, the ending violates two earlier assumptions which had been built into the story. First, Baley himself (misleadingly, it turns out) had said earlier, "You don't think there are two murderers, do you? If Gladia was responsible for one crime, she must be responsible for the second attempt, also" (p. 505). But according to the ending, there *are* two murderers, Leebig and Gladia. Asimov through Baley has intentionally misled us, and I'm not at all sure that that sort of thing is any more legitimate than having the hero say nothing at all about his plans, theories, and actions.

Second, Baley himself (again misleadingly, as it turns out) had also reassured everyone, "It is easy to show that, whoever committed the murder, Mrs. Delmarre did not" (p. 537). If this is not deliberate obfuscation, it is at least having Baley use the term "murder" in a very strict way: she bashed in his head, but she didn't murder him because Leebig set her up to do it. The responsibility for her action was his, not hers. I'm not sure that such hair-splitting over the word "murder" is legitimate. She did so do it, despite Baley's misleading assertion and proof to the contrary.

The novel is rushed to a conclusion once Leebig commits suicide. There is a touching (literally and emotionally) farewell scene between Baley and Gladia. I assume this is here in order to establish some sort of further motivation for Baley's shielding of her—"further" because we have already seen that he thinks her morally innocent. There is no farewell scene between Baley and Daneel, a curious oversight, it seems to me, considering the importance of their relationship in both Robot Novels. Then, abruptly, Baley is back on Earth for a seven-page summing up with the man who had assigned him the case originally. Three things come out in this scene: (1) Earth must start colonizing again (which was also one of the conclusions of *The Caves of Steel*), (2) Gladia killed her husband, and (3) Baley wants to go to Aurora next (which demonstrates that Asimov clearly had a sequel in mind). And the novel ends with a short scene showing Baley's discomfort at being back in the City. Man must move out among the stars, etc.

This rush-to-conclusion may simply be the result of Asimov's recognizing that once the crime has been solved a mystery story must end as quickly as possible. But there is an air of hastiness about the whole thing, as if he wanted simply to have done with

it. It was at this stage in his career that he decided to get out of
fiction and into nonfiction primarily, and perhaps this enters into
it. (Very early in the novel, Baley is made to think, "If we don't
like it, let's do something about it. Let's not just waste time with
fairy tales" [p. 366].)

Perhaps Asimov's hastiness in ending the novel can be accounted for by a vague dissatisfaction with it on his part. In the
above discussions of the climactic scene and the concluding snippets, I have pointed out some possible reasons for dissatisfaction.
Let me cite a few more. For one thing, Daneel's role in this novel
is in some respects even less satisfactory than it was in *Caves,*
where at least he stood alongside Baley throughout. Here, for
nearly one third of the novel, Daneel is absent. Baley—and Asimov?—simply doesn't want to be encumbered by him. Daneel is
given an excellent—though wrong—solution to the murder, but
basically Asimov does not use Daneel to good effect. The lack
of a farewell scene between the two may be a kind of admission
of this.

As we have noted often before, Asimov likes to heighten reader
interest by concealing certain relevant information. He likes to
have his heroes do things for unexplained reasons of their own.
We must simply be patient, and sooner or later it will all be made
clear. This technique is in itself neither good nor bad. It depends
on how it is used and on the effect of that use on the novel as a
whole. I think that in *The Naked Sun* its use harms the novel on
at least two occasions. The first instance begins immediately after
the attempted poisoning of Gruer. Baley says, "It could be done
very easily. And I'm sure I know exactly how" (p. 438). Then
the whole thing is forgotten for over sixty pages (which in itself
is bad enough) to be revealed eventually as a relatively minor
point in an interview Baley was having with a suspect concerning another matter entirely! We are first asked to wait too long,
and then the solution is given to us in the wrong context.

The second instance occurs when Baley gives Daneel the slip
and goes off on his own for nearly sixty pages of data-collecting
and suspect-interviewing. Only when he rejoins Daneel does he
say why he has been insisting on seeing rather than viewing and
why he had to be without Daneel. (Daneel's response is perfectly
apropos—of both Baley and Asimov: "You did not explain this"

[p. 523].) In other words, for over sixty pages we don't have the faintest idea what's going on or why.

In the first instance, Asimov hides how Baley thinks the poisoner did it—and then tells too late and in a relatively minor scene. In the second instance, he hides Baley's motives for sixty pages of activity. I don't see that the concealment technique contributed anything valuable to the novel in either case.

A third reason for discontent—besides Daneel's lack of a role and the misuse of the technique of concealment—is that here (as was not the case in *Caves*) the plot does not always provide sufficient excuse and reason for exploring the setting. "Getting the feel of the planet" can be used to justify doing anything, I suppose, but it is not sufficient reason for doing any particular thing. After a while, in Lije's perambulations without Daneel, we begin to ask, Why does he want to go there? and Why does he want to know that? The long discussion of Solaria's cultural history in Chapter 10 is interesting, but it seems too much like a mere background-inserting conversation. The tour of the farm in Chapter 11 is again interesting, but again it feels like a digression. Of course, if Asimov had not decided to conceal from us what Baley was after, perhaps they would seem to fit better. As they stand, on first reading they are filler, and only in hindsight do they become relevant and then only in a very general way.

Finally, here again, as in *Caves*, Asimov shows that tendency to let Baley overlook an obvious question for the sake of orderly development of the plot. The novel is almost finished before Baley thinks to ask anyone about Gladia's presumed motive for killing her husband. Since throughout the novel all the Solarians had insisted to Baley that Gladia had to be the murderer, why didn't Baley ask someone about this sooner than page 507? The answer seems to be because the novel as plotted demanded that this bit of information be revealed now and no earlier.

The Naked Sun is not so good as *The Caves of Steel*. By choosing *Caves* as his best novel, Asimov implicitly seems to agree with that evaluation. It does, however, have two major points in its favor. It continues Asimov's examination of the Three Laws of Robotics in new and interesting directions: the ability of robots to obey the Three Laws depends on what they know, so that a clever human being can play on their ignorance to murder and to wage war. Also, *The Naked Sun* shows us once again Asimov's ability to construct in detail an alternate setting for consciousness and the habitual ways of thinking that would develop in that setting. These are no mean feats, and I think that for most sympathetic readers of science fiction, they completely overbalance whatever technical flaws the novel might have. The craftsmanship of *The Naked Sun* may not be up to that of *The Caves of Steel*, but both novels show us Asimov's imagination at work sustaining a vision and helping us live in that vision for a while. That's what science fiction is all about, and these two examples show us why Asimov is as revered as he is.

Asimov himself tells us what happened during and immediately after the writing of *The Naked Sun:*

> While I was writing *The Naked Sun,* it became perfectly clear to me that what I was working on was the second novel of a trilogy.
>
> In *The Caves of Steel* I had a society heavily overweighted in favor of humanity, with the robots unwelcome intruders. In *The Naked Sun,* on the other hand, I had an almost pure robot society with only a thin leaven of humanity barely holding it together.
>
> What I needed to do next was to form the perfect topper to my vision of the future by setting the third novel of the trilogy in Aurora, and depicting the complete fusion of man and robot into a society that was more than both and better than either.
>
> In the summer of 1958 I even started the novel, and then, somewhere in the fourth chapter, between one page and the next, something happened. . . .
>
> In the fall of 1957, when Sputnik One went up, I began brooding about the overwhelming importance of science popularization. It seemed to me that the American public deserved understanding of science and that it was the burning duty of writing scientists to try to give them that understanding. [P. 555]

As a result, he became a science popularizer and his output of science fiction was drastically reduced. This third period in his science fiction career, the period of the novels, was over. His next period was to be marked by anthologies of shorter fiction culled from the magazines, and it is to these anthologies and to this short fiction that we now turn.

Asimov's Collections

The Martian Way and Other Stories (1955)
Earth Is Room Enough (1957)
Nine Tomorrows (1959)
Asimov's Mysteries (1968)
Nightfall and Other Stories (1969)
The Early Asimov (1972)

CHAPTER SEVEN

Asimov's Collections I

Setting aside the stories that have already been treated—his Robot Stories, his Foundation Series, and his novels—Asimov produced between 1941 and 1969 ninety-three science fiction stories. Of those ninety-three sixty-seven have appeared in the six collections that mark this fourth period in his career. Because of their availability, I intend to concentrate on these sixty-seven stories, but I will not totally ignore the twenty-six that he has not (as yet) put into collections of his own.

The Early Asimov (1972)

In *The Early Asimov* Asimov prints all nine of the non-Robot and non-Foundation stories he had printed between 1939 and *Pebble in the Sky* in 1950, and he prints them in the order in which they were written rather than the order in which they were printed. (The greatest discrepancy in this regard occurred with "Author! Author!" which was written in the spring of 1943 and not printed until the first month of 1964. This certainly serves as a reminder that the date of a story's publication is not always a good indication of where that story falls in an author's career.) In examining the nine stories in *The Early Asimov* which appeared after "Nightfall," we will be examining the nonseries stories Asimov wrote in the second period of his science fiction career, the 1940s.

The first story Asimov wrote after "Nightfall" was "Not Final!" Set in the not-too-distant future, "Not Final!" concerns human scientists on Ganymede who make radio contact with intelligent life forms on Jupiter, who turn out to be extremely hostile to the human race and who therefore decide to rise up off the surface of Jupiter and exterminate the vermin of humanity. ("Victory Unintentional" was the Robot Story sequel to "Not Final!") The story looks to a variety of Asimov's other works in a variety of ways. As in the Foundation Series, the "action" consists mainly of a series of conversations. The story consists of five scenes: (1) two men sit and talk (pp. 340–41), (2) two men walk and talk (pp. 342–47), (3) two men sit and talk (pp. 348–50) and a third joins them (pp. 350–52), (4) three men stand and talk (pp. 352–55), (5) two men talk, one standing, one sitting (pp. 355–56). So far as what we are asked to visualize is concerned, the plot is that two men talk awhile in a room; get up, put on space suits, and walk across the surface of Ganymede; go into another room to talk some more; and are taken by a third man to see a lab experiment. The last scene is a conversation between two men on a spaceship, neither of whom has appeared in the story before. Clearly, the action of the story is not in what happens, in what the characters do. Written in June of 1941, "Not Final!" shows Asimov developing the ability to have conversation carry the story, an ability he would put to good use in August when he wrote the first story in the actionless Foundation Series.

As the two men are walking across Ganymede, one looks up and sees Jupiter. "At first, Orloff absorbed the gibbous disk in silence. It was gigantic, thirty-two times the apparent diameter of the Sun as seen from Earth. Its stripes stood out in faint washes of color against the yellowness beneath and the Great Red Spot was an oval splotch of orange near the western rim" (p. 344). Asimov does exactly this sort of astronomical scene-painting elsewhere (for example, in the Lucky Starr series). He often permits his characters to be impressed by the awe-inspiring sights that space travel has made available to them.

The story also demonstrates that understanding of how scientists work which characterizes Asimov's fiction from "Marooned Off Vesta," whose solution hinged on a physical property of water which the student Asimov had just learned in chemistry class, through the first part of *The Gods Themselves,* with its realistic portrayal of the jealousies and motivations of research scientists. One of the conflicts in "Not Final!" is between the true scientist, who uses theory and mathematics to learn what the results of an experiment will be before it is actually performed, and the technician, who putters around at random with little or no idea of what will happen. In this story, ironically, the true scientist demonstrates that the Jovians cannot create a force field strong enough to lift them off their planet, while the technician builds such a ship by trial and error—and at the cost of an arm and an eye.

"Not Final!" is a well-cobbled, neatly put together story. I take it to be a typically "Asimovian" story. As in "Homo Sol," the early Asimov is speaking in his own voice. He found that voice early and has spoken in it with remarkable consistency ever since. One knows what one is getting when he picks up an Asimov story: "Homo Sol" and "Not Final!"

Asimov wrote two fantasy stories with Frederick Pohl, "The Little Man on the Subway" three months before he began "Nightfall," and "Legal Rites" two months after "Nightfall" and immediately after "Not Final!" Speaking of collaboration, Asimov points out that these two stories with Pohl were "the only pieces of fiction I ever wrote in collaboration, and I didn't really enjoy the process. I'm essentially a loner and like to take full responsibility for what I write. In the case of 'Legal Rites' it seems to me that the beginning is mostly Pohl's rewriting; the trial scene is mostly mine; the ending—I don't remember" (p. 384).

"The Little Man on the Subway" is about a subway conductor named Cullen whose train gets shunted onto a track where stations have names like Seraph Road and Cherub Plaza, and whose last huge station is ruled by a god named Crumley, who makes Cullen a Disciple. Cullen then gets involved with some rebel Disciples who—oh, forget it. It's an awful story.

"Legal Rites," on the other hand, is a pleasantly amusing story about a ghost who goes to court to establish his legal rights to the property he haunts—and wins the case! Trial scenes by their very nature are largely conversation, and conversation is a forte of Asimov's. The lengthy trial in "Legal Rites" is especially good.

"Author! Author!" is a pleasant surprise from among Asimov's works. Like the two stories he wrote with Pohl, it is fantasy rather than science fiction, and it therefore lacks the scientific element usually associated with Asimov. It is tempting to read autobiographical elements into this story, since its central character is an idolized writer of popular fiction, here named Graham Dorn instead of Isaac Asimov and here a writer of detective stories about one Reginald de Meister rather than science fiction stories about Elijah Baley.

For me, the first scene in the story is a curiously familiar one. I was present one evening when Asimov, after a public lecture, sat in an upholstered sofa a bit too low for him, balancing a tiny napkin and an even tinier paper cup of red punch on one knee and three coin-sized cookies on the other. He was doing an excellent job of being the lion for a group of people who wanted to lionize him. And the conversation sounded remarkably like Graham Dorn's twenty years earlier:

—Oh, Mr. Dorn, do you work from inspiration? I mean, do you just sit down and then an idea strikes you—all at once? And you must sit up all night and drink black coffee to keep you awake till you get it all down?

—Oh, yes. Certainly. (His working hours were two to four in the afternoon every other day, and he drank milk.)

—Oh, Mr. Dorn, you must do the most awful research to get all those bizarre murders. About how much must you do before you can write a story?

—About six months, usually. (The only reference books he ever used were a six-volume encyclopedia and year-before-last's World Almanac.)

—Oh, Mr. Dorn, did you make up your Reginald de Meister from a real character? You must have. He's oh, so convincing in his every detail.

—He's modelled after a very dear boyhood chum of mine. (Dorn had never known *anyone* like de Meister. He lived in continual fear of meeting anyone like him. He had even a cunningly fashioned ring containing a subtle Oriental poison for use just in case he did. So much for de Meister.) [Pp. 398–99]

Dorn has decided to quit writing detective stories and to try his hand instead at a "serious" novel. (That similar thoughts have occasionally occurred to Asimov is clear from his continual denials that he is even the least bit interested in writing Great Literature about the Eternal Verities.) The gimmick in the story is that Reginald de Meister does not want his creator to abandon him, and so de Meister enters Dorn's world in order to prevent it. Reality, it appears, is what people believe, and Dorn has made so many people believe in de Meister that de Meister is real.

So the character appears in the author's world, and Asimov has a lot of fun with the situation. For example, during their first conversation, de Meister attempts to convince Dorn that Dorn had better keep on writing de Meister mysteries. Dorn rebels.

> Reginald de Meister's eyes turned icy, and Graham suddenly remembered the passage on page 123 of *The Case of the Broken Ashtray:*
>
> *His eyes, hitherto lazy and unattentive, hardened into twin pools of blue ice and transfixed the butler, who staggered back, a stifled cry on his lips.*
>
> Evidently, de Meister lost none of his characteristics out of the novels he adorned. Graham staggered back, a stifled cry on his lips. [Pp. 404–5]

Dorn's publisher is happy to hear that de Meister is real on the grounds of good publicity: "What other writer has a real detective? All the others are fictional. Everyone knows that. But yours —*yours* is real" (p. 410). When de Meister meets June Billings, Dorn's fiancée, Dorn remembers a line in every one of his novels:

> *There was a certain fascination about de Meister that appealed irresistibly to women.*
>
> And June Billings was—as it had often, in Graham's idler moments, occurred to him—a woman.
>
> And fascination simply gooed out of her ears and coated the floor six inches deep.
>
> "Get out of this room, June," he ordered.
>
> "I will not."
>
> "There is something I must discuss with Mr. de Meister, man to man. I demand that you leave this room."
>
> "Please go, Miss Billings," said de Meister.
>
> June hesitated, and in a very small voice said, "Very well."
>
> "Hold on," shouted Graham. "Don't let him order you about. I demand that you stay."
>
> She closed the door very gently behind her. [P. 418]

To top it all off, de Meister sees to it that Dorn literally cannot write anything but de Meister stories. Dorn's problem is how to get rid of de Meister. How does one uncreate a character who exists because you convinced readers he was real?

Dorn revises his latest de Meister manuscript to give the detective a shrewish wife, who then appears in the story because the secretary typing the manuscript believes in her. To escape, de Meister disappears. And everyone else lives happily ever after.

"Author! Author!" is a pleasant, wittily told story which probes the relationship between fiction and reality. It is closer to *Six Characters in Search of an Author* than to *The Caves of Steel*. One could even consider it a very short and hesitant step in the direction of "serious" literature. I think it—despite excessive imagery like that fascination gooing out of ears and covering the floor six inches deep—one of Asimov's better stories, even though it is in no way "Asimovian."

The next story Asimov wrote was an inconsequential piece of material called "Death Sentence." It is reminiscent of the kind of story in which you learn on the last page that those two stranded colonists are called Adam and Eve, or the one in which those funny-looking creatures whose strange habits you've been laughing at are Earthmen. In "Death Sentence" an albino scientist named Theor Realo has spent the greater part of his professional life seeking a world established by the Ancients in prehistoric times and peopled, as part of an experiment in psychology, with organic robots. These robots would be dangerous to the Galaxy if they escaped their home planet. (Campbell's influence is clear.) When the decision is made to destroy the robot world, Realo dashes off to warn its inhabitants. He is heading toward one of their major cities—New York, they call it.

Despite some interesting features—the albino scientist is a pattern for the Mule, for example, and the infighting among the scientists and bureaucrats prefigures that in the first part of *The Gods Themselves*—still, the triteness of the story's ending hurts it. (Yes, I know it was written thirty years ago, but even if it weren't trite then, it can be nothing else to someone reading it today.)

It also contains a major flaw—or at least a mistake in presenta-

tion that unnecessarily misleads the reader. In the opening scene
Realo says, "I've lived on Dorlis twenty-five years" (p. 427). He
also says he knows the robot world exists because "I've been there
these last twenty-five years!" (p. 428). Therefore, Dorlis is the
robot world, right? Wrong. When he leaves the scientific expedition working on Dorlis to confirm his findings, he goes to "a dust-
speck of an isolated world" which is clearly *not* Dorlis. We live
with those scientists on Dorlis a long time before we learn that
Dorlis is not the robot world. We have been misled, and that is a
storyteller's mistake in craftsmanship that should not have been
allowed to stand. "Death Sentence" is not up to either "Homo
Sol" or "Not Final!" as good nonseries Asimov, though its subject
matter and procedures are more typical of him than "Author!
Author!"

Between 1943 and 1948 Asimov wrote only two stories that
were not part of either the Robot Stories or the Foundation
Series: "Blind Alley" (written September–October 1944) and
"No Connection" (written May 1947). "Blind Alley" is a curious
story necessarily marred by the kind of story it is. For one thing,
it is really one of the Foundation Series even though it was not
printed in any of the three Foundation collections. The events
of the story are dated 977–78 Galactic Era, Trantor is mentioned
as the center of government, and the Galaxy is entirely occupied
by human beings. When I asked Asimov about it, he replied,
"'Blind Alley' was not really written as a Foundation story. I
used the Galactic Empire background because that was convenient, but I was eventually sorry that I did, because there is
just no room for any non-human intelligent species in the Foundation universe" (personal letter, November 15, 1973). But in
the story the nonhumans leave the Galaxy precisely because there
is no room for them. Probably more pressing than the reason
Asimov gives is that "Blind Alley" makes no mention of Hari
Seldon and his Plan. It is not in the main line of the Foundation
Series in exactly the same way that "Robot AL-76 Goes Astray"
was not in the main line of the Robot Stories and so was left out
of *I, Robot*.

Even more curious than its being an unacknowledged Foundation story is that it features aliens. The central character is a
bureaucrat named Loodun Antyok, and his problem is what to

do with/about the nonhumans on Cepheus 18. He decides to
help them escape the humans-only Galaxy of the Empire by
emigrating to the Megallanic Clouds. To accomplish this goal
without bringing any blame on himself—the nonhumans weren't
supposed to escape—he must skillfully manipulate others into fil-
ing reports and making suggestions each of which will fit together
and enable the nonhumans to gain independence. The story,
then, alternates between Asimovian conversation and unreadable
examples of bureaucratic reports. Since these reports are meticulously reproduced as a part of the story, the readability of the
story cannot but be marred by them. Even so, the major theme of
the story is clearly developed. As Antyok himself puts it, the story
shows "how a capable administrator can work through red tape
and still get what he wants" (p. 465).

By the way, Asimov points out that "Blind Alley" was the
first of his stories ever to be anthologized—by Groff Conklin in
1946 in *The Best of Science Fiction*—and therefore it was the
first time he learned that a story could earn more for its author
than the amount he gets for its original sale and publication. That
he learned that lesson well is clear from the six anthologies of his
own stories which he put together between 1955 and 1972, and
that give this particular chapter and the following one the title
"Asimov's Collections."

Like "Death Sentence," "No Connection" is not important
Asimov. It imagines a future world in which bears have evolved
into the dominant species on at least a part of Earth, and men
have metamorphosized into creatures called Eekahs. Like the
scientists in "Homo Sol," the bears are stubbornly independent
and loners, and like the human beings in "Homo Sol," the Eekahs
are dangerously militaristic and can band together to achieve
their ends. As the seventeenth- and eighteenth-century Europeans considered the North American continent unoccupied
even though hundreds of thousands of Indians lived there, so
the Eekahs consider the lands of the bears uninhabited and
theirs for the taking. As in H. G. Wells's *The War of the Worlds*,
though less directly, the lesson of "No Connection" is that a superior technology—especially one whose members are willing to
organize in order to accomplish certain aims—will always defeat
an inferior technology. The central character, an archaeologist

bear, sees "no connection" between these threatening Eekahs and his own scientific specialty, the Primitive Primates who built an advanced technological civilization only to destroy it. But the connection is obviously there for the reader, and it accounts for the way the Eekahs will eventually destroy the bears' culture and civilization. The story employs some interesting concepts— Asimov does an especially good job with the building up of the bears' social patterns and their habitual ways of thinking and behaving—but it is weak in conflict and its resolution is understood rather than demonstrated.

The last two stories Asimov wrote in this pre-*Pebble in the Sky* period are both significant, not so much for themselves as for their connections—prefigurings, if you will—with later and more famous Asimov works. "The Red Queen's Race" (written in the early summer of 1948) is actually a first version of his later very fine novel *The End of Eternity*, and "Mother Earth" (written in the early fall of 1948) marks his first use of an overpopulated Earth in conflict with fifty Outer Worlds, a conflict in the background of both his Robot Novels and the best of the Lucky Starr juveniles.

"The Red Queen's Race" is set toward the end of the twentieth century. The end of the Third World War in 1965 is mentioned, and a major figure in it was a part of the Manhattan Project in his youth. But the story demonstrates that Asimov had not begun to extrapolate into the future. The population of the United States is given as 160 million, and the "future" is really the world of the 1940s with a few gadgets added. In other words, the story makes no more attempt than the Foundation Series had to show that life might be different in the future. It's today, not tomorrow.

"The Red Queen's Race" is also one of the few stories Asimov has written in the first person. (He much prefers third.) The story is composed of an introduction and four scenes. The four scenes are actually four conversations, and, as we have seen time and again—e.g., "Not Final!" the Foundation Series, "Blind Alley" —one of Asimov's most distinctive traits is his preference for moving a story via discussion rather than action. He prefers the cerebral story to action-adventure.

But two things about "The Red Queen's Race" are especially important in Asimov's career. For one, it is Asimov's first science fiction mystery story, and it is for his science fiction mystery stories as much as for "Nightfall," the Robot Stories, and the Foundation Series that Asimov is known today. As early as "Marooned Off Vesta" Asimov had Warren Moore doing a kind of detective work in trying to figure out how to remove the threat to his life. The science fiction hero as problem-solver is very close to the detective. Given Asimov's interest in popular fiction and in rational thought, it is certainly only natural that he should eventually try his hand at mystery stories. And given his early career as a science fiction writer, it is also natural that he should begin with a mystery story in the science fiction idiom. Curiously, Asimov didn't include it in *Asimov's Mysteries* "because I never thought of the story as a mystery. To me it was a 'time paradox' story" (personal letter, November 15, 1973).

Second, "The Red Queen's Race" is Asimov's first extant time-travel story. "The Cosmic Corkscrew" was also a time-travel story, but it is no longer extant, and he had also touched on the idea briefly in a short-short called "Time Pussy," to be discussed later. Still, "The Red Queen's Race" was his first fully developed time-travel story. Admittedly, Asimov's name is not as closely connected to time-travel stories as it is to science fiction mystery stories, but one of his best novels, *The End of Eternity*, is a brilliant example of the type, and "The Red Queen's Race" plays with the identical ideas as *The End of Eternity*. Overstating the case, one could say that the short story is a rough draft of the novel.

Eternity, the organization existing outside time, had been founded because Vikkor Mallansohn had worked out his equations in the twentieth century. Yet Mallansohn was a time traveler himself, and so the equations were given to the twentieth century rather than produced by it. The whole novel details Eternity's attempt to found itself, and the key is a book called the Mallansohn memoir. Almost everyone in the novel is working to supply the proper causes so that the effect will be the Mallansohn memoir as Eternity found it. One other thing: Eternity had the power—and arrogated to itself the right—to effect reality changes. That is, through an action taken by one of its technicians, reality as experienced by people in history could be changed. In fact, some people who had been alive in one reality would not even exist in another.

Many of the same ideas, in a far less sophisticated state, are to be found in "The Red Queen's Race." An eccentric scientist named Elmer Tywood causes a chemistry text to be translated into Attic Greek. Then he sends the book back in time to the Greeks in an apparent attempt to establish a technological civilization at a much earlier time in human history. In other words, he seems to be trying to effect a reality change. Asimov was drawing here on material presented by L. Sprague de Camp in his two-part article for the September and October 1941 issues of *Astounding*, an article entitled "The Sea-King's Armored Division."

Once they figure out what Tywood did and why (the mystery story elements in the story), the narrator and his boss begin to worry about their place—and the places of everyone they knew —in the new reality Tywood seemed to be trying to establish. For reasons made clear in the story, there is a time lag of twenty days between Tywood's sending the book back and the characters' noticing(?) any change in their present. Here is how the narrator describes it:

> All humanity was virtually under sentence of death. And while that was merely horrible abstraction, the fact that re-duced it to a thoroughly unbearable reality was that I was, too. And my wife, and my kid.
>
> Further, it was a death without precedence. A ceasing to exist, and no more. The passing of a breath. The vanishing of a dream. The drift into eternal non-space and non-time of a shadow. I would not be dead at all, in fact. I would merely never have been born.
>
> Or would I? Would I exist—my individuality—my ego—my soul, if you like? Another life? Other circumstances? [P. 518]

The story moves forward in two successive thrusts. First, the problem of what Tywood did and why must be solved, and second, they must decide how to face and/or remove the threatened reality change. In the detective story the I-narrator solves the first problem. In the time-travel story (if one can so divide the story) one Professor Mycroft James Boulder removes the threat from the reality change. Boulder was the Classical scholar who had translated the text into Greek for Tywood, and he "took care that only such passages as would account for the queer scraps of knowledge the ancients apparently got from nowhere would be included" (p. 524). In other words, Boulder supplied the proper causes for the known effects so that no reality change would take place. "This is the world in which the Greek chemistry text was sent back" (p. 524). Tywood succeeded and thus established the world we live in. He prevented, not effected, a reality change. (And he also supplied an explanation for the phenomena discussed in de Camp's article.)

"The Red Queen's Race" and *The End of Eternity* clearly both play games with the same pieces: a book transferred in time (the chemistry text; the Mallansohn memoir), cultural changes initiated from the future (Greek science; Mallansohn's equations), causes rigged to explain previously known effects (Democritus' atoms and Hero's steam engine; Mallansohn's recorded memories), and reality changes (the establishment-preservation of our contemporary world; the acts of the technicians and the eventual destruction of Eternity). Had Asimov told *The End of Eternity* straight, it would have been one of the great science fiction novels. As it is, the concepts in it—first formulated and used in "The Red Queen's Race"—make it one of Asimov's most memorable performances. "The Red Queen's Race," as a first step to *The End of Eternity*, is surely one of Asimov's most important short stories.

I might add here that Asimov himself was not aware of the close relationship between the two stories. When I asked him about it, he replied that *The End of Eternity* "was *not* a conscious rewriting of 'The Red Queen's Race' in that I did not consciously think of RQR when writing EOE. Of course, I had my own brain working both times, and I do tend to think in certain patterns, as does everyone" (personal letter, November 15, 1973). One other thing: I also asked him about the hard-boiled detective who is the narrator of "The Red Queen's Race." He said, "I don't know where that hard-boiled detective in 'The Red Queen's Race' came from. When you mentioned him, I had to look up the story before I believed it."

Even though "Mother Earth" anticipates the Robot Novels, its

relationship to them is not so close as that between "The Red
Queen's Race" and *The End of Eternity*, and therefore "Mother
Earth" is not as important a story as "The Red Queen's Race"
was. Primarily, "Mother Earth" and the Robot Novels share the
same setting: an overpopulated Earth in conflict with fifty Outer
Worlds, including Aurora, the first planet colonized and therefore named for the dawn of interstellar colonization. But the
story and the novels do not share similar ideas and actions. If
"The Red Queen's Race" and *The End of Eternity* are two games
of chess using the same board, pieces, and strategies, with White
winning one game and Black the other, then "Mother Earth" is
a game of checkers and the Robot Novels are games of chess,
both played on the same boards, but with completely different
pieces and strategies. "Mother Earth" is not a first version of the
Robot Novels; it is a first use of their settings.

The story itself is not new in Asimov. As in several of the
Foundation stories and as in "Blind Alley" a master statesman-
administrator in a series of conversations manipulates people
and events to get the result he wants. In "Mother Earth" an
Earth politician named Moreno, against much opposition, ma-
neuvers Earth into losing a conflict with the Outer Worlds. But
as one character asks in the story's first paragraph, "Are you sure
that even a professional historian can always distinguish between
victory and defeat?" (p. 525). As a result of the isolation forced
on Earth by the victorious Outer Worlds, Earth faces "a century
of rebuilding and revitalization, and at the end of it, we shall
face an outer Galaxy which will either be dying or changed"
(p. 559). If the Outer Worlds are dying, Earth can build a Terrestrian empire; if changed, Earth and Outer Worlds will learn
to get along because, for complicated reasons explained in the
story, racism will be dead. In either case, "out of the grand intellectual mixture, Mother Earth will finally have given birth not
to merely a Terrestrian, but to a Galactic Empire" (p. 559). This
sounds as if the Earth-vs.-Fifty-Outer-Worlds background of the
Robot Novels is a stage on the way to the Galactic Empire of the
Foundation Series, but Mother Earth is not radioactive, and I
still think that the presence or lack of an atomic war clearly dif-
ferentiates Asimov's two alternate futures one from the other.

"The Red Queen's Race" and "Mother Earth" were the last two

stories Asimov wrote before the publication of *Pebble in the Sky,*
an event by which I have marked the beginning of his third period and therefore the end of his second, that extending from
"Nightfall" all through the forties to the publication of his first
hard-cover book. In this second period he had fulfilled his youth-
ful ambition: he had become a respected and steady contributor
to Campbell's *Astounding.* Besides the handful of stories just
examined, he had written "Nightfall," the Robot Stories collected
in *I, Robot,* and the Foundation Series, all for Campbell's
Astounding and all still read and enjoyed today.

His third period was marked by his novels, and I have de-
lineated it as *Pebble in the Sky* (1950) through *The Naked Sun*
(1957). His decision to turn from science fiction to science nonfiction was made in late 1957, but due to prior commitments and
publication lags, its effects were not felt by readers until late
1958. So far as his short fiction is concerned, his third period may
be said to extend through to the publication of the appropriately
titled "Lastborn" ("The Ugly Little Boy") in the September 1958
issue of *Galaxy.* In the nine years from *Pebble in the Sky*
through "Lastborn" Asimov published an incredible sixty-three
stories and thirteen novels. Clearly, the early and middle fifties
were Asimov's most prolific period as a science fiction writer. Two
comparisons are instructive. As recounted in *The Early Asimov,*
in his first eleven years of trying he had published sixty stories,
and in the eleven years from 1959 through 1969 he published
only twenty-one stories and one minor novel, *Fantastic Voyage*
(1966). The drastic tapering off of his science fiction output is
obvious after 1958.

Having examined the nine nonseries stories from 1941 through
1950 in *The Early Asimov* collection, I now intend to comment
on many of the stories in his five other collections: *The Martian
Way and Other Stories* (1955), *Earth Is Room Enough* (1957),
Nine Tomorrows (1959), *Asimov's Mysteries* (1968), and *Nightfall and Other Stories* (1969). The existence of the first three collections is indicative of the demand for Asimov in the fifties, that
of the last two and of *The Early Asimov* (1972) of his possible
return to the field in the late sixties, early seventies. These five
collections make available to us fifty-eight of the eighty-four stories he published in the twenty years from 1950 through 1969.

I will also have some things to say about some of these remaining yet-to-be-collected stories. (The fiction that Asimov has published since 1969 will be dealt with in "Conclusions: The Most Recent Asimov.")

The Martian Way and Other Stories (1955)

Four stories appear in *The Martian Way and Other Stories*. The first, "The Martian Way," has been one of Asimov's most critically acclaimed stories. In *In Search of Wonder* Damon Knight refers to it as "one of the best science fiction novellas ever published" (p. 93), and in 1972 the Science Fiction Writers of America voted it into *The Science Fiction Hall of Fame*, Vol. II.

Its plot is relatively simple. The central character is clearly Ted Long, a resident of Mars and a member of a group called Scavengers because, in little two-man spaceships, they spot and retrieve the spent stages of the Earth-Mars rockets. In the political sense his opponent is John Hilder, a Grounder (i.e., Earthman) politician who hopes to become Global Co-ordinator. The initial situation is presented quickly and efficiently via conversations, activities, and flashbacks early in the story: humanity has spread among the minor planets; in order to keep their spaceships and their society operating, Mars and its Scavengers drain off a small percentage of Earth's water. The problem is Hilder's campaign against the Wasters (of water), which leads to the threat of forcing the colonists on Mars to return to Earth. The conflict involves the removal of that threat. One solution suggested and set aside is the smuggling of water from Earth's night side. The actual solution is going to the rings of Saturn for an alternate water supply, as those rings are made up of huge chunks of ice. The resolution finds Mars independent of Earth and ready to lead mankind out among the stars.

Several things are of interest about this story line. First, as in the Foundation Series Asimov is displaying his skill at setting up a politically oriented story. The problem is not only a personal one for particular crew members but a political one on which hangs the future of human civilization on the inner planets—indeed, the future of man's expansion through the Galaxy. The actions of the story are therefore significant in human history. Second, the Scavengers are of different races and

nationalities, but they work together. Science fiction transcends
the artificial boundaries of nation-state and race. Ted Long, Mario
Esteban Rioz, Richard Swenson, and Hamish Sankov achieve
the common goal together. Third, Ted Long's well-thought-out,
rational approach solves the problem far less violently than the
first-suggested power play of going in and taking what they
want. Fourth, the solution works because the environment of the
Martian colonists—encapsulated, artificial, stringent—has prepared those colonists for much longer space voyages than Earthmen could have made. The trip to Saturn and back takes well
over a year, whereas the longest Earthmen could stay in space
was six months, and then only with much difficulty. With its emphasis on setting, science fiction is about the relationship between
man and his environment.

Asimov likes to refer to a successful prediction in this story.
The men had to occupy themselves somehow on their year-long
journey to Saturn. He has them fill their off-duty hours experi-
encing the pleasant euphoria of space-floating, what today we
call space-walking. Long before anyone had actually done it,
Asimov here predicted that it would be fun, and he was the first
to make that suggestion.

Actually, he seems to have scored on some other predictions,
too. At a time when science fiction's Venus was a cloudy water-
world perhaps crawling with slimy prehistoric life, and long before the *Mariner* flybys of Venus, Asimov put into "The Martian
Way" the sentence "Venus has no water at all because it is too
hot" (p. 23). At a time when science fiction was concentrating
on gigantic spaceships that took off and landed all in one piece
(see the movies *Destination Moon* and *When Worlds Collide*)
Asimov assumes the use of multistage rockets ejecting their first,
second, and third stages into space to be retrieved by the Scavengers. And he also looks back to our present—which was his future when he wrote—in such statements as "Our ancestors burned
the oil of Earth madly and wilfully" (p. 23) and "He knows all
too well what selfish men can do to Earth's resources. He knows
what happened to Earth's oil during the Time of Troubles, for
instance" (p. 42). Ah yes, adolescent escape literature which
twenty years before it happened was trying to get people to see
the coming of the energy crisis.

There is one other subject that I would like to develop here at some length, and that is narrative point of view. I want to examine Asimov's handling of this element in the first short scene of the story. A good number of Asimov's stories begin with the central character being named and put into action in the first sentence. In "The Martian Way" the first subject-verb combination is "Mario Esteban Rioz watched." One's first assumption, then, is that we are about to read a story using third-person limited point of view.

Here is the entire first paragraph:

From the doorway of the short corridor between the only two rooms in the travel-head of the spaceship, Mario Esteban Rioz watched sourly as Ted Long adjusted the video dials painstakingly. Long tried a touch clockwise, then a touch counter. The picture was lousy.

So that first assumption seems correct: we stand with Rioz and we see what he sees. In the next paragraph, in fact, we drift into Rioz's mind: "Rioz knew it would stay lousy," and we are told why: "They were too far from Earth and at a bad position facing the Sun." That this is Rioz's thinking is then reinforced: "But then Long would not be expected to know that." Next, we are given an exact description of Rioz's posture as he stands there watching and thinking—and us with him. Surely the narrative point of view is third-person limited, to Rioz, except that the second paragraph ends with this sentence: "Then he jerked into the galley like a cork popping out of a bottle." Agreed that it's a descriptive image, but what does it describe? Why is an action "into" described in terms of an action "out of"? Is Rioz coming or going? Where is the galley? The language is imprecise and confusing because it does not firmly control the reader's visual imagination. Even more importantly (keeping narrative point of view in mind), if the remainder of the first two paragraphs was seen through the eyes and thoughts of Rioz, who is seeing and reporting on this? Exactly where is our center of visualization (narrative point of view) situated in relation to Rioz, Long, the doorway, and the galley? Hasn't it, in fact, come unstuck from Rioz?

The next two sentences-paragraphs explain away part of the difficulty:

"What are you after?" he asked.
"I thought I'd get Hilder," said Long.

Now we know Rioz popped into (not out of) the galley, and we can correct or clarify our visualization of the sequence of events. But the point is that we should not have to.

"Rioz propped his rump on the corner of a table shelf." (What's a "table shelf"? What does one look like? What's it for?) Back to narrative point of view: Are we doing this with Rioz from inside, or are we watching him do it from outside somewhere? Where?

A brief exchange of statements establishes that power is in short supply, and watching Hilder is considered by Rioz to be a waste of power. Are we saying these words with Rioz and listening with him to Long's statements, or are we listening to both of them?

Next we get two paragraphs of physical description introduced this way: "Their eyes met challengingly." (Challengingly? How exactly do eyes do that?) The rest of this paragraph is a description of Rioz, evidently as seen by Long, else why the "their eyes met" introduction? And the next paragraph is Long's description as seen by Rioz. So in the first of these two paragraphs the narrative point of view has definitely come unstuck from Rioz and lodged in Long, just as earlier it had left Rioz for an unspecified location during that "into/out of" sentence.

The passage continues for some more irritated conversation between the two, culminating in Rioz's turning down the thermostat to save energy. All this is being given us either from inside Rioz or from some neutral observation point outside them both, like a camera filming the scene.

Finally we get, "Rioz stepped through the door, and Long stared after him for a long moment." (Long for a long?) The scene's last few short paragraphs are then all from the point of view of Long. Rioz, whom we started out thinking was going to be the third-person limited narrative point of view, is no longer even present.

The obvious thing for us to do is to fall back on omniscient narrative point of view, and that's exactly what I intend to do.

After all, we begin inside one character, watching and thinking with him. Then we are outside him, watching him enter the room. We listen to a conversation between two characters, and we move inside one's head to look at the other, and inside the other's head to look at the one. Then we're outside both for some more conversation until the one we were with first leaves, and we spend the rest of the scene with the second.

I do not object in principle to an omniscient narrative point of view, but I do think that in this case the point of view does not fulfill its function of helping us to accurately visualize a scene. It moves from person to person and from place to place under the demands of exposition rather than of a clear, visual imagination. To put it baldly, we are being told what we need to know for the story line, not shown what we need for accurate imaginative participation in a real scene. Damon Knight praises Asimov in this story for "writing compactly and with enviable control." In this first scene, at any rate, I don't find the control as firm as it might be.

One final example. After Rioz has left, Long settles back to watch the speech despite the poor picture on the TV screen. He watches "the slow dissolution of the curtain" as Hilder is revealed. Is this "dissolution of the curtain" the effect of seeing a real curtain open on a bad TV picture, or is it an electronic feat achieved by future television technicians? What am I supposed to see as I read that image? There is a failure of visual imagination—of communication—from writer to reader here, it seems to me.

I have been willing to spend this much time on this one scene for two reasons: first, to present an extended example of the kinds of information paying attention to narrative point of view can yield, and second, to show that Asimov's visual imagination—or at least his ability to re-create what he sees in the minds of his readers—is not always without fault.

But I don't want to end this discussion of one of Asimov's best stories on a negative note. I want to end it out near Saturn with those heroic Martian Scavengers.

Saturn grew until at last it rivaled and then surpassed the Sun. The rings, set at a broad angle to their trajectory of approach, swept grandly about the planet, only a small portion being eclipsed. Then, as they approached, the span of the rings grew still wider, yet narrower as the angle of approach constantly decreased.

The larger moons showed up in the surrounding sky like serene fireflies. . . .

Saturn filled half the sky, streaked with orange, the night shadow cutting it fuzzily nearly one quarter of the way in from the right. Two round little dots in the brightness were shadows of two of the moons. [Pp. 49–50]

There is no failure of the visual imagination or its communication here. As I have remarked before, the sense of wonder in science fiction is often sight, the wonders of the universe spread out before awe-filled human observers. As in the above-quoted example, Asimov often does as much as a worker-in-words can do to present that vision.

Because of its emphasis on the relationship between environment and consciousness, science fiction often gives its readers fresh insights into things as they are. The second story in the collection *The Martian Way and Other Stories* is based entirely on such a shift in perspective. Two boys, named Slim and Red, find two alien creatures alongside a crashed spaceship and decide to cage them for a circus. After some trials and tribulations in a Tom Sawyerish atmosphere, the two aliens escape and head home. You guessed it: They are heading toward Earth, and Slim and Red are tentacled monsters. But the point is that you cannot judge sentient life by externals. As readers we lived with—inside —Slim and Red for a while, we sympathized with them, we laughed and worried for them. So they turn out to be tentacled monsters, so what? All sentient life forms are brothers under the skin. While the story "Youth" may be neither very original nor very interesting, its theme is certainly significant.

"The Deep," the third story in the collection, plays games not with physical features, but with social patterns, especially the family. Here the aliens come to us, and we see ourselves as others see us. We are found revolting and not worth communicating with, not because of our hideous external appearance, but because we center our lives around the begetting, bearing, and raising of our own children. The aliens are horrified to find that among us "Each creature would know the identity of its own child. Each child would have a particular father." When one alien expresses the foolish hope that they might learn from us, he is brutally put down: "Learn what? . . . To know our parents and make friends of our children?" And they decide "there can never be any meeting of minds. The difference is so fundamental, so innate" (p. 136).

Like "Nightfall," like so much science fiction, the theme of the story is obvious: given different environments, other consciousnesses will evolve thinking other things "perfectly natural." It's a lesson we all need to have reinforced periodically—that the way I think is not the only way there is to think—and "The Deep" does a good job of reinforcing it.

Unfortunately, Asimov has succumbed in this story to a certain amount of homocentricity. An alien mother, against all their social customs (and all the odds of storytelling) knows the identity of her child, is concerned over what happens to it, and protects, helps, even loves it all she can. We are meant to sympathize with her, I suppose, because she is so . . . you know, *human.* This element in the story seems intended to indicate that mother love is universal and natural, and as such it works against everything else in the story. It is a false note in an otherwise interesting presentation of an alien psychology, one different from our own and therefore one providing an altered perspective and a fresh insight into our own.

Just as "Youth" reminded us that our shape is not necessarily *the* shape, so "The Deep" helps us see that our social patterns with regard to the bearing and rearing of children are not necessarily *the* patterns. What is "only natural" varies from one environment to another.

"Sucker Bait," the last of the four stories in the collection, is another (along with "The Martian Way") of Asimov's best. There are a variety of reasons for this. For one thing, the science fiction story is firmly built on an accurate scientific puzzle. Over a century earlier a colony of more than a thousand people had died mysteriously on the planet Troas (nickname: Junior). It becomes imperative that the government discover why they died, and a scientific expedition is sent out. After considering several possible explanations—unfriendly aliens, disease, even psychological disorders—the correct answer is eventually found: beryllium poisoning. Unfortunately, the solution may have come too late for the members of the expedition. So while the pattern of the story is familiar (see "Marooned Off Vesta" discussion, p. 10), in that it focuses on threat-data-solution, that solution brings worry, not joy, and the ending as a result is more ambiguous than usual.

The story is also an excellent example of that science fiction game called world-building. Junior is a character among planets and within the story. Because it occupies one of the two Trojan points of a double-star system, it has a distinctive astronomical situation. The mention of Trojan points gives Asimov the opportunity to work into the story a neat little "history of a scientific term" lecture such as he loves to give.

Seen from space, its unusual aspect makes Junior an excellent example of "sight as science fiction's sense of wonder."

North and south, a third of the way to the equator, lay the icecaps, still at the start of their millennial retreat. Since the *Triple G.* was spiraling on a north-south great circle . . . , each cap in turn was laid out below them.

Each burned equally with sunlight, the consequence of Junior's untilted axis. And each cap was in sectors, cut like a pie with a rainbowed knife.

The sunward third of each was illuminated by both suns simultaneously into a brilliant white that slowly yellowed westward, and as slowly greened eastward. To the east of the white sector lay another, half as wide, which was reached by the light of Lagrange I only, and the snow there blazed a response of sapphire beauty. To the west, another half sector, exposed to Lagrange II alone, shone in the warm orange red of an Earthly sunset. The three colors graded into one another bandwise, and the similarity to a rainbow was increased thereby.

The final third was dark in contrast, but if one looked carefully enough, it, too, was in parts—unequal parts. The smaller portion was black indeed, but the larger portion had a faint milkiness about it. . . . Moonlight, of course. [Pp. 166–67]

Later, given an opportunity to look at photographs of that view, some members of the expedition "groaned inwardly at the thought of having placed comfort before a chance to see the original of *that*" (p. 169). To see *that*. What there is waiting out there for us to see!

In building up its "personality" Asimov also gives us Junior's geological era: retreating ice caps; cold, moist climate; islands and coastlines to be gradually inundated as the ice caps melt over the next million years. Its life forms include gigantic (six feet across) flowers and a variety of other strange plants and lower animals. Since there is no intelligent life, there can be no architecture, technology, social patterns, civilization, items often used to create a unique world. What there is is fitted together so carefully that the data of unoccupied Junior are consistent and fully available to us. For me, however, the planet beneath that data never quite comes alive, never takes on imaginative reality. It resembles reality only in the way a chess game resembles a medieval battle: intellectually, without any of the textures and sounds of life. Junior is the location of a puzzle to be solved. It is not a real place.

A third element that contributes to the story's success—besides its accurately constructed scientific problem and setting—is the character of its problem-solver. Mark Annuncio is distinctive physically and intellectually. Physically, "he had mouse-brown hair with nothing but silken straightness to it; a narrow, receding chin, a small mouth, and a pointed nose. All he needed were five or six delicate vibrissae on each side of the nose to make the illusion complete. And he was below average in height" (p. 141). Intellectually, he is a specially trained member of the Mnemonic Service: he stores an incredible number of facts and he can call them up via random association in toto. He knows, for example, the percentages of the elements (by weight) in the planetary crusts of 21,854 planets. It is his ability to call up and link together randomly stored bits of data that enables him to solve the problem. Being told the beryllium content of Junior's crust causes him to remember—and later to quote verbatim—a passage in "a very old book about poisons" concerning beryllium poisoning. Annuncio's special abilities and his special training render him unable to get along with his fellows on the expedition. His

attitudes toward them, their attitudes toward him, help enrich the personal relationships in the story and make it more interesting.

In its scientifically accurate puzzle and its technically proficient world-building, if not in its central character (though one should recall the stunted Mule of the Foundation Series and the albino Theor Realo of "Death Sentence"), "Sucker Bait" shows distinctively Asimovian traits. I have also mentioned the little "history of science" lecture and the visual portrait of Junior as seen from space.

"Sucker Bait" brings to mind other things we have seen in Asimov. For example, specific mention is made of the planet Aurora, which figured as a prominent part of the backgrounds of "Mother Earth" and the two Robot Novels and which was to have been the setting of the third Robot Novel. "Sucker Bait" also contains an element that is actually a development of the astronomical situation in "Nightfall": "Colored suns, mind you. Colored suns. Do you know what that means? It means that a human being, yourself or myself, standing in the full glare of the two suns, would cast two shadows. One blue green, one red orange. The length of each would naturally vary with the time of day" (p. 190). In other words, where "Nightfall" probes in detail the spectacular effects of a once-every-two-thousand-years occurrence, "Sucker Bait" at least raises in a peripheral manner the question of the effect of normal, everyday color shifting (due to multiple suns).

In "Sucker Bait" I hear nostalgic (for me) remnants of the breezy style of the Foundation Series. One character is described as speaking, for example, "with the peculiar emphasis men of small appetite use when speaking to men of hearty appetite, as though a poor digestion were something that came only of rigid virtue and superior intellect" (p. 146). Once he started writing seriously and with an eye to eventual hard-cover publication, Asimov abandoned this ability of his to be incisive and amusing with language. It reappears only occasionally in his later stories.

Another technique Asimov likes to use is present here. In fairly complex stories he likes to present a few scenes from the point of view of a minor character or even a bystander in the story. This lets us see the central character through different

eyes, and it lets us get inside and learn more about a side character. Such a fresh slant on people and events cannot help but enliven a story.

I have promised not to get into sources and influences very much in this study, but I do want to make one or two observations here. Mark Annuncio and the Mnemonic Service remind me a lot of Elliott Grosvenor and the Nexial Department that A. E. van Vogt was writing about in the early fifties. And though Asimov didn't care for Campbell's insertion of mental science in *Astounding* in the fifties, one can't help but wonder how much of Campbell is behind such statements as "In the machine-centered civilization that filled the Galaxy, it was difficult to learn to appreciate the achievements of naked mind without a long apprenticeship" (p. 162).

Furthermore, I tend to see these attitudes and examples of Campbell and Asimov in the background of what many people (including myself) take to be the outstanding science fiction novel of the sixties: Frank Herbert's *Dune*. I see them especially in the Butlerian Jihad, which swept the Galaxy clean of technological thinking machines and forced the development of mental powers on the part of the Mentats, the Guildsmen, and the Reverend Mothers. Isn't Mark Annuncio a Mentat, and therefore a literary predecessor of Paul Muad-Dib? Note, too, that the Martian way, in Asimov's story of the same name, was developed on a desert world as a result of the deprivation of water and resulted in an almost messianic sense of purpose on the part of the Martian colonists.

One final thing about "Sucker Bait": its theme. The scientists on the expedition are experts divided from one another by their professional expertise. Time and again, one scientist defers to another's "professional opinion." The effect of all this is to compartmentalize knowledge. The theme of the story is best put by a character who recognizes all this and says, "Don't you think . . . it's time we worried less about professional opinion and more about over-all co-ordination?" (p. 192). Anyone who has read much of Asimov's nonfiction or heard him speak knows that this is a central preoccupation of his: the need for the co-ordination and integration of knowledge. In fact, it was largely

in response to the depth of his feeling of this need that he quit science fiction in 1957–58 and became primarily a science writer. "Sucker Bait" is therefore an important story in Asimov's career because it shows his awareness in the early fifties of the issue that was to draw him away from the field in the late fifties.

Earth Is Room Enough (1957)

"The Dead Past," which I take to be far and away the best story in this collection, appeared in 1956, two years after "Sucker Bait." It shares with the earlier story Asimov's continued interest in the nonspecific generalist as an integrator of the knowledge of overly specific specialists. Set in the mid-twenty-first century, the story extrapolates two major trends from today's world: the growing importance of the science writer to a place of respect and affluence, and the growing control of scientific research by a bureaucratic central government. As happens often in Asimov's shorter fiction, these two changes seem to be the only ones that have occurred over a period of more than a hundred years. We are actually being asked to consider today with only a few changes rather than to live in a real future world imaginatively and totally constructed.

Considering that in the mid-fifties Asimov was already succumbing to the urge to go into straight science writing, the prestige and financial success given that profession in this story can surely be considered wishful thinking on his part. His justification for the new role of the science writer is this: Scientists are not expected to cobble their own shoes or tailor their own shirts. They don't know how. Furthermore, as they demonstrate over and over again, they don't know how to write, either. So why should they be expected to produce their own papers and reports? A literate generalist—someone who has managed to go through college while keeping his mind pure of the taint of specialization—is the obvious answer. And since these people can relate (in both senses of the word) what the ignorant-of-everything-else specialists learn, they are given prestige and money. What an idyllic view of one's future occupation!

The other extrapolation was of the growth of government control of scientific research. This came about because, more and

more, such research had to be funded by the government through grants.

When science was young and the intricacies of all or most of the unknown was within the grasp of an individual mind, there was no need for direction, perhaps. Blind wandering over the uncharted tracts of ignorance could lead to wonderful finds by accident. But as knowledge grew, more and more data had to be absorbed before worthwhile journeys into ignorance could be organized. . . .

No one would advocate running a factory by allowing each individual worker to do whatever pleased him at the moment, or of running a ship according to the casual and conflicting notions of each individual crewman. It would be taken for granted that some sort of centralized supervisory agency must exist in each case. Why should direction and order benefit a factory and a ship but not scientific research? [P. 19]

As a result of this recognized need for control, a key attitude develops, one that I assume most readers would not sympathize with: "Curiosity is an occupational danger with scientists" (p. 31). So the story seems to have a standard villain: the bureaucratic government which stifles and thwarts free inquiry on the part of curious scientists.

Naturally we cheer our heroes as they pursue their unauthorized research. It's the free individual versus big government, right? Well, as it turns out, that's not exactly right. Ironically, the free individual cannot in this instance get the job done. Eventually it takes three "specialists" each contributing his own expertise to accomplish the task. In other words, our "hero" turns out to be a three-man research team, a project of its own.

The first member of this team is mild-mannered Arnold Potterley, Ph.D., a college teacher of history. He is the most interesting and complex person in the story. He also enables the historically inclined Asimov to work in a lot of fascinating material on ancient Carthage. Potterley and his wife, Caroline, had had a little girl, Laurel, who at the age of three had been burned to death in a house fire. Potterley carried with him for twenty years the fear that he had caused the fire and therefore the death of his only child by failing to completely extinguish a cigarette when he went in to check on her that night. As a result, when he learned that the Romans had accused the Carthaginians of infanticide by throwing babies into a fiery furnace shaped like the god Moloch, he took it upon himself to prove the Carthaginians innocent. As one character in the story puts it, "Somehow, this explained the reason for Potterley's rabid, irrational desire to boost the Carthaginians, deify them, most of all disprove the story of their fiery sacrifices to Moloch. By freeing them of the guilt of infanticide by fire, he symbolically freed himself of the same guilt" (p. 47). Asimov's personal interest in the past and Potterley's motivation in the story are beautifully fused in a psychological concern and insight rare in Asimov.

To prove the Carthaginians innocent Potterley turns to chronoscopy. In the mid-twentieth century a scientist named Sterbinski had used the newly discovered neutrino to build a device for viewing and listening to the past. His work had been absorbed into the government bureaucracy, and "The Dead Past" begins with Potterley requesting time on a chronoscope in order to study ancient Carthage. When his request is denied, he must try to build his own chronoscope. Potterley furnishes the research team its first motivation for action.

But he does not have enough knowledge to build one. Fortunately, Jonas Foster, a new young scientist in the Physics Department, still has enough intellectual curiosity to wonder about the chronoscope and about the government's suppression of its development and use. The project—the actual building of the chronoscope—becomes his task. But he needs more data and some materials. Fortunately, his uncle Ralph Nimmo, a successful science writer, has access to the data outside Foster's specialty, which specialty fortunately allows Foster to design and build a cheaper and better chronoscope than Sterbinski's. In fact, combining his design with materials bought at a corner store, anyone could build and operate a chronoscope. (The "fortunatelys" in this paragraph mark places where Asimov's preplanning is obvious. Take away any of these three things and the story will not happen.)

The plot of the story is clear. Potterley's goal is to prove the Carthaginians (and indirectly himself) innocent of burning infants to death. Foster's intellectual curiosity leads him to build a chronoscope to prove he can do it and to prove that the free scientist can accomplish more than one encumbered with the restrictions that barnacle government control of research via grants. And Nimmo wants to help his nephew get a good start in life. The three together make up a research team whose goal it is to create a chronoscope despite government prohibition. The conflict is in their attempts to get everything together to build the chronoscope, the solution is its building, and the resolution is the establishing of a world with cheap time-viewing available to everyone.

In the telling of the story Asimov uses a technique that needs some discussion here. The first third of the story seems hopelessly muddled in the same way that almost all of *The Currents of Space* was: too much flashbacking in order to present necessary exposition. Here, however, the flashbacking does follow a pattern. First, he presents us with a person in a given situation, then he flashes us back to events in that person's earlier life (sometimes with flashbacks inside of flashbacks), and finally he brings us back to finish the original situation. This happens with Potterley (pp. 11–16), Foster (pp. 16–21), Caroline (pp. 21–24), and Nimmo (pp. 29–30). It does seem a bit of a muddle, but a lot is being accomplished, including an incredible (for Asimov) description of Caroline Potterley:

> Caroline Potterley had once been an attractive woman. There were occasions, such as dinners or university functions, when, by considerable effort, remnants of the attraction could be salvaged.
>
> On ordinary occasions, she sagged. It was the word she applied to herself in moments of self-abhorrence. She had grown plumper with the years, but the flaccidity about her was not a matter of fat entirely. It was as though her muscles had given up and grown limp so that she shuffled when she walked while her eyes grew baggy and her cheeks jowly. Even her greying hair seemed tired rather than merely stringy. Its straightness seemed to be the result of a supine surrender to gravity, nothing else. [P. 21]

By giving us the outside of this woman, Asimov has given us her inside as well. Her physical description is also her psychological portrait, and this sort of efficiency and insight is also rare in Asimov.

By its end "The Dead Past" has taken an utterly unpredictable turn. Our heroes do succeed in beating the tyrannical government and building a chronoscope of their own. This is what we have spent the story wanting them to do. But then re-entering the story is the government agent who had originally turned down Potterley's request to time-view ancient Carthage (hiss, hiss; boo, boo). He raises two things of considerable importance. For one thing, he criticizes the attitude of all three—and therefore also of us readers—toward the government: "You all just took it for granted that the government was stupidly bureaucratic, vicious, tyrannical, given to suppressing research for the hell of it. It never occurred to any of you that we were trying to protect mankind as best we could" (pp. 54–55). And it is true that one assumption shared by the three heroes and we readers was that the government wasn't likely to know what it was doing. Why do we make this assumption?

The second thing the government agent brings up is the key question, "But when does the past really begin?" (p. 52). This in turn leads to the realization that "the dead past is just another name for the living present" (p. 53) when one focuses a chronoscope on a past only one one-hundredth of a second gone. In other words, by inventing a cheap chronoscope and by distributing its details to the public, our three heroes have destroyed privacy. As the agent says, "What kind of a world we'll have from now on, I don't know. I can't tell, but the world we know has been destroyed completely" (p. 55). Asimov has shrewdly taken assumptions we know in our bones are right—free inquiry is good, bureaucratic government is bad—and shown us that, *in this instance,* they are faulty assumptions. Imagine: The government knew what it was doing. What a revolutionary idea! And the scientist who wanted to create something just to satisfy his intellectual curiosity turned out to be a villain for doing it.

Perhaps even more surprising (considering Asimov's choice of a future career for himself) is another idea developed in the story: some knowledge *ought not* to be integrated. This is awfully close to that old science fiction cliché "There are some things man was not meant to know." Asimov is here looking at the dark side of science, and he sees Frankenstein's monster lurking there. Of course, the world we know in one sense always ends with a new invention. The world we live in differs from past worlds because of the invention of the automobile, antibiotics, and radio. Each of these things destroyed a world. Will the chronoscope destroy our world any more effectively and thoroughly than the automobile destroyed Wyatt Earp's? And will Potterley, Foster, and Nimmo be any worse a set of villains than, say, Henry Ford, Jonas Salk, and Louis Pasteur?

One other perhaps: Perhaps what we really need is a novel from Asimov constructing in detail what that new world (with no privacy) would be like. Then we could more easily decide whether our heroes in "The Dead Past" did a "good thing" or a "bad thing," and we could also decide better whether Asimov has in fact written a Frankenstein story here. Regardless of its sequel possibilities, "The Dead Past" surely ranks with "The Martian Way" and "Sucker Bait" as outstanding Asimov.

With few exceptions the other stories in *Earth Is Room Enough* are gimmicky trifles which strike one once and are then easily forgotten. (Three of the exceptions, "Kid Stuff," "The Immortal Bard," and "Dreaming Is a Private Thing," I intend to discuss in a different context later, and so I leave them out of consideration here.) "Satisfaction Guaranteed" is fairly well done, but as a Robot Story it also appeared in *The Rest of the Robots* and I discussed it there (see pp. 51–52). "Jokester" is a minor variation on the "Earth is property" theme, of which "Breeds There a Man . . . ?" in *Nightfall and Other Stories* is a better example (see pp. 235–36), and "Someday" is a variation of the superior "The Feeling of Power" in *Nine Tomorrows* (see pp. 215–16).

The gimmicky nature of *Earth Is Room Enough* is illustrated by "Gimmicks Three," in which a man gets out of a pact he made with the devil by traveling in time and preventing himself from signing the pact, and by "The Last Trump," in which the Archangel Gabriel delays blowing the Last Trump and ending the world in 1957 because it was not made exactly clear to him from what event he was to measure the 1,957 years. Both stories are about technicalities, ingenious perhaps, but trifles.

Short-shorts are notorious for depending entirely on their gimmicks, and five of the stories (counting "The Immortal Bard") are short-shorts. In "The Watery Place" three aliens in a flying saucer from Venus are sent back to their watery home by a hick sheriff who thought they said "Venice." In "The Message" a time-traveler from the thirtieth century asserts his presence at World War II in Italy by writing "Kilroy Was Here." In "Hell-Fire" the figure of Satan is detected in super-slow-motion pictures of an atomic bomb explosion. And in "The Fun They Had" children of the future envy children of the present their school system. None of these stories does anything more with its central ideas than merely present them. Of the four cited above, "The Fun They Had" is the best because it lets us see our present social patterns from a different perspective. And the image of Satan in the atomic blast is a memorable one. It would probably make a better painting than short story. This is further evidence of the visual quality of Asimov's imagination.

The remaining two stories in the collection, "Franchise" and "Living Space," are also essentially gimmick stories, but here they are saved from trivialness by being more fully developed and by depending on better gimmicks. In "Franchise" Asimov presents a *reductio ad absurdum* of present trends in the projecting of the results of elections. Today, on the basis of early, scattered returns from certain preselected precincts, the radio and television networks are able to give us accurate predictions of election results hours before the last voter has voted. Asimov narrows this sample down to one person and eliminates entirely the necessity for all those other people to bother voting at all. The history books thereafter refer to the election not by the name of any prominent candidate, but by the name of that year's voter. It is a memorable gimmick but not a memorable story.

The best gimmick in the collection (outside of the chronoscope in "The Dead Past") is to be found in "Living Space," where science has solved the Earth's overpopulation problem by opening up parallel worlds for human occupancy. Since there are so many parallel Earths, each person or family can have one of his own simply by registering for it and paying rent. Everything seems ideal for a while, but then people from other populated parallel Earths begin to occupy Earths we are using.

This is bad enough when these others are Nazis from a German Earth, but when a man "complains that his home is surrounded and that there are things staring through the glass roof of his garden . . . purple things with big red veins, three eyes and some sort of tentacles instead of hair" (p. 111), there is nothing to do but end the story. It is a great gimmick, but it isn't really developed into a full-fledged story. The gimmick *is* the story.

Nine Tomorrows (1959)

Asimov himself ranks "The Ugly Little Boy" and "The Last Question" one-two as the two best short stories he has written. I have discussed "The Last Question" among the Robot Stories (see pp. 53–54), and I will discuss "The Dying Night" and "I'm in Marsport Without Hilda" in the context of the other Asimov collection in which they can be found, *Asimov's Mysteries* (see pp. 223–28). Without a doubt "The Ugly Little Boy" is a top-notch story, right up there with "The Martian Way," "Sucker Bait," and "The Dead Past." But I would like to make a very few remarks about the other five stories in the collection before getting to it.

The first story, "Profession," is a long and fully developed story that simply doesn't work for me. Its theme is good, and we have seen it already in several other of Asimov's stories: in the future a way is found to separate creative generalists from the majority of people better off specializing in something. That way involves forcing the creative person to step forward and proclaim, "Hey, wait a minute. I have value, too. I can create." That realization must come from within and cannot be forced on anyone.

But two things go wrong in this story. The first is the assumption that specialists cannot create. The second is the whole context into which the sorting-out process is put: the Olympics. There are contestants vying against one another for professions in front of huge audiences of relatives and friends. The whole thing is so forced that one comes away wondering exactly the same thing the central character does: "Why do they call them the Olympics?" (p. 74).

"The Feeling of Power" is a very neat gimmick story that would have been at home in *Earth Is Room Enough* had it been written in time. In fact, one story in the earlier collection, "Someday," could almost be taken as a first version of "The Feeling of

Power." In "Someday" some children teach themselves to read and write squiggles on paper so they will have a secret written language in which to communicate with one another. With this small beginning, perhaps someday the art of creating written literature will return. In "The Feeling of Power" one man "reinvents" mathematics, a task done by computers for so long that people have forgotten how to add, subtract, multiply, and divide. The application is obvious to the military society of the time. Missiles are directed by computers. If men could learn to compute, manned missiles could be developed, and with such a weapon the war against Deneb might be won. The ironic gimmick of taking our ideas of progress and applying them to what we would call retrogression lets us see that progress is after all a relative thing, and that mere change is not necessarily progress: it may simply be change. In "The Feeling of Power" Asimov brilliantly and entertainingly gets us to laugh at our own assumptions about the term "progress."

"The Gentle Vultures" and "All the Troubles in the World" are both minor stories. In "The Gentle Vultures" representatives of an alien race wait on the moon for Earthmen to initiate the atomic war that will destroy them and allow the aliens to colonize the planet. As they wait, they discuss Earthmen, their technological progress, the Cold War, and in doing so allow us to see ourselves from outside. Finally, they realize the atomic war will not come, and they go back home to wait for the Earthmen to spread into the Galaxy and take over. As in such earlier stories as "Homo Sol," Earthmen are seen as different, dangerous, and ultimately invincible.

"All the Troubles in the World" is interesting largely because it is an Asimov computer story, and so fits in to the Robot Stories to a limited degree. It is set in a future where everyone has access to a gigantic computer named Multivac, into which they pour all their troubles and thus attain solace. But Multivac has to retain all those troubles. Eventually it tries to commit suicide. This story is about that first suicide attempt. It is clear that there will be others and that eventually Multivac will indeed learn how to kill itself. Then the world as its inhabitants know it will be radically altered not as a result of adding a technological device (as in "The Dead Past"), but as a result of taking one away. It's

an interesting story which works only to the extent that one
grants that a computer would ever want to commit suicide in the
first place. Of course, Asimov thinks of his robots and computers
as conscious, and those of his readers who at least think so while
they read the story will have no trouble with this element in it.

"Spell My Name with an S" (how many times must Asimov
have been misspelled Azimov!) is another "Earth is property"
story that I prefer to discuss with "Jokester" and "Breeds There
a Man . . . ?" later (see p. 236).

This brings us to the outstanding story in *Nine Tomorrows*,
"The Ugly Little Boy," published under the title "Lastborn" when
it appeared in the September 1958 issue of *Galaxy*. The ugly
little boy of the title is a Neanderthal child brought via time
travel into a contemporary laboratory as a publicity stunt to raise
money for a nearly bankrupt research firm called Stasis, Inc. Its
director, Dr. Gerald Hoskins, hires a nurse, Edith Fellowes, to
care for the boy during his stay in our time. The narrative point
of view is third-person limited, to Miss Fellowes. She is also the
story's central character, in two senses: she is the person we are
with most (a misleading standard) and she is the problem-solver
in the story. Into her life comes the problem of caring for Timmie
(the Neanderthal boy) to the best of her ability. She must clean
him, clothe him, teach him, and protect him. The story is about
how she does all these things, especially the last.

In a minor way, her opponent in doing all these things is Timmie himself. At first force is necessary to get him bathed and
dressed. A certain amount of conflict is present in any student-
teacher relationship, and there is some between Miss Fellowes
and Timmie, too. She also tries to help Timmie learn to get along
with another child, Jerry, the son of the director, but in this she
fails.

Ultimately, however, the conflict comes down to a difference
in attitudes toward Timmie on the parts of Miss Fellowes and
Dr. Hoskins. He considers Timmie the subject of an experiment;
she considers him a human being. Toward the end of the story
this difference surfaces very clearly. At one point, for example,
Dr. Hoskins says to her, "I'm sure you must realize that we cannot maintain the Timmie experiment forever," and she replies,
"But you're talking about a boy. Not about a rock—." Dr. Hos-

kins's impersonality even toward people then surfaces: "Even a boy can't be given undue importance, Miss Fellowes" (pp. 224–25).

In the story's final scene Dr. Hoskins's dispassionate attitude is made even clearer. When she tries to kidnap Timmie in order to protect him—and taking him out of the stasis field which holds him in the present would demand a prodigious amount of expensive energy—she is stopped by Dr. Hoskins.

> She said pleadingly, "What harm can it do if I take him, Dr. Hoskins? You can't put energy loss ahead of human life?"
> Firmly, Hoskins took Timmie out of her arms. "An energy loss this size would mean millions of dollars lost out of the pockets of investors. It would mean a terrible setback for Stasis, Inc." [P. 230]

Even more damningly, Asimov has Dr. Hoskins argue, "Timmie stands in the way of expansion! Timmie is a source of possible bad publicity; we are on the threshold of great things, and I'm sorry, Miss Fellowes, but we can't let Timmie block us. We cannot. We cannot" (p. 232).

Asimov has chosen to use dramatic character presentation, but even so he is controlling our attitudes, getting us to decide in favor of Timmie and Miss Fellowes and against Dr. Hoskins, in favor of compassion and humanity and against objectivity and scientific impersonalness. I would go so far as to suggest that Asimov is setting compassion against reason—almost emotion against reason—and uncharacteristically (remember "Marooned Off Vesta" et al.?) coming out on the side of compassion-emotion.

"The Ugly Little Boy" is an antiscience story by Isaac Asimov. This makes it as nontypical and surprising as the antiprogress, Frankenstein elements in "The Dead Past." It is instructive that these two of his best stories do not develop the ebullient, optimistic, science-science-über-alles Asimov of the popular image. There is more to the man than that.

In some ways, "The Ugly Little Boy" is not only compassionate but also sentimental. Asimov likes to tell about the way his mere recounting of the plot in public can reduce audiences to tears. It is a story with a primarily emotional rather than intellectual impact, and it is therefore not typical of Asimov. Yet he considers it his best story. Why should the rational, scientific, intellectual Asimov be so attracted to such a sentimental, emotional, admittedly tear-jerking story?

I suggest that the story means more to him than it does to the average reader. It has personal overtones in it which resound inside its author in ways that cannot reach other readers. Let me venture into a type of criticism I do not often give much credence to myself. For lack of a better term, I call it Freudian. I suggest that we try reading the story as a sort of emotional allegory. Timmie, the ugly little boy, the misfit in a world he never made, is Asimov himself. Timmie's home, Stasis Room One, from which he cannot escape, is Asimov's attic study, his office, or even his own private inner life. The outside world is the one you and I live in, and Jerry is you and me, the nonunderstanding outsider. Miss Fellowes—note her name—represents a wish fulfillment for a mother figure, a female helper and companion. Dr. Hoskins is the intellectual, demanding life Asimov has chosen for himself and is here having second thoughts about, even condemning as too impersonal. The ending, in which Miss Fellowes returns with Timmie to his savage Neanderthal world to die, represents a retreat from reality with the mother-female figure. Note that that retreat is a place of pain and death, indicative of guilt feelings on his part over the very desire to get away.

When Asimov read this interpretation in an earlier printed version, his reaction was "Your psychological interpretation of 'The Ugly Little Boy' may not be altogether wrong. I am a claustrophile and like to be in enclosed places. Maybe Timmie does somehow represent me in my attic (or hotel room, now). I can't judge that, though. It's for others to say" (personal letter, October 10, 1972).

He also gave an interesting account of his reasons for liking the story so much:

> The reason I like it so much even though its sentimentality is so opposed to my usual rigidly cerebral style, is that it is one of the stories in which I-showed-them. I have certain things I prefer to do because I prefer to do them, and I am perpetually being accused of doing them because I can't do

anything else. (Like the people who say Picasso draws figures in distorted fashion because he can't make them lifelike.)

Well, I got tired of hearing that I can't handle human emotion, so I wrote a story intending to handle it. . . .

Okay, I set about to prove that I could write a moving story and I did and no one can ever say I can't. And when I choose to write cerebral stories, that's *choice*. [Personal letter, October 10, 1972]

In the same letter he cites as examples of other "stories in which I-showed-them" *The Gods Themselves*, the second part of which handles both aliens and sex, two things people had thought Asimov wasn't good at, and "I'm in Marsport Without Hilda" for its human ribaldry. And I have already cited *The End of Eternity* as a novel that Asimov says he wrote "in a deliberate attempt to be different . . . to insert more emotion and a heroine who was as explicitly sexual as I could manage" (personal letter, November 15, 1973; see p. 148). In other words, Asimov could be more versatile than he is, and he is able to cite "The Ugly Little Boy," "I'm in Marsport Without Hilda," *The End of Eternity*, and *The Gods Themselves* to prove it.

Whatever the reasons, Asimov prefers "The Ugly Little Boy" to "Nightfall," the story his fans and fellow writers invariably choose as his best.

CHAPTER EIGHT

Asimov's Collections II

Asimov's Mysteries (1968)

Asimov cites *The Caves of Steel* (written in 1953) as his first science fiction mystery story. The central character in "Author! Author!" was a popular writer of detective fiction, but the story he is in is not itself a mystery. And I quoted earlier his remark about "The Red Queen's Race": "I didn't include it in *Asimov's Mysteries* because I never thought of the story as a mystery" (see p. 192).

Asimov's first three science fiction mystery short stories all had as their central character that curious combination of Asimov's own personal idiosyncrasies and Norbert Weiner's physical features, Dr. Wendell Urth, extraterrologist. Published in *F+SF* these three stories were "The Singing Bell" (January 1955), "The Talking Stone" (October 1955), and "The Dying Night" (July 1956). Ten years later he wrote a fourth Wendell Urth story for the all-Asimov issue of *F+SF*, "The Key" (October 1966). In between, in 1956, he wrote a story in which he almost used Urth again, "The Dust of Death." It is to these five stories that we must now turn our attention.

Asimov often speaks of R. Austin Freeman's Dr. Thorndyke series in connection with his own writing of mystery stories. I asked him if he considered Dr. Thorndyke to be Dr. Urth's literary godfather:

> The Wendell Urth stories were influenced by R. Austin Freeman only in that he specialized in describing a crime and then showing the detection (like the TV program, "Colombo.") I did that in my first Wendell Urth story. Actually,

the great influence on my mystery stories was Agatha Christie. When I write stories I write Christie—in the mystery field, anyway. I am now doing a series of mystery stories for Ellery Queen's Mystery Magazine. I have so far written eight and sold eight and, to my way of thinking, they are pure Christie. [Personal letter, August 8, 1972]

I quote the entire passage so that readers more expert in Agatha Christie than I am will know Asimov's attitude and will be able to form their own evaluations of it. What concerns me more is the remark about Freeman's technique of "describing a crime and then showing the detection." This structural pattern is present to one degree or another in all five of the stories we are about to look at. In fact, the stories divide so neatly into two parts, crime and detection, that Asimov is able to print them with a row of asterisks separating the one part from the other. Urth himself, as the detective, only appears in the last part of the four stories he is in.

In "The Singing Bell" the crime is murder on the moon. We watch Louis Peyton murder Albert Cromwell and take for himself a large supply of Singing Bells, worth hundreds of thousands of dollars. Then we sit with Inspector H. Seton Davenport as he goes over the details of the case with Urth. Finally, Peyton is brought to Urth and he is betrayed by his inability to function correctly in Earth's gravity after having spent over two weeks on the moon.

Two things are especially noteworthy in this story. First, Wendell Urth does not solve the murder: the police already knew the murderer's identity, but they lacked evidence. Nor does Urth furnish the evidence they require: he only establishes reasonable grounds for the psychoprobe which will get the evidence necessary for conviction. In supplying those, Urth does his job, and that's a bit different from the usual detective story and from the Dr. Thorndyke pattern Asimov professes to be following.

Second, as in "Marooned Off Vesta," the givens of the story are rigged so that the story can happen. Peyton spends one month of every year in complete isolation from the rest of humanity. Asimov tells us he does this because he hates humanity and needs an annual retreat, but I am not convinced. I think this bizarre and implausible pattern is established because much of the story depends on it. "Why does he do that?" "Because if he didn't there would be no story." For me, it is too contrived and artificial.

In "The Talking Stone" smugglers from the asteroids are detected and accidentally killed before they can reveal the location of an asteroid so rich in uranium that the silicone life form that exists there is over a foot long instead of the more normal inch or two. The crime story is ended with the deaths of the smugglers, and the story's second half is transmuted into solving a puzzle rather than a crime: where are the co-ordinates to the location of the uranium asteroid written down?

After going over the report brought him by Inspector Davenport, Urth has all the clues we readers have, and with them he solves the puzzle. The solution is a neat variation of Poe's "The Purloined Letter," and I leave it to interested readers to look it up.

One of the more interesting things about the story is the way Asimov's readers forced him to do some rethinking about it. They objected to the unfeeling way he treats the death of the silicone life form. (Since that life form could communicate with humans, it had to join the smugglers in death so that no one would be alive who could reveal the asteroid's location. Then there would be no puzzle to solve and no story.) Asimov writes:

> As I reread the story now, I must admit the readers are right. I showed a lack of sensitivity to the silicony's rather pathetic death because I was concentrating on his mysterious last words. If I had it to do over again, I would certainly be warmer in my treatment of the poor thing.
> I apologize.
> This shows that even experienced writers don't always do the Right Thing, and can miss something that is bobbing up and down right at mustache level. [P. 37]

Here we see Asimov giving a bit of criticism of one of his own stories. Admittedly it is a minor point, but it is nevertheless a good example of how a writer thinks when shaping even such minor parts of his stories.

The third Wendell Urth story was "The Dying Night." Three

classmates from different observatories in different parts of the solar system meet a former classmate on Earth at an astronomical convention: Talliaferro from the moon, Kaunas from Mercury, and Ryker from Ceres. The fourth classmate, Villiers, has invented a matter transmitter and is about to reveal its details. One of the three classmates breaks into his room, reads then destroys the paper, and leaves Villiers dying of a heart attack. The body is discovered by one of the convention's organizers, Mandel. In the second part of the story, Mandel takes the three suspects to Wendell Urth's apartment, where Urth solves the crime. As in "The Singing Bell" that solution is based on the criminal's being given away by habits acquired while living out of the Earth's environment.

It should be noted that none of these three Wendell Urth stories follows the Dr. Thorndyke pattern exactly. In "The Singing Bell" Urth did not solve the crime or supply evidence against the criminal. In "The Talking Stone" the crime story is transposed into a puzzle story which Urth does solve. And in "The Dying Night" we do not see the criminal commit the crime. In fact, we do not know his identity until Urth points it out. Only in following the two-part division of crime and detection do the stories follow the Thorndyke pattern. Perhaps Christie *is* more of an influence than Freeman.

Of "The Dust of Death" Asimov tells us,

> Originally I had planned to make this another Wendell Urth story, but a new magazine was about to be published and I wanted to be represented in it with something that was not too clearly a holdover from another magazine. I adjusted matters accordingly. I am a little sorry now and I played with the thought of rewriting the story for this volume and restoring Dr. Urth, but inertia rose triumphant after all. [P. 96]

It seems appropriate, therefore, to discuss this story, however briefly, in the context of the Wendell Urth stories. In "The Dust of Death" Asimov sticks more closely to the Dr. Thorndyke pattern than he had in the first three. Edmund Farley murders the great Llewes by arranging an explosion in Llewes's laboratory. Though the details of how the explosion was arranged are kept from us until the second part, the identity of the murderer is not. The role usually assumed by Urth in the second part is here filled by two men working together in conversation, Jim Gorham, one of Llewes's other employees, and Inspector Davenport of the first three Wendell Urth stories. The placement of this story among the Urth stories is clear.

As in "The Singing Bell" and "The Dying Night" the killer is given away by a mistake he made which was caused by his having been in an environment different from Earth's long enough for certain ways of thinking to become habitual. Asimov's early mysteries, then, are all based on a theme he had used earlier, most notably and successfully in "Nightfall" and the Robot Novels: environment shapes our consciousness.

With "The Key" Asimov is writing a science fiction mystery once again for *F+SF*, and so Wendell Urth can return as the detective. Despite containing what strikes me as a major technical flaw, "The Key" is the best of the Wendell Urth stories, primarily because it is the richest. Let me cite the technical flaw first. Three opportunities to reveal background material present themselves: first, when the events occur; second, when Inspector Davenport and his superior, M. T. Ashley, discuss the case; and third, when Davenport and Ashley take the case to Urth to be solved. The "now" of the first opportunity is framed by two pairs of identical sentences placed eleven pages apart: "Karl Jennings knew he was going to die. He had a matter of hours to live and much to do" (pp. 178, 189). In a fashion reminiscent of *The Currents of Space*, between those two pairs of sentences Asimov gives us a long flashback explaining why Jennings is about to die, which flashback in turn contains several short flashbacks into how Jennings and his murderer, Strauss, met and came to be on the moon together. Flashbacks within flashbacks.

But that is not the problem. I think that in this instance the flashbacks are well handled. They work here. The problem is that given the second opportunity for presenting this material—the conversation between Davenport and Ashley—that same material is indeed re-presented, with the addition only of the three-by-five card which turns out to be the key to the mystery. In other words, the first eleven pages of the story are irrelevant or the great majority of the Davenport-Ashley conversation is irrelevant.

The exposition, therefore, is repetitious and inefficient. Begin the story on page 189 under the asterisks, and nothing is lost. Fortunately, Asimov does forgo using the third opportunity to retell it all and instead reports that "Davenport condensed the tale, giving it in crisp, telegraphic sentences" to Wendell Urth (p. 201).

Perhaps this is as good a place as any to mention a minor problem in the story. An agent named Ferrant reconstructed the conversation between Jennings and Strauss which forms the first ten pages of the story. He then passes that reconstruction along to his superiors, so that the authorities come to know as much as he did. But Ferrant turns out to be one of Strauss's compatriots. Why, then, did he not destroy, conceal, or distort that evidence? Asimov should not have made one of the bad guys a source of information for the good guys.

"The Key" is the best of the Wendell Urth stories because of its richness, its texture. Let me explain through examples. On this two-hundred-years-in-the-future Earth live 6 billion people. Though the population is stable (due to the perfection and widespread use of uterine inserts), many people in that future world feel a decrease in population is in order. Asimov has said elsewhere that he thinks a population of 1 billion would be ideal, and one of the characters, Strauss, begins by mentioning that figure when he and Jennings discuss population reduction. But Strauss continues to reduce the ideal number, finally settling on a mere 5 million. Furthermore, he adds a racist element by insisting, "I want my ethnic group, *our* ethnic group, to prevail. I want the Earth to be inherited by the elite, which means by men like ourselves. We're the true men, and the horde of half-apes who hold us down are destroying us all" (p. 186). Thus "The Key" raises important demographic issues. What ought the population of the Earth to be? Who is to decide? How can our present population growth be halted? How can we decrease the Earth's population and at whose expense?

Furthermore, "The Key" to a certain extent exemplifies the maxim that in Asimov there are no villains. Strauss's plan to reduce the Earth's population from 6 billion to 5 million at the expense of everyone who is not like himself is certainly extreme and Hitler-like. But as Ashley explains, "Have you never felt that it would be wonderful to get rid of the unintelligent, the incapable, the insensitive, and leave the rest? . . . Convince yourself that the end is important enough, that the danger is great enough, and the means will grow increasingly less objectionable" (p. 190). Strauss and the others like him had so convinced themselves, and, in their own eyes at least, they were reasonable men working for the good of humanity as they saw it.

The story is also enriched in a typically Asimovian way when Urth, during his explication of the solution, delivers a three-paragraph-long history-of-science lecture on how a certain crater on the moon came to be named (p. 206). Asimov tells us that one of the reasons he deserted science fiction for science popularization was so he could write such passages unencumbered by the necessity to work out plot lines and characterization and other of the paraphernalia of fiction.

There is also, I suspect, a bit of wishful thinking at one point in "The Key." Jennings and Strauss had found on the moon an alien artifact, nicknamed "the Device," which made telepathy possible for Jennings but not for Strauss. Urth puts it this way: "I think the Device can be actuated by love, but never by hate" (p. 208). Wouldn't it be marvelous if all the products of technology could only be activated and used by men with good hearts and good intentions? If guns would work only for the police and never for the criminals? The research scientist need never again feel guilty, because the products of his research would always be put to good uses by good men. (Of course, Strauss thought he was doing the right thing in trying to rid the Earth of 5.5 billion people. His heart was pure.) Machinery that acted only out of love on the part of its operators would probably create as many problems as robots constructed never to harm human beings. Hmmmmmmmm. . . .

Finally, "The Key" is enriched in a quite accidental way for anyone reading it after having seen the movie *2001: A Space Odyssey*. *2001* grew out of an Arthur C. Clarke story called "The Sentinel," about an alien artifact found on the moon. By a curious coincidence(?) Jennings hides the Device from Strauss by burying it in the crater, Clavius, the same crater in which the alien monolith is dug up in *2001*.

Earlier, in connection with the robot mystery novels *The Caves of Steel* and *The Naked Sun,* I discussed Asimov's primary contribution to the development of the science fiction mystery. Briefly: He put the science fiction into the setting and the mystery into the plot. This is much easier to do in a novel, where one has room to develop setting in greater detail. In a short story the background information must be much more rigorously concentrated on that which is relevant to the story line. As a result, it is easier for the backgrounds of a series of separately conceived short stories to become confused. In "The Singing Bell" Asimov casually mentions, as a part of the science fiction background to the story, that Peyton's food supply "came pushing over the mass-transference beam within the hour" (p. 4). Yet in "The Dying Night" Villiers is killed for his paper introducing mass transference. Again, in "The Singing Bell" the moon is fairly well colonized and patrol ships scurry over it, but in "The Key" only a few expeditions have been there. The backgrounds of the Wendell Urth stories don't quite fit together. This is a typical problem with a series of short stories sold over a period of time and only collected later. Another prime example would be Ray Bradbury's *The Martian Chronicles,* and it is a tribute to Asimov's thoroughness that the Foundation Series is as homogeneous as it is.

Asimov's Mysteries contains four other stories that deserve some comment here: "I'm in Marsport Without Hilda," from the period 1950–59, and three others from his next period, 1959–69, "Anniversary" (the sequel to "Marooned Off Vesta"), "Obituary," and "The Billiard Ball." I take all four up here, despite this not being strictly the chronological place for them, because I want to keep the mystery stories together.

"I'm in Marsport Without Hilda" is another of those rarities among Asimov's work, a story in the first-person narrative point of view. It is also a story that Asimov wrote in response to a challenge by an editor. It seems that the editor suggested that Asimov didn't write love (i.e., sex) scenes because he couldn't, whereas Asimov insisted it was because of his "natural purity and wholesomeness." So Asimov wrote "I'm in Marsport Without Hilda" (which contains neither love nor sex) to prove his point. You figure it out.

Oh, the narrator makes a date with a luscious young thing, and we see her seminude on the videophone occasionally. But video-

phoning and good (or bad) intentions is all we get. The narrator
never takes us or himself physically into her presence. In the
course of the story, the narrator distinguishes the villain from
two other suspects by telling all three "ribald" stories: "I tried to
make it unnecessary for them to imagine—the way I told it they
were *there*. . . . I kept it up, with loving, careful detail" (pp.
121–22). But we are not given any of those details. In other
words, Asimov has a character say he said sexy things, but he
does not have a character say sexy things, much less do anything
sexual. The reaction of the guilty party to this extemporaneous
pornography is described this way: "Ferrucci's breathing speeded
up and the beads of sweat came out on his forehead" (p. 122).
Asimov can't get himself up to another perfectly natural male
reaction to explicit sexual descriptions. The atmosphere of "I'm in
Marsport Without Hilda" is rather the unhealthy one of adolescent sniggering than the healthy one of normal adult relationships. It actually reinforces rather than refutes the editor's
original judgment. One conclusion to be drawn from all this is
that sex—at least, sex in his fiction—embarrasses Asimov. It is a
blind spot in his ability to look at the human condition and see it
straight and whole. The parents of junior high school sons and
daughters need not be concerned when they discover their curious offspring reading a story by Asimov.

"Marooned Off Vesta" was published in the March 1939 issue
of *Amazing Stories*. Twenty years later, for the March 1959 issue,
Asimov obligingly wrote a sequel. In the sequel, "Anniversary,"
Warren Moore, Mark Brandon, and Mike Shea meet at Moore's
house twenty years after their rescue to reminisce and celebrate.
Comparing and contrasting certain elements in the two stories
reveal some interesting things about Asimov's development as a
writer in between.

The initial situation in "Marooned Off Vesta" was wildly improbable, and in "Anniversary" Asimov has Moore remark about
it: "It was just a lucky thrust in a lucky direction and at a lucky
velocity that put our section of the wreck in orbit" (p. 151). The
initial situation in "Anniversary" is to a point perfectly natural.
Moore and Brandon met every year to celebrate their rescue. But
this is the first year Shea had joined them, and he joins by coincidence. On his way to retirement in Arizona he just happened

to look up the other two on the twentieth anniversary. He had forgotten it himself. As it turns out, Asimov the plot-constructor could not let Shea be present at any earlier anniversary, because he has information that would certainly come out whenever he attended one, information crucial to the story Asimov wants to tell. He had, for plot purposes, to attend only this one. Therefore, while there is a wild improbability in the initial situation of "Marooned Off Vesta," there is at least a slight one in "Anniversary." Still, neither story would be at all without its particular improbability, and I guess that in itself is enough to justify them.

In "Marooned Off Vesta" the problem is literally a matter of life and death: they must find a way to get down to Vesta in order to survive. In "Anniversary" the problem is more sedate: they want to become famous again, to find a way out of being marooned in oblivion. In the earlier story Shea furnishes Moore with the data he needs to save their lives; in the latter one Shea (and Multivac) furnishes Brandon with the data Brandon needs to make them famous again. Shea has much the same role in both stories, while Brandon not very plausibly has changed from panicked bystander to rational problem-solver, and Moore inexplicably has changed from rational problem-solver to calm bystander.

Note that all the differences here are in the direction of a slicker, more placid story: the initial situation is less improbable; the problem is less significant (no longer life and death); the characters are less emotional (in the sense that no one is panicked and frightened any longer).

Given the situation, the solution in "Marooned Off Vesta" was completely logical. The solution in "Anniversary" depends on a wild coincidence: once a thin line of reasoning has led them to look for something, it turns out that Warren Moore had that something all along among his souvenirs. Where the wildly improbable had occurred before we joined the story line of "Marooned Off Vesta," it is used to set up the solution in "Anniversary."

Finally, in contrasting the rational Moore with the emotional Brandon, "Marooned Off Vesta" could be read as a nice little allegory on reason versus emotion. That is, "Marooned Off Vesta" has a significant theme. Nothing significant is included in "Anniversary." In fact, its concentration on the goal of becoming famous again lends to the story a certain air of corrupt vanity. The only thing "Anniversary" has going for it is that it is less melodramatic and "pulpy" in its diction.

On any grounds that I can see (other than its more smoothly commercial style), "Anniversary" is an inferior story to "Marooned Off Vesta."

"Obituary" is an unusual story in the Asimov canon in that it is I-narrated by a woman. This narrative point of view was forced on him by the story itself. Let's see if we can roughly reconstruct the process.

The plot evolved this way. After reading in the New York *Times* the obituary of a fellow science fiction writer, Asimov got to wondering what his own obituary would eventually be like. Of course, he would never know because no one gets to read his own obituary. Then he decided to write a story about someone who did. The challenge was to think of some way this would (seem to) be possible. For a science fiction writer, one obvious solution would be time travel. A man alive now goes into the future and reads his own obituary there. But on the one hand, this had been done before, and on the other, it still isn't a story. The exact technique for the time travel had to be worked out, and complications enough to make an original story had to be thought up.

The time-travel device itself turned out to be reminiscent of the "kettles" in *The End of Eternity.* Called a "crucible" here, "it was a small but deep container made out of thick metal and rusted in spots on the outside. It was covered by a coarse wire netting. . . . Inside it was a white mouse with its paws up on the inner side of the crucible" (p. 162). Whatever is under the netting is moved into the future, duplicated, and returned, along with the duplicate, to the present. The hitch is that when any animate matter is duplicated it (a) returns to the present inanimate and (b) disappears when the moment of duplication is reached (again), leaving only the living original. This gives Asimov what he needs, both a dead man and that man still alive. Thus Asimov has his "possible" way for a man to read his own obituary.

Having worked out the time-travel device, he next must work it into a story. The man who invents such a device would of course become famous, so Asimov has him a vain scientist seeking fame. In order to heighten the importance of this experiment, Asimov also makes his scientist unsuccessful, a loser named Lancelot Stebbins. Asimov next makes Lancelot so desirous of fame that he wants to spring his discovery on the world in as spectacular a way as he can imagine, so he has Lancelot arrange to have the dead duplicate found with cyanide crystals scattered about, leading investigators to think that he (it?) died of cyanide poisoning. He also has Lancelot arrange that the moment of duplication be three days after the moment of his apparent death. That is, on the third day he will rise again, to claim his publicity and glory.

As it now stands, the story would be about a successful publicity stunt. It would be like telling "The Ugly Little Boy" from the point of view of Dr. Hoskins and ending it with the successful capture of Timmie out of the Neanderthal past, with its attendant fame and fortune for Stasis, Inc. Asimov deepened "The Ugly Little Boy" by developing a concern for Timmie as a human being and by letting a conflict grow around that issue.

In "Obituary" Asimov does not go that far. But he does make Lancelot an obnoxious husband who dominates his wife to the extent that in one scene he spits on her. Since he is a loser and everything always goes wrong for him, she confidently expects his elaborate plan for fame will go wrong, too. Since she must help him duplicate himself, she fears she will be the cause of this failure. And when he threatens to kill her if she allows anything to go wrong—well, what can she do? On the third day, when the duplicate disappears and her living husband steps out of the room where he has been hiding and reading his obituaries, she gives him a cup of warm tea flavored with cyanide. She then puts his corpse into the coffin where the duplicate had been, and *voilà!* she has removed the threat to her life.

The wife is the story's central character, its problem-solver. Her motivation for interfering in her husband's experiment and killing him is all-important. Asimov can give us her motivation best by letting us share her thinking. In this way "Obituary" forces Asimov to tell a first-person story with that person being a woman. Very unusual in Asimov, but surely technically necessary here.

In many ways, "The Billiard Ball" is a complementary story to "Obituary." Both are first person narrated rather than Asimov's more usual third person. Both feature contrasting main characters, one dominant, one submissive. Both end with the submissive character successfully—i.e., without getting caught—murdering the dominant one. And in both stories the murders are carried out against a backdrop of a fantastic technological device, in "Obituary" a time machine, in "The Billiard Ball" an antigravity device. The major difference is that in "Obituary" the I-narrator is one of the two main characters, the browbeaten, submissive wife, while in "The Billiard Ball" the I-narrator is a third party, outside the conflicting pair, looking in and becoming suspicious a murder has been committed without actually being able to prove it.

Asimov finds the story memorable because "it is the only story I know of to combine the mystery form with Einstein's General Theory of Relativity" (p. 209). Personally, I find more instructive a remark made by the I-narrator when describing his job: "My job was to find human interest in the Two-Field Theory for the subscribers to *Tele-News Press*, and you get that by trying to deal with human beings and not with abstract ideas" (pp. 210–11). What better advice could any beginning science fiction writer hope to be given?

Nightfall and Other Stories (1969)

Nightfall and Other Stories contains twenty stories. Only one, "Nightfall," was first published before 1950, and of the remainder only five are from the sixties. This means that the backbone of the collection is made up of stories from the fifties, even though Asimov had already anthologized four out of every seven stories he had published in the fifties in *The Martian Way and Other Stories, Earth Is Room Enough, Nine Tomorrows,* and *Asimov's Mysteries.* Therefore, *Nightfall and Other Stories* is put together largely from leftovers. Personally, I find it the least interesting of Asimov's collections. It begins strongly, of course, with "Nightfall," holds up well with some good early stories like "Green Patches" and "Breeds There a Man . . . ?"—even "Hostess" and "C-Chute" have their interest—then settles into a run of

rather bland stories until it ends with several short-shorts from
the sixties. The real meat of the book is in its first five stories.

"Nightfall" has already been discussed at some length (pp. 19–
29), so let's turn our attention immediately to "Green Patches."
This story is of some importance in Asimov's career. During the
forties, Asimov had sold regularly to Campbell and *Astounding*,
so regularly that he began to fear that he was "a one-editor
author." This fear had partly motivated his writing of "Grow Old
with Me" (later to be rewritten as *Pebble in the Sky*) for Sam
Merwin, Jr.'s *Startling Stories* in 1947. The story of that fiasco has
been told earlier (pp. 111–13). This same fear manifested itself
in 1950 when Horace Gold was putting together the first issues
of *Galaxy* and asked Asimov for some stories. "I hesitated, for I
was not at all sure that Mr. Gold would like them and I was wondering whether I could bear rejections that would serve as 'proof'
that I was not a real writer but only a one-editor author" (p. 37).
Asimov sent Gold "Darwinian Poolroom" and "Green Patches,"
Gold took them both, and Asimov was able to consider himself
a real writer, one whose work editors liked and bought.

"Green Patches," called "Misbegotten Missionary" in its magazine appearance, is particularly interesting when viewed from the
perspective of "Whose story is it?"—that is, who is its central
character? The narrative point of view shifts back and forth from
a small alien creature, six inches long with two tiny green patches
on it and with little suction cups at each end, to a group of human
explorers centering on Dr. Weiss, the ship's biologist. The story
line follows a success or a failure, depending on whether one
thinks of Weiss or the alien as its central character.

From the point of view of Weiss and the Earthmen, here is the
plot line. Initial situation: The crew of an Earth explorer ship in
its normal course of duties had landed on Saybrook's planet, been
absorbed into the alien life form there, and committed suicide
rather than bring themselves (i.e., that alien life form) to Earth.
Problem: A second ship is sent to find what had happened and
why. Conflict: It learned that all individual life forms on Saybrook's planet were actually linked to one another via a communications system located in the two green patches of fur every
living thing there had, and therefore no such thing as an independent individual could exist. All life forms would become part

of this larger life system. How to prevent it and return safely to Earth? Solution: The ship is thoroughly cleansed of all alien life forms, and the one that had sneaked aboard and disguised itself as a six-inch section of wire is electrocuted when the device it had made itself a part of is activated upon landing on Earth. Resolution: Life as we know it is saved. Restoration of status quo. (Note that, viewed this way, the solution in the story does not come about as a result of anything any of the men think, say, or do. Their efforts were inadequate. The happy ending just happens. *Deus ex machina.* Mankind lucked out.)

From the point of view of the alien, here is the plot line. Initial situation: All forms of life happily united and in communion with one another around the planet. Problem: An alien ship lands filled with life forms that are not united to one another, that are actually fragments of life. The unified life forms naturally want to help these fragmented aliens achieve unity among themselves. Conflict: A life form is smuggled aboard, disguises itself as a section of wire, and awaits arrival at the aliens' home planet (Earth) where it can begin to help them. Solution: It is accidentally electrocuted. Resolution: The Earthmen will have to continue in a state of anarchy for a while. (Note that the alien life form is not villainous and evil. It is trying to help humanity. This is one of those stories that can be cited in support of the generalization that "in Asimov there are no villains.")

A. E. van Vogt's story "Black Destroyer" had appeared in the same issue of *Astounding* as Asimov's "Trends." "Black Destroyer" was innovative in being told largely from the point of view of the alien monster Coeurl as it prowled its desolate planet seeking new energy off which to feed and finally coming into conflict with the crew of a human explorer ship. That story by van Vogt opened up a whole new vein in science fiction, and Asimov's "Green Patches" is one of the results, as was "Nightfall" in its own way. What's it like to be an alien, with motivation of one's own which sometimes may innocently bring one into conflict with members of the human species? On the pattern of "Black Destroyer" "Green Patches" presents a sympathetic alien working at cross-purposes with humanity. It is marred only by its *deus ex machina* ending.

"Breeds There a Man . . . ?" is an excellent example of a kind of science fiction story of which "Jokester" and "Spell My Name with an S" are less good examples. This is the story in which "we are owned." In "Jokester" an inquirer uses Multivac to learn that all jokes are extraterrestrial in origin, that they are intended to help the aliens who "own" us learn about human psychology, and that "these outer intelligences are to us as we are to rats" (p. 160). In "Spell My Name with an S" one alien bets another that he can cause a class A effect with a class F stimulus and wins by preventing a nuclear war by causing a scientist to start spelling his name with an S instead of a Z, the point being that we are controlled and manipulated to suit the whims of outsiders.

As with "Green Patches," "Breeds There a Man . . . ?" yields interesting results when approached via the question Whose story is it? After first reading it, one's instinctive reaction is to think of its central character as being Dr. Elwood Ralson, the brilliant but erratic scientist who, while inventing the projector whose force field results in a defense against nuclear weapons, discovers that we are owned by aliens who do not want us to make defenses against nuclear weapons and who will destroy the Earth before they permit us to do so. After all, Ralson solves the two most important problems in the story, how to build the projector and why we never built one before, and shouldn't that make him the central character?

Unfortunately for this approach, the story is not really about Ralson's efforts to solve those two problems. Our time and attention in the reading of the story is kept on the efforts of others to keep Ralson at work, not being with him while he works.

Others might suggest Dr. Oswald Grant as the central character because the narrative point of view is fastened mostly to him and because we learn what and as he does. But he is doing no more than acquainting himself with Ralson's ideas and then incidentally passing them along to us. He is a passive observer and an interlocutor, not a doer.

Actually, the people who cause this story to be are those hidden, unnamed establishment figures known in the story by that universally present pronoun "they" (as in "When are *they* going to fix this street?"). The action in "Breeds There a Man . . . ?" is caused by the political authorities who want Ralson to develop that defensive shield.

Initial situation: a world with atomic weapons and no defense against them. Problem: Develop a defense. Conflict: Keep the scientists at work until one is developed. Solution: the projector. Resolution: a world with atomic weapons and a defense against them. Using this approach, Ralson's second discovery, that we are owned, is an unsought-for—and disbelieved—by-product of the real conflict. It is not what the story is about.

What I mean to suggest by all this is that our instincts are probably right: it *should* be Ralson's story. But Asimov's roundabout way of telling it has obscured that fact. We are placed at the periphery of the story, where it seems to be about a successful government project whose success is marred by the death of one of the team, rather than at the center of a story about a researcher who learns more than he expected and dies for it. It's Ralson's story, not the faceless theys. We should share his growing awareness and fears, not be told about them secondhand by Dr. Grant. In my opinion Asimov's storytelling instincts played him false in this instance.

The other two of the first five stories in *Nightfall and Other Stories* are "Hostess" and "C-Chute." "Hostess" is told in third-person limited narrative point of view, with the third person being a woman, Rose Smollett. Although she is alert and intelligent, she is not particularly attractive and didn't marry until thirty-four. This has made her insecure, and throughout the story she worries about why her husband, Drake, married her. In that sense, this is Rose Smollett's story. Not only is she the narrative-point-of-view character, but she solves her problem by finding out eventually exactly why Drake married her.

But the story is complex because it is not simply about Rose's problem. Two other characters are involved, and arguments could be constructed showing that the story is each of theirs, too. There are five intelligent races in the Galaxy, and a representative of one, Dr. Harg Tholan, becomes a house guest in the Smollett apartment. He comes to Earth to solve a problem of his own: he wants to locate the source of the Inhibition Death, which causes the members of his race to stop growing and therefore to die quickly. (Asimov was involved in cancer research at the Boston University School of Medicine at the time he wrote this story, and his notion of the Inhibition Death is in the story often dis-

cussed in terms of cancer. It clearly developed as an imaginative result of his day-to-day work.) Dr. Tholan solves his problem when he discovers that the Death is caused by a parasitic sixth intelligent race to which Earthmen had become adapted over the centuries. (This also allows us to see what was most likely the original seed of the story, Asimov's imaginary answer to the question of what causes cancer: "If for any reason the parasitic intelligence . . . does leave the human body . . . growth does take place, but not in any orderly fashion. We call the growth cancer" [p. 190].)

The third problem-solver in "Hostess" is Drake, Rose's husband. He is a hard-boiled detective working in Missing Persons (and therefore the story could be considered at least partly a mystery story). The parasite within him controls him completely, so that Drake's (i.e., the parasite's) problem is how to remain undiscovered, how to destroy the evidence that Dr. Tholan has unearthed. He-it solves the problem by killing Dr. Tholan, by explaining away that event to his wife, and by disappearing.

Dr. Tholan wants to know what causes the Inhibition Death: parasites on humanity that can be spread among the stars by runaway, "missing" persons. Drake wants to protect the parasites from Dr. Tholan's knowledge: he kills Dr. Tholan and runs away. And Rose wonders why Drake married her: the parasites reproduce in their own way during the first year of marriage. She has been used, and the title "Hostess" becomes a grisly pun. (Had Asimov reversed the roles and then called the story "Host," the pun would have been too obvious.) So in "Hostess" we are given three different characters, each with his own motivation and problem to solve, and the three are neatly woven into a readable story that grew out of Asimov's research into cancer.

Two other elements in it should be mentioned. First, Rose spends a considerable amount of time in the story accumulating data and constructing logical explanations for what she finds. In other words, she is a Balkis-type character in a short story, when previously we had seen this sort of character almost exclusively in Asimov's novels (see pp. 124–26, 133–35, 139). In a short story the first explanation is usually the correct one, otherwise the story wouldn't be short. Note for comparison that in *The Caves of Steel* Lije Baley is able to construct three different detailed ex-

planations of the murder, but that was because the novel length allowed it, was even caused by it. Finding Rose doing it in a short story is unusual.

Second, given the assumptions of the story, Asimov is able to construct a beautiful (in the sense of breathtakingly ingenious) explanation of the Garden of Eden myth:

> Was it only a coincidence or was it some queer racial memory, some tenuous long-sustained wisp of tradition or insight, stretching back through incredible millennia, that kept current the odd myth of human beginnings? She thought to herself, there were two intelligences on Earth to begin with. There were humans in the Garden of Eden and also the serpent, which "was more subtil than any beast of the field." The serpent infected man and, as a result, it lost its limbs. Its physical attributes were no longer necessary. And because of the infection, man was driven out of the Garden of eternal life. Death entered the world. [P. 91]

This reading of the biblical episode is so apropos to the context of the story that the act of creative imagination that made possible the joining of the two is, for me, enough to justify the existence of the story. It is the most unexpected and memorable thing in the story.

"C-Chute" is interesting largely as a study of the different reactions among a small group of men to their being taken prisoners of war. The most interesting of all is Randolph Mullen, a small, retiring, ineffectual bookkeeper who has been away from home for seventeen years and has been captured on his way back. It is Mullen who goes outside the spaceship, tricks one alien into opening the air lock and thereby killing itself, enters the chlorine-filled control room, and in hand-to-hand combat kills the second alien. This transformation from milquetoast to hero is awe-inspiring and perfectly natural when one considers the motivation. When asked why he did it, Mullen can only reply quietly, "Haven't you ever been homesick?" (p. 164). Homesickness as a motivation for heroism. It rings so true that one can only applaud Asimov's insight here.

The other stories in the collection are only of marginal interest. In "In a Good Cause" Asimov hides the central character from us

until the end, but the price he pays is to have the story preach an anti-alienism that is foreign both to him and to science fiction. The aliens, by the way, are the four-legged, nonoxygen breathers of "Hostess" reused. "Sally" is a moderately famous story about old but intelligent automobiles put out to pasture (so to speak) who band together to protect the human who loves and cares for them. The idea itself is fascinating, but when it is put into action via a chase scene toward the end, it becomes simply ludicrous. Perhaps the best of these "other" stories is "It's Such a Beautiful Day," about a schoolboy in a world in which people habitually matter-transmit themselves from one indoor location to another who develops an unhealthy (his mother thinks) obsession with the out-of-doors. It is a slight situation, but Asimov develops it in a way that could be called tender. He is in full control of his medium in such stories.

Uncollected Stories

There remain twenty-six stories from the periods 1950–57 and 1958–69 that are not yet available in collections edited by Asimov. A quarter of these are short-shorts, and this demonstrates in its own way that Asimov has a strong inclination toward stories with a trick or snap ending. Many depend on puns, as in "Dreamworld" (*F+SF*, November 1955) and "A Loint of Paw" (*Asimov's Mysteries*). Others work on the same principle he used in such short stories as "Youth": the reversal of readers' assumptions, as in "Exile to Hell" (*Analog*, May 1968). His finest short-short, "The Immortal Bard," does appear in one of his collections, *Earth Is Room Enough*, and I will discuss it shortly (see pp. 251–52). Here, I would simply like to suggest that the short-short form can seldom be made to yield much of value. "The Immortal Bard" strikes me as the exception that puts that rule to the test.

Even some of Asimov's short stories linger mistakenly in the memory as having been short-shorts. Examples would be "Darwinian Poolroom," the first story he wrote for Gold at *Galaxy* (October 1950), "Button, Button" (*Startling Stories*, January 1953), "Rain, Rain Go Away" (*Fantastic Universe*, September 1959), and "The Holmes-Ginsbook Device" (*If*, December 1968). "Darwinian Poolroom" is an I-narrated conversation about evolution that ends in the speculation that man may be inventing

simultaneously the nuclear bombs with which to destroy himself and the thinking machines with which to replace himself. In "Button, Button" an authentic signature of one of the signers of the Declaration of Independence is brought into the present, but the parchment missed out on over 150 years of aging and everyone therefore declares the signature to be a very good fake. In "Rain, Rain, Go Away" those foreign-looking next-door neighbors with the funny accent who are so afraid of clouds literally dissolve when caught in an unexpected thundershower. And "The Holmes-Ginsbook Device" features the development in the twenty-first century of a new way to package and distribute data, a device named after its inventors, a "book." Clearly, Asimov likes unexpected, trick endings, and he uses them in both his short-shorts and his short stories.

The three best of Asimov's uncollected stories are "Belief," (*Astounding*, October 1953), "Each an Explorer" (*Future #30*, 1956), and "Ideas Die Hard" (*Galaxy*, October 1957). "Ideas Die Hard" contains several elements that by now we are used to finding in an Asimov story. For example, it concentrates on conversation rather than activity, it discusses the beauty of Earth as seen from space, and it contains history-of-science materials (particularly material about evidence for a flat versus a round Earth, including references to Galileo, Columbus, and pendulums). Considering its original date of publication (1957), there is in it a remarkable anticipation of one line of argument used in today's space program: "It was decided that a manned vehicle was needed so that manual correction could be introduced to compensate for the small, cumulative failure of the imperfect automation" (p. 130).

This story, too, reflects Asimov's delight in the surprise ending. A two-man crew is sent out on what they—and we—think is the first mission to circumnavigate the moon. When they begin to circle behind the moon, they see that it is propped up with two-by-fours and canvas. The snap ending is that the trip was merely a simulation so that the crew's psychology could be studied. The reader is misled along with the crew into making a whole set of erroneous assumptions, so that "Ideas Die Hard" fits the pattern of stories like "Youth" and "Exile to Hell."

"Belief" was written for Campbell in the period when Campbell was high on psi. In that sense, it was tailored for a market, written to please the enthusiasms of an editor by a writer who didn't share those enthusiasms, and perhaps this is at least partially why Asimov has not included "Belief" in any of his collections. The descriptions of the relationships among the college teachers are not so well done as usual in Asimov, either. He seems to be playing with other people's stereotypes rather than writing out of his own personal experience here.

At the same time, the theme of the story—what it teaches—is a significant one. Basically, "Belief" demonstrates the concept of "the burden of proof." A college teacher of physics discovers one day that he has the power to levitate. With some difficulty, he convinces his wife, but he realizes he could never prove it to others. They would always wonder how he really did it, and they would think him crazy. Eventually, he arranges matters so that he doesn't have to prove his ability to others, but rather for their own sakes they have to find out how he does it. He shifts the burden of proof from himself to them and thus solves his problem. As one of the characters puts it toward the end, "In other words you had made your levitation his problem and not your own" (p. 99). Though perhaps overly long, especially in its middle sections, "Belief" so clearly demonstrates its theme that it must be considered one of Asimov's more successful stories.

The last story I want to look at in this section, "Each an Explorer," uses some typically Asimovian elements in a fascinating new way. Fundamentally, it is "Sucker Bait" and especially "Green Patches" in a different guise. A two-man explorer ship locates a new planetary system and settles down on one of its two Earth-like planets to collect data which might be useful for later colonization. They find plant life (which was common), they find animal life (which was much less common), and they find intelligent animal life (which was unheard-of). They then discover that the intelligent animal life has been made subservient to and by a species of telepathic plants, and the explorers rush back to Earth to warn it of the danger, carrying spores of the thought-controlling plants with them. In "Green Patches" we accidentally survived. In "Each an Explorer" we are doomed.

"Each an Explorer" does not belong to its two narrative-point-of-view characters. The alien, telepathic plants are the story's problem-solvers. Their powers have perfectly adapted them to any environment containing animals because they can force those animals to care for the immobile plants. When the new animals arrive from space, the plants easily control the thoughts of those animals, too, and so the plants are able to spread their species among the stars, each spore an explorer.

The nagging problem with the story is that from the time our two explorers land in the system until the time they leave they behave in a completely irrational and implausible way. For example, they find valuable "Gamow hyperspatial sighters" marked "Model X-20, Gamow Products, Warsaw, European Sector," and they ask no questions because they are too interested in the monetary value of the instruments and in finding more of them. Initially forced to land by malfunctioning atomic motors, they scarcely notice when those motors begin to work again. One reads this section skeptically, noticing flaw after flaw in its construction.

Intriguingly enough, the last part of the story has Asimov going over all these flaws and explaining them away one by one. (Well, it's never really made clear why the telepathic plants tinkered with the hyperatomic motors in the first place, since the explorers were about to land anyhow, nor are we told how telepathic plants can interfere with the operation of inanimate machines. But let that go for now.) The point is that implicitly the last part of the story does a job of practical criticism on the first part. It's Balkis of *Pebble in the Sky* again, going over Asimov's story line and detecting the flaws in it and explaining them away. Only here the explanations are the correct ones, where Balkis's were incorrect even though better than the correct ones. It's self-criticism in an Asimov story, a look into the mind of the storyteller as he works on his plot construction, and it is therefore extremely fascinating reading.

But one thing nags at me: I'm not sure that in this case it's legitimate. The implausible events are caused by the unnatural telepathic plants, a sort of *deus ex flora*. They could have been called upon to explain anything. Isn't this like putting your characters through a series of wildly impossible experiences—and then having one of them wake up? "Oh boy, what a dream! Well, that explains that." Only it isn't an explanation. It's a way to avoid an explanation. I feel somehow that Asimov's telepathic plants are a bit too close to it-was-all-a-dream. However one feels about this particular issue, "Each an Explorer" certainly stands out for a variety of reasons as one of Asimov's better stories.

Critical Stories

Many practicing writers occasionally write stories about writers writing stories. After all, fiction is about human activity, and one human activity is certainly the creating of fiction. Besides, who would be in a better position to describe and comment on this activity than a writer himself? Furthermore, the writing of fiction is accompanied by the reading and eventually the criticizing of fiction. A writer without readers or critics is a part-time writer who doesn't sell.

Asimov has written a handful of stories about writing and/or criticism, and (probably because I am writing a critical book about his fiction) I find these stories particularly attractive. There is a context into which these few stories must be put, however. For one thing, Asimov does not consider himself a conscious artist. He considers himself a storyteller: he thinks of a story idea, sits down at his typewriter, and lets the story tell itself through a little man who sits inside him. In one letter to me, for example, he remarked, "My stories are not deeply thought out in advance but to a very large extent tell themselves" (August 7, 1973). In another he said, "I myself know very little about writing in any formal way and haven't the faintest idea as to why I do things one way rather than another, start in such a fashion, choose to center my story about a particular character" (October 10, 1972). In *Opus 100* he says, "I tell anyone who listens that there is a little man inside me that does the writing, that he is quite beyond my control, and that I just sit there at the typewriter and read what comes out in utter fascination" (p. 298).

Just as he is not interested in the theoretical side of writing before the fact, so he is not interested in literary criticism. He refuses, for example, to review science fiction books. He does review nonfiction science books, and he has done reviews for *TV Guide*, especially reviews of science fiction series. He has produced numerous introductions and prefaces which tend to be biographical, autobiographical, and/or descriptive (rather than critical and evaluative) in nature. And he has written one of the best descriptive essays on science fiction, "Social Science Fiction" (in R. Bretnor's *Modern Science Fiction*, 1953). An excellent sampling of this sort of thing is available in his own *Is Anyone There?* "Part III: Concerning Science Fiction."

In a study of his fiction, however, what I want to get at is the criticism Asimov writes implicitly in some of his stories. Three such stories have already been mentioned: "Author! Author!" in which the mystery writer Graham Dorn is confronted in the flesh by his most popular creation, Reginald de Meister; "Someday," in which children while away time listening to a machine called a Bard piece together stories from its supply of stock characters and situations; and "Jokester," in which our civilization's store of jokes is kept up by alien joke-writers. Of these three, "Author! Author!" is the best by any standard and especially in the present context. Asimov shows us a writer of popular fiction who is self-conscious and a little pretentious. Dorn plays the literary lion at a tea, treats his fiancée with disdain, and announces to his editor that he is about to write a "serious" novel. Asimov is here having fun at the expense of readers who insist on lionizing writers, women who think writers are "romantic," and the old-fashioned, snobbish point of view that used to distinguish between "popular" and "serious" literature. More significant is Dorn's confrontation with de Meister. Literally, de Meister is straight out of the pages of popular fiction. As a result, he doesn't belong in the "real" world, and Asimov has a lot of fun with the incongruity that results from putting him there.

In *Nightfall and Other Stories* appears "The Up-to-Date Sorcerer," in which Asimov himself performs on Gilbert and Sullivan the kind of practical criticism I am trying to do on him. That is, he criticizes the endings of two Gilbert and Sullivan stories and suggests a better ending for one of them. As his title indicates, his story is a reworking of *The Sorcerer*. In both stories a highly moral love potion, which does not affect married people, is accidentally used to transfer the affections of a young lady from her fiancé to an older man. The problem is how to right things between the young people. In Gilbert and Sullivan's version the older man commits suicide, which nullifies the effects of the potion, etc.

In Asimov's version the suicide is seen as ineffective, partly because the effect of the potion would not change with the death of the "loved" one. The young man—and Asimov behind him—continues to analyze the ending of *The Sorcerer:*

> "As a matter of fact, between ourselves, it was a very poor ending for the play, perhaps the poorest in the canon. . . . It was pulled out of a hat. It had not been properly fore-shadowed earlier in the play. It punished an individual who did not deserve the punishment. In short, it was, alas, completely unworthy of Gilbert's powerful genius." [P. 296]

The characters then seek for analogues to the situation in other Gilbert and Sullivan stories, and discuss *Ruddigore,* in which a man was under a curse "which compelled him to commit one crime or more each day. Were one day to pass without a crime, he would inevitably die in agonizing torture." He breaks the curse through the application of reason: "If he deliberately re-fused to commit a crime, he was courting death by his own act. In other words, he was attempting suicide, and attempting sui-cide is, of course, a crime—and so he fulfills the conditions of the curse." This gives Asimov's characters the clue they need, and they draw this conclusion: "Gilbert obviously believes in solving matters by carrying them to their logical conclusions." The cor-rect solution to *The Sorcerer* and the one used by Asimov in "The Up-to-Date Sorcerer" is, then, "Marriage. . . . Once each couple is married, the amatogenic principle—which does not af-fect married people—loses its power over them. Those who would have been in love without the principle remain in love; those who would not are no longer in love—and consequently apply for an annulment" (p. 297).

In this way Asimov performs the practical criticism of showing what he thinks is wrong with Gilbert and Sullivan's original end-ing to *The Sorcerer,* of showing what is right in a comparable second ending (to *Ruddigore*), and of showing how to apply the second (correct) ending to the first (incorrect) one. "The Up-to-Date Sorcerer" provides a fascinating insight into Asimov's critical mind at work.

Two of Asimov's stories that deal explicitly with the writing of fiction are "The Monkey's Fingers" (*Startling Stories,* February 1953) and "Kid Stuff" from *Earth Is Room Enough.* "The

Monkey's Fingers" has not been reprinted as yet, but, especially
in the present context, it is a delightful little story. A science fiction writer named Marmaduke Tallinn is trying to convince Lem-
uel Hoskins, science fiction editor for Space Publications, that a
recently submitted and partially rewritten story of his deserves to
be published. But they cannot agree on the placement of one
block of material. Marmie has written the story so that its political and sociological implications are discussed by the characters
after the climactic scene so that its pace won't be interrupted by
such exposition, while Hoskins wants the politics and sociology
written into a scene that does interrupt the climactic one on the
grounds that the readers would quit reading after the excitement
is over. Which is correct?

Fortunately, Marmie has a fan, Dr. A. R. Torgesson, who is also
a trained scientist with a cybernetically enhanced monkey named
Rollo. Given a passage from a work, along with certain other
background information, Rollo can type the complete work word
for word as it should be written. Well, almost word for word. For
example, to test him, they have Rollo type up Hamlet's "To be or
not to be" speech, and instead of "to take arms against a sea of
troubles" Rollo types "to take arms against a host of troubles."
Dr. Torgesson explains:

> "Shakespeare *did* write 'sea.' But you see that's a mixed
> metaphor. You don't fight a sea with arms. You fight a host
> or army with arms. Rollo chose the monosyllable and typed
> 'host.' It's one of Shakespeare's rare mistakes." [P. 80]

If one wishes, one can take this as Asimov (tongue in cheek?)
correcting Shakespeare.

In any event, Torgesson reads Marmie's story to Rollo all the
way to the disputed passage, then he lets Rollo finish it. Rollo
does so by inserting the sociopolitical passage where the editor
said it ought to be. This forces Marmie to fall back on inspiration
and intuition. Picking up with the Shakespearean "mistake,"
Marmie argues,

> "Shakespeare just happened to know when to *break* the rules,
> that's all. Little Rollo is a machine that can't break the rules,
> but a good writer can, and *must*. . . . I know that I must

break the rules to maintain the profound emotional impact of the ending as I see it. Otherwise I have a mechanical product that a computer can turn out." [P. 82]

One can't tell where Asimov stands in all this. Marmie expected the rules of craftsmanship to support him. Only when they didn't was he forced to defend inspiration. Whether Asimov favors the rules or inspiration, one can't tell from this story. Still, there is some nice inside by-play in this conflict between a science fiction writer and his editor over the placement of material in a science fiction story.

A second story in which Asimov deals explicitly with the writing of fiction is "Kid Stuff." Jan Prentiss writes fantasy (not science fiction this time) for a living, but he is slightly ashamed of it so he hasn't told the neighbors what he does. One day a telepathic fairy shaped like an insect appears on his desk and prepares to kidnap him so it can use his brain to focus its own psychic energy. Jan plies the insect-fairy with richly alcoholic eggnog, confusing it enough so that when it tries to take over his son's mind, it can't. "He assumed that all children believe in fairies, but he was wrong. Here in America today children *don't* believe in fairies. . . . The elf just never realized the sudden cultural changes brought about by comic books and television" (p. 92).

Superficially, the story is about a threat to a family removed by clear thinking (not muddied by alcohol). More importantly, it's about the cultural change mentioned above. And in its frame, Jan Prentiss learns to respect his work a bit more as a result of what has happened: "Next time I see Walt Rae, I think I'll just drop a hint that I write the stuff. Time the neighbors knew, I think." This part of the story is certainly about that vague sense of guilt that hangs over some writers of popular fiction and makes them, like Graham Dorn, want to write some serious stuff. Such writers have been told so often that they write ephemeral trash that they have begun to believe it. Asimov knows better, and luckily so did Shakespeare, Dickens, Dostoevsky, and other writers of popular fiction. Maybe there's hope for Jan Prentiss, too.

The two most significant stories that Asimov has written in this context, however, are both to be found in *Earth Is Room*

Enough, "Dreaming Is a Private Thing," about the creative writer himself, and "The Immortal Bard," about the importance of the literary critic to the creative writer.

"Dreaming Is a Private Thing" is a beautiful little story in five scenes. It's a procedural story in which an executive faces four crises in a day's work. The pattern of the story is not initial situation-problem-conflict-solution-resolution. Rather, the five scenes are carefully arranged so that by the time the reader is finished he has learned through an extremely efficient presentation about a whole new entertainment industry, its problems, and the men who live and work in it. Perhaps the tight organization of this story—and others—owes something to Asimov's experiences as a university professor and lecturer.

The executive in the story is also its narrative-point-of-view character (third-person limited), Jesse Weill, head of Dreams, Inc. In the first scene one of his talent scouts, Joe Dooley, brings in a boy, Tommy Slutsky, who seems to have a talent for "dreaming." Weill checks the boy and agrees with Dooley's estimate. Then he haggles with Tommy's father over contract terms. In this scene we are shown how young dreamers are recruited—not told, shown. In the second scene a government agent, John J. Byrne, of the Department of Arts and Sciences, discusses with Weill a new problem the government faces: illicit pornographic dreamies, cheaply made, raw and crude. Their existence may force the government into censorship, especially as it was an election year and morality always makes good campaign fodder. The process of convincing Byrne that the porno dreamies are privately and amateurishly made is also the process of informing the reader what dreamies are, how they are made, etc. In other words, the second scene is dramatic exposition, something Asimov has always done particularly well. (In one sense, of course, the whole story is dramatic exposition.)

In the third scene Francis Belanger, an employee of Dreams, Inc., tells Weill that the competition, Lustre-Think, is setting up Dream Palaces where several hundred people can all share the same simplified third-person dream in contrast to Dreams, Inc., which supplies very complex first-person dreams to individuals. (In a sense, this is the old "serious" versus "popular" literature debate again in a futuristic disguise, with Asimov building a story that implicitly favors the serious over the popular. A curious stance for a man who denies serious literary and artistic pretensions.)

So far we have been shown how dreamers are located, what dreaming is, and what the competition is doing. In the fourth scene we actually meet a full-grown, practicing, famous dreamer, Sherman Hillary. Hillary is the future's equivalent of the creative writer. And he has come to announce that he is quitting. He is tired of being a dreamer (writer). "It's gotten so I don't go out any more. I neglect my wife. My little girl doesn't know me. . . . I'm tired of things like that, Mr. Weill. I want to be a normal person and live in this world" (p. 189). Weill tries unsuccessfully to argue him out of it—"You dream for a hundred million people every time you dream"—but eventually he accepts the resignation and Hillary leaves.

In the fifth and last scene Asimov has Weill succinctly and poignantly sum up Hillary's plight, and the plight of all the dreamer-writers like him. Weill knows Hillary cannot quit, and he explains why he will be back:

> "A fine day I've had. I had to argue with a father to give me a chance at new talent, with a government man to avoid censorship, with you to keep from adopting fatal policies, and now with my best dreamer to keep him from leaving. The father I probably won out over. The government man and you, I don't know. Maybe yes, maybe no. But about Sherman Hillary, at least, there is no question. The dreamer will be back."
>
> "How do you know?"
>
> Weill smiled at Belanger. . . . "Listen. When I was a youngster—there were no dreamies then—I knew a fellow who wrote television scripts. He would complain to me bitterly that when someone met him for the first time and found out who he was, they would say: Where do you get those crazy ideas?
>
> "They honestly didn't know. To them it was an impossibility to even think of one of them. So what could my friend say? He used to talk to me about it and tell me: Could I say, I don't know? When I go to bed, I can't sleep for ideas danc-

ing in my head. When I shave, I cut myself; when I talk, I lose track of what I'm saying; when I drive, I take my life in my hands. And always because ideas, situations, dialogues are spinning and twisting in my mind. I can't tell where I get my ideas. Can you tell me, maybe, your trick of *not* getting ideas, so I, too, can have a little peace.

"You see, Frank, how it is. *You* can stop work here anytime. So can I. This is our job, not our life. But not Sherman Hillary. Wherever he goes, whatever he does, he'll dream. While he lives, he must think; while he thinks, he must dream. We don't hold him prisoner, our contract isn't an iron wall for him. His own skull is his prison, Frank. So he'll be back. What can he do?" [P. 191]

Does anyone doubt about whom he is speaking? "Dreaming Is a Private Thing" is Asimov's analysis, in science fiction terms, of what it is like to be a creative writer.

"The Immortal Bard" is his estimate of the relevance of criticism—especially academic criticism—to the work of the creative writer. It takes only two pages, and that is one clue right there. "The Immortal Bard" recounts how a university teacher and physicist, having invented a time machine, has been able to bring important men from the past into the present and talk with them. The English instructor to whom he tells all this is shocked to hear that the physicist had brought Shakespeare into the present and that Shakespeare had read and evaluated some of the works of criticism devoted to his plays. His reaction was "God ha' mercy! What cannot be racked from words in five centuries? One could wring, methinks, a flood from a damp clout!" (p. 163). It turns out that the physicist had even enrolled Shakespeare in the English instructor's Shakespeare class, but it was a mistake and Shakespeare had to be returned humiliated to 1600. Shakespeare flunked the Shakespeare course.

In other words, academic criticism has nothing whatever to do with what writers do. This should come as no shock to anyone. Academic criticism is intended to train a reading audience, not the writers themselves. Readers are into literature for entirely different reasons than writers are, and criticism intended for the one is not likely to be very helpful to the other. A mechanic has a completely different interest in cars than has a tourist, so a mechanic would no more read a tour guide to find out about cars than a tourist would read a factory manual to learn where the best sight-seeing is.

Still, as an associate professor in a department of English, I do wince a bit at a story in which Shakespeare cannot pass a modern Shakespeare course. Because I think Asimov is right.

ship, tools. I call narrative techniques. Having already applied them to individual stories—which is the best way to put them to use—let me here generalize on their use in Asimov's fiction. The narrative point of view is almost always third-person limited, with that person being the central character of the story. Even when he is working with a large cast of characters in a novel, say, and must move about among them, each scene tends to be narrated solely from the point of view of one of its participants, rather than from the point of view of an omniscient outside observer. Asimov lets us see fictional events the way we see life: through the experience and observations of only one person.

Generally, the central character of a story is named and put into action in the first sentence. That is, the subject in the first sentence we read will be the central character's proper name, and its verb will let us see that person doing something. (When he does not put his central character in motion before us in the very first sentence, he will do it very, very shortly thereafter. It won't do to let the reader wait too long before finding out who the central character is, whom to identify with.) His central characters are usually white middle-class males on the sunny side of forty, because the market he writes for is composed largely of such people.

The problems these people have to solve generally involve the making of decisions rather than the performing of actions. At least, even in a basically action-adventure story, decision-making is shown to take precedence over doing things. Very often this decision-making is done by two or more people in conference. This tends to change the story from the personal to the political. It also has the advantage of externalizing the decision-making process and thereby giving the reader something to watch and listen to. Interior monologues are not as available to us in everyday life as conversations. This emphasis on conversation and decision-making, instead of on activity for its own sake, gives Asimov's fiction a certain cerebral quality, which is one of its most distinctive traits.

The stories usually begin very soon after a problem has arisen. The initial situation and the problem are passed along to the central character—and, in the process, to the reader—by someone who thoroughly understands both. Asimov is excellent at the

CONCLUSIONS

The Most Recent Asimov

"Asimovian." I have used the adjective myself, and I have seen it used by others. What others mean by it I cannot say. But I would like to suggest in some detail what I have found the term to mean. There will of course be exceptions in the Asimov canon to everything that I say, but I intend to generalize from specific examples, and I think that what I have to say will cover the majority of instances.

On matters of style: The typical Asimov sentence is short and clear. His sentences tend to gain length not by the accumulation of dependent clauses, but by the addition of simple sentences: not "The boy who hit the ball ran around the bases," but "The boy hit the ball, and then he ran around the bases." His verbs tend to be colorless, non-meaning-bearing linking verbs, and the meanings of the sentences tend to be carried by their nouns, adjectives, and adverbs. He does not like to use figurative language, so he almost never uses images, metaphors, similes. (His preference for linking verbs instead of meaning-bearing verbs is directly related to this, because linking verbs are not imagistic. They do not require that you see something. Meaning-bearing verbs do carry this requirement. The visualization is the meaning they bear.) Typically, one does not notice Asimov's language, unless one is aware how difficult it is to write this clearly. Lovers of language will say that he is no stylist; lovers of communication will admire and envy him. I think Asimov's language represents in a quintessential way the language science fiction writers aspired to during the Golden Age, the Campbell years of the forties.

I have used a variety of tools in discussing Asimov's craftsman-

The Most Recent Asimov

"Feminine Intuition." *F + SF*, October 1969

"Waterclap." *If*, April 1970

"2430 A.D.—Too Late for the Space Ark." *IBM Magazine*, October 1970

"The Greatest Asset." *Analog*, January 1972

"The Computer That Went on Strike." *Saturday Evening Post*, Spring 1972

"Mirror Image." *Analog*, May 1972

"Take a Match." *New Dimensions II*, ed. Robert Silverberg, 1972

The Gods Themselves. 1972

dramatic form of exposition. It is another form of conversation, and he knows how to move stories through conversation. He sometimes uses the flashback for exposition, but he is less consistently good at this method. He tends either to allow the time sequence to become a bit muddled (e.g., *The Currents of Space*) or to become redundant by using both dramatic exposition and the flashback to pass along the same material (e.g., "The Key").

The conflicts in an Asimovian story usually involve difficulties in the way of accumulating data, in interpreting that data, and in deciding what to do as a result of the data and its interpretation. A calm, reasoned approach, rather than a hastily-arrived-at emotional one, provides the solutions to the stories. The resolutions generally mark a return to the status quo. In this sense, he is a conservative writer. The most important Asimovian theme is the importance of science (data-collecting) and reason (data-evaluating and decision-making).

Asimov's stories are set in the immediate and far future, and on Earth and distant planets circling other suns. He seldom sets stories in the past, on alternate worlds, in other dimensions, or in countries other than the United States or future extensions of the United States. His backgrounds are meticulously worked out and scientifically accurate. One leaves an Asimov story with the feeling of having lived for a while somewhere else. This ability of his to provide his settings with that "lived in" quality is another of Asimov's most distinctive features.

Unfortunately, his characters do not share as much as they should in the convincingness of his settings. One does not leave an Asimov story convinced that he has lived for a little while with real people. The characters tend to do and think what they must for the sake of the story rather than for their own sake. In his fiction at least, his interest in people is theoretical not personal, general not particular. Asimov's fiction reflects an interest in the physical, chemical, biological, and astronomical phenomena that life makes available for study, not in the experience of living itself. Put another way, his fiction is concerned with the lowest common denominator of human experience—the common environment of all our separate consciousnesses—rather than in those separate consciousnesses themselves. It focuses on what is generally true of and for us all rather than on what is specifically true of and for only one person. His fiction shows no interest in and scarcely an awareness of two extremely personal elements in all men's lives, religion and sex. As a result, his people are depersonalized to the extent of being dehumanized. I might use an aphorism to describe Asimov's characters: they are not people, they are story parts.

Fiction humanizes and specifies the general. I find it very instructive when Asimov admits he gave up science fiction for science writing so he could write directly about science without the bother of considering people and people's behavior. (I assume that this is at least partly what Asimov meant in *Opus 100* when he said, "I loved science too much. I kept getting the urge to explain science without having to worry about plots and characterization" [p. 16]. What is characterization but people? What are plots but the behavior of people?)

Besides these narrative techniques of style, narrative point of view, plot, theme, setting, and character, three other things strike me as being usually present in an Asimovian story. Asimov loves everything about science, including its history (and he loves history, too). Present in many of his stories are informative little history and history-of-science lectures of the kind he does at greater length in *F+SF*. Second, his fiction is filled with astronomical views, what it looks like to be out among Jupiter's moons or Saturn's rings or in orbit about a newly discovered planet of a distant star. Once again, in science fiction the sense of wonder is sight, and Asimov wants us to share that sense of wonder with him: the sublimity and the beauty of what there is to see out there. Third, Asimov's fiction reflects his delight in the surprise ending, the story that goes *click!* at the end. He loves the challenge of fooling the reader, of leading him to the unexpected, and so he is very adept at writing short-shorts and longer stories that one mistakenly remembers as being short-shorts because all one recalls is the punch line.

For me, all of the above is included in the term "Asimovian."

But the adjective implies a steady state. Asimov has written fiction since 1938. Is that fiction all of a piece, or has he developed in any specific ways through the years? While I was doing the reading and writing of the earlier chapters in this study, I could maintain a feeling of change, of growth and development in

Asimov's fiction. I was able to discern four periods in that career, and I could think of him as moving from one period to the other. I could move from the early stories to the Robot Stories to the Foundation stories to the novels.

But movement is not necessarily development, a change of setting is not necessarily a growing, an opening up of new markets is not necessarily a maturing. And when I read all those collected and uncollected stories, what I notice is that some are better than others and some not so good, and that there is no chronological pattern to which is which. Realistically, I can see only two major changes in Asimov's career. The first was in 1938–39 when he changed from science fiction fan to science fiction writer, and the second was in 1957–58 when he changed from science fiction writer to science writer.

During his career as a science fiction writer, however, I can detect only two relatively minor developments. One of these was in his style. His early stories abound in the violent diction of the pulps. There is more emotion of a nonrealistic sort in that early fiction. As he wrote, he mastered the medium of clear, unemotional language. A second development was in the kinds of backgrounds he used. The backgrounds of the early stories are imitated from contemporary science fiction. As he wrote, he began to put together his own backgrounds based on contemporary science. Except for these two developments—in style and in settings—"Marooned Off Vesta" and "The Callistan Menace" are just as "Asimovian" as "Take a Match" and much of *The Gods Themselves*. Asimov found his voice early and has been speaking in it ever since.

In the future Asimov will probably continue what he has been doing since 1958, writing primarily straight science books and articles with an occasional foray into science fiction because he loves the field and doesn't want to disengage from it entirely. Still, I sense in his most recent fiction not only a tentative return to the field but a return of a certain kind. The writing of *The Gods Themselves* required a major commitment of time and energy, and it was a major commitment to a work of fiction. He has also returned to the subject matter of his earlier successes. "Feminine Intuition" featured a retired Susan Calvin called upon to return to her former job briefly. "Mirror Image" reunited Lije Baley and

R. Daneel Olivaw. A new positronic robot story, "That Thou Art Mindful of Him," appeared in the May 1974 issue of F+SF. And he has been trying to work on a new story in the Foundation Series. Somehow I wouldn't be surprised to hear that the little man inside him has set to work on a sequel to "Nightfall" (telling perhaps what happened to the people secure in the Hideout) and/or the once-begun-but-never-finished third story in the Robot Novels.

Whether or not Asimov indeed begins to produce science fiction in quantity again, he has, I think, to choose between two kinds of story that he has in him to write. I do not expect him to turn to drastic stylistic experiments, to try to develop an imagistic style and strong verbs. He will continue to write like Asimov. The choices lie in his subject matter. He could continue to do what he has been doing of late: mining old material. The old familiar series, the old familiar settings, the old familiar characters. Supplying nostalgic trips for his many fans.

Or he could follow up in the direction I see him hesitantly looking in a couple of his most recent stories. To do this would require two major changes in attitude on his part, changes I don't believe he is ready to make. The first would be to take fiction seriously, and the second would be to write fiction about those things that are important to him. The two are clearly interrelated: if he took fiction seriously, of course he would use it to say those things that are important to him.

The first change carries in it the assumption that he does not now take fiction seriously. I don't think he does. For Asimov, fiction is merely entertainment, merely a way of passing time harmlessly. He downgrades "the eternal verities" and has little use for critics who see deep meaning and significance in his work. (Or in Shakespeare's, as "The Immortal Bard" made perfectly clear.) When Sputnik went up in the fall of 1957, and Asimov felt compelled to do what he could to close the science gap between the United States and the Soviet Union, what did he do? Considering his oft-expressed idea that science fiction bends the minds of young readers toward science, we might have expected him to double—nay, quadruple—his output of science fiction as his way of recruiting scientists. Instead, when a serious job was to be done, he turned to nonfiction, to science popularization.

What things does Asimov think are important? In his public appearances on television and radio, at universities and science fiction conventions, even in newspaper and magazine interviews —in short, in his nonfiction—we can see what is on his mind these days. Let me cull my examples from one interview with him, this one published in *Boston* (December 1969) and called "Scientific Inquiry: A Boston Interview with Isaac Asimov" (pp. 51–54, 82–90).

If you *really* want an example of useless scientific work . . . that can lead only to terrible destruction, and which, to my way of thinking, no scientist with a conscience should engage in, it is the matter of chemical and biological warfare. There is nothing as far as I know in CBW that can help scientific theory in any way, or that can have any constructive use. . . . It is a universal human insanity. . . .

[When asked whether he was optimistic over science and its ability to solve mankind's problems, he replied:] I'm afraid I am not. . . . Never at any time have we managed to get people to look at humanity as a single unit, to look at the world as indivisible. . . . We live in an age of planetary problems and for the first time planetary problems have become matters of life and death. By a planetary problem I mean a problem that cannot . . . be solved on any basis smaller than the entire planet. For instance, overpopulation. There is no way in which the United States . . . can solve the overpopulation problem because if the United States reaches a population plateau and the rest of the world continues breeding recklessly, we're in trouble anyway. . . . Either the entire planet solves it, or no one solves it. The same is true of the problem of the stripping of the earth's resources, . . . the problem of pollution, . . . the problem of nuclear war. . . . We have got, somehow, to get it into our heads that the really important things on earth today are good for everybody or bad for everybody. There is no distinction. We cannot afford enemies any more. . . . Within a generation or two human society will be in total destructive disarray. Heaven knows how bad it will be. The most optimistic view I can take is this: Things will get so bad within a dozen years that it will become obvious . . . that we must, whether we like each other or not, work together. We have no choice in the matter. . . . Technologically, we can stop overpopulation, but we have to persuade people to accept the technology. . . . Babies are the enemies of the human race. . . . Let's consider it this way: by the time the world doubles its population, the amount of energy we will be using will be increased sevenfold which means probably the amount of pollution that we are producing will also be increased sevenfold. If we are now threatened by pollution at the present rate, how will we be threatened with sevenfold pollution by, say, 2010 A.D., distributed among twice the population? We'll be having to grow twice the food out of a soil that is being poisoned at seven times the rate.

Where in his fiction are all these things central?

Admittedly, the general theme of his stories has always been the ability of human reason to solve problems. But what problems has human reason been set to solving in his most recent fiction? In "Feminine Intuition" Susan Calvin reasons out where certain robot-accumulated data can be found after the robot is accidentally destroyed (when a meteor collides with an airplane!). In "The Greatest Asset" a wise old bureaucrat reasons that a brilliant young scientist ought to be allowed to work on a hopeless project because "man's greatest asset is the unsettled mind." In "The Computer That Went on Strike" a computer programmer reasons out that Multivac has quit answering questions because its programmers don't say "Please?" In "Take a Match" a generalist high school teacher solves the technical and human problems involved in saving a spaceship trapped in a thick black cloud. They are all Asimovian stories teaching the value of reason, yes, but that reason is applied to trifles which are completely beside the point of Asimov's main concerns. His stories actually serve to distract us from the real problems which he sees all around us. He cannot take his fiction seriously if he insists on using it in such inconsequential ways at a time when he sincerely believes civilization as we know it is breaking down.

In his fiction Asimov is cheerfully optimistic. In *The Caves of Steel* the overpopulation problem has been solved, as have the problems of the stripping of the Earth's natural resources, of pollution, of nuclear war, of uneven distribution of wealth, of nationalism. In the Robot Stories man's technological devices open up the solar system and then the Galaxy. In the Foundation Series man has successfully spread his civilization throughout the Galaxy. But we know that *really* he is pessimistic about our civilization's surviving this century. Where in his fiction do we find an emphasis on the things he is really concerned about?

I do not wish to be misunderstood here. I am not saying that Asimov ought to turn to the writing of what he calls tomorrow fiction, the attempt to let readers live with characters in stories that show what tomorrow will probably be like, a sort of fictionalized futurism. On the one hand, Asimov will write what he likes and he doesn't need me to point his way for him. On the other, one can write about real problems and issues in today's world without writing tomorrow fiction. The main action of H. G. Wells's *The Time Machine* takes place hundreds of thousands of years in the future and is not intended to show what that tomorrow will really be like. Yet the novel is directly applicable to Wells's contemporary society. I am trying to be descriptive, not prescriptive, and what I am saying is that in some of his most recent fiction Asimov seems to me to be moving in the direction of taking fiction seriously and of writing about things that really concern him. I see him doing this primarily in two works, and therefore, for me, they are the most important things he has written lately, *The Gods Themselves*° and "Waterclap."

On January 24, 1971, Asimov was in the audience at a science fiction convention in New York City when Robert Silverberg referred to plutonium-186. Later, Asimov pointed out to Silverberg that plutonium-186 was an impossible isotope, but he offered to write a five-thousand-word story about it anyway. The story was to be called "Plutonium-186." Thus, unknowingly, did Isaac Asimov begin *The Gods Themselves* (1972), his first science fiction novel in fourteen years.

He describes how he went about planning the story: "I had to think of something that would make possible (or at least seem to

° The following material on *The Gods Themselves* appeared in a slightly altered form in *Extrapolation*, Vol. 13, No. 2 (May 1972), 127–31.

make possible) the existence of an impossible isotope, then think of complications that might ensue, and then of the resolution of those complications" (p. 7). Very early in the story a quantity of plutonium-186 has been discovered, and the characters are faced with exactly the problem Asimov had had to solve, how to account for the existence of this impossible isotope. The character's solution in the story shows us the writer's solution at his desk. A very minor character is made to say, "You know, what we need is a little bit of fantasy here. Suppose. . . ." A little later, a major character, Frederick Hallam, elaborates this "little bit of fantasy," and in so doing answers that perennial question asked of science fiction writers, "Where did you get that crazy idea?" What Hallam says, in effect, is (a) the small container of plutonium-186 does in fact exist, (b) its production in our universe was impossible, and therefore (c) it was sent to us from a parallel universe with a different set of physical laws. As a result, *The Gods Themselves* could be classified as a "parallel worlds" novel.

Next, Asimov had to "think of complications that might ensue." He decided to make the parallel universe a source of energy for us, just as our universe was a source of energy for it. What he calls Electron Pumps are set up, and the world's energy problems are solved. Only—and here's the conflict that makes this a story—one character, Peter Lamont, becomes convinced that the energy exchange will lead to the detonation of the sun. It becomes his task to convince the Establishment that the Pumps must be turned off. Basically, the conflict is between Lamont and the Establishment, especially as represented in Hallam, "the Father of the Electron Pump."

"Plutonium-186," then, is an ecological story on a grand scale. It is a story developing exactly those themes about which Asimov has spoken so pessimistically in his nonfiction. We are doing too little too late. Overpopulation, hunger, disease, pollution, fuel shortages, inequitable distribution of wealth—things will get a lot worse before they get any better, and they may never get any better. The resolution of the conflict in "Plutonium-186" is in accord with this thinking. Peter Lamont is unable to convince anyone in authority that the sun will soon nova because of the unchecked use of the Electron Pumps. A friend of his quotes the German playwright Schiller as saying, "Against stupidity the gods themselves contend in vain," and then advises Lamont, "Let it go, Pete, and go your way. Maybe the world will last our time, and, if not, there's nothing that can be done anyway. I'm sorry, Pete. You fought the good fight, but you lost" (p. 72). And Lamont is left alone, sitting in a chair and thinking of the end of the world, and blinking back the tears.

"Against stupidity the gods themselves contend in vain." "You fought the good fight, but you lost." Where is the cheerful, slick-magazine optimism in this? This is Asimov looking at the world straight and telling us what he sees, in fiction. He is not playing intellectual games or merely being entertaining. He is saying something important, to him and to us.

One of the most interesting things about "Plutonium-186" as a work of fiction is the way it reveals Asimov's years as a writer of science fact. This is most obvious in the little informative lectures scattered through the story. They read exactly as though they were written for his series of articles in *F+SF*. More importantly, "Plutonium-186" reads like an account in the history of science. This is most clearly seen in the way Asimov gives us the exposition of the story, "exposition" here still referring to the way the writer chooses to present the past of the story to his readers. The writers' creeds all say, "Put the reader where the action is." "Show, don't tell." But often in his exposition Asimov decides to reconstruct rather than to visualize (or to make real). He asks his reader not to participate in events, but to evaluate sources and decide what probably happened. This sounds as though it shouldn't work, but it does. Remember that the basic conflict is between Lamont and Hallam, and that Lamont wants Hallam's Electron Pumps turned off. Part of Lamont's strategy is an *ad hominem* attack on Hallam: he tries to discredit Hallam, and to do that he must search for the truth in the past. Asimov's method of exposition parallels Lamont's method of attacking Hallam. Thus, treating the past of the story as an episode in the history of science is an appropriate and innovative way of reflecting the conflict between Lamont and Hallam.

Unfortunately, Asimov had promised Silverberg a five-thousand-word story, and "Plutonium-186" had grown into a twenty-thousand-word novelette (largely, I suspect, because of Asimov's interest in the science fact/history of science aspects of his presentation). So Asimov wrote "Take a Match" for Silverberg's *New Dimensions II* and decided on his editor's advice to use "Plutonium-186" as the basis of a novel.

Note that the original story, although too long for its original market, was complete. Asimov had thought of something that would make the impossible isotope at least seem possible, he had thought of complications arising therefrom, he had thought of an appropriate resolution, and he had summed up the theme of the story in a quotation from literature. Where will the rest of the novel come from?

In the story so far, the "men" of the para-universe have contacted us and shown us how to build our halves of the Electron Pumps (without somehow solving the problem of how to communicate back and forth about any other matters, a difficulty that Asimov leaves unexplained). The obvious gambit for a continuation would be to tell the story from the point of view of the men in the para-universe. This suggests the possibility of a three-part novel: (I) "Plutonium-186," (II) the para-men, and (III) men and para-men together solving their problems. The aliens are clearly associated in Asimov's mind with the middle phrase of the Schiller quote, "the gods themselves." In "Plutonium-186" Lamont has fought against the stupidity of the Establishment and failed. What more natural than to retitle the first section "Against Stupidity"? Only now a problem arises: The last part of the quote doesn't fit very well, because in the expanded version the solar system is eventually to be saved. It will not ultimately be a "vain" contest. So Asimov simply adds a question mark to the last title, and the three parts of *The Gods Themselves* are given the titles "I. Against Stupidity," "II. The Gods Themselves," and "III. Contend in Vain?"

While he was planning and working on "The Gods Themselves," Asimov was very much aware of two forces working on him. He explains them as follows:

> [1] I've often been told I can't handle extra-terrestrials and that that's why my Foundation stories deal with all-human galaxies. Not so!
>
> In *The Gods Themselves*, I set the second part in the parallel Universe and deliberately told a story of extra-

terrestrials and not only managed to do so, but also managed (in my own opinion and according to many letters I have received) to create the best extra-terrestrials ever created. . . .

[2] Also when I finished the first part of the book (as an independent novelette with no intention of doing more at the time), Doubleday urged me to make a novel of it and showed a copy to a paperback editor while I was thinking. I was told the paperback editor said, "Couldn't he put sex into it?" and Doubleday said, austerely, "Of course not. Asimov never does."

So I did. I put sex into the second part. It is all sex and, I think, sex seriously and decently handled as an integral part of the plot and with no holds barred. It just happened to be extra-terrestrial sex. [Personal letter, October 10, 1972]

As a result of this dual challenge to handle aliens and sex as he never had before, Asimov wrote the brilliant middle section of *The Gods Themselves*. In this section he takes us elsewhere and allows us to live there for a while. It is a detailed study of consciousness as it developed and lives in a vastly different environment from our own. Perhaps, as much as anything else, it leaves behind an awe-full respect for life and sentience.

But no science fiction alien can ever be entirely different from ourselves. They spring out of and are thus rooted in the human imagination. In one sense what Asimov has done is return to a certain type of medieval allegory, the type represented by *The Romance of the Rose*, in which the allegorical abstractions are abstracted from the human psychology. The family groups of three—exemplified here in Dua, the female, and Odeen and Tritt, the males—are abstracted from each of us. The medieval allegorist might have called Dua, Emotion; Odeen, Intellect; and Tritt, Common Sense. In these days of unisex and women's lib, it is interesting that Dua, the female, creates an environment in which Tritt, the male, can conceive and rear the children. Asimov does not present simply Male-Intellect-Logic versus Female-Emotion-Intuition. (Fill in whatever other dualities you are used to.) Instead, each of us has within him a Dua, an Odeen, and a Tritt, and "The Gods Themselves" can be read profitably, I think, as a reminder that our natures are not dual but complex.

"Against Stupidity" and "The Gods Themselves" mesh together very well. In the first part we are with our fellow human beings, receiving cryptic messages; in the second we are with the para-men, sending those messages. One slightly jarring note is that initially we are led to believe that the para-men's continued use of the Pumps is the result of stupidity on their part parallel to our own, whereas we learn that they know they are about to destroy our solar system but they don't care. They are motivated not by stupidity, but by maliciousness. This blunts the original theme of "Against Stupidity"–"Plutonium-186."

"Contend in Vain?" does not fit in very well at all with the earlier two sections. The Schiller quote that was so appropriate to the pessimistic "Plutonium-186" no longer fits the more conventional story in which the hero saves the universe, marries the girl, and lives happily ever after. This incongruity is what Asimov was recognizing when he put the question mark in "Contend in Vain?" (Try to read Schiller's statement as a question. The strained falseness of the last three words exactly suits the whole last section of the novel in its relationship with what has gone before.) Worse yet, the breathtaking and promising ending of "The Gods Themselves" has been ignored. When the para-man Estwald stepped forward and said, "I am permanently with you now, and there is much to do . . . ," we were led to believe that he would do something. We expect that in Part III Lamont and Estwald would join in an honest effort to solve the mutual problems between the two universes.

Instead, the men of the para-universe are never brought onstage again. They are slipped into the background as a permanent but impersonal threat which is finally neutralized by conjuring up another para-universe (a pocket-frannistan?) to balance theirs out. The para-men deserve far better than to be so abruptly dropped because there is simply too much preparation in the second part for their continued use.

Admittedly, by itself and with a less awkward title, "Contend in Vain?" is a very good piece of writing. In it we have once again the politically astute Asimov of the Foundation Series, the one who substitutes talk for action because he knows that decision-

making is more important than mere activity. And we have once again the Asimov of *The Caves of Steel*, so good at constructing the details of a future human society down to its attitudes, architecture, and games (the future society here being located on the moon).

Nevertheless, in context "Contend in Vain?" does not work. Surprisingly—I would have said impossibly earlier—the first two sections are so good that they make the typically Asimovian last section look weak. "Against Stupidity" has its history-of-science expository structure in which we are asked to reconstruct probable events rather than participate in actual ones (a technical innovation) as well as its honest and realistic—and pessimistic—appraisal of where we as a civilization stand (an innovation in subject matter). "The Gods Themselves" has its successful treatment of aliens and sex and its implicit demonstration that all consciousness is companioned by all other consciousness. But I cannot forgive Asimov for "Contend in Vain?" Besides abandoning the brilliantly conceived para-men, conjuring the pocket-frannistan of another parallel universe with which to solve the novel's problem, and pasting on a happy ending, he has in it abandoned those things that are important to him as detailed in his nonfiction. (By the way, it's not the happy ending I object to, it's the pasting on. Had Estwald and Lamont working together solved their mutual problems, I would not have objected to *that* happy ending, and it would have been right in keeping with Asimov's other work, too.)

The three separate parts of *The Gods Themselves* are all very good stories. Put together they do not form a unified whole. Put together in their particular order, they also show Asimov backsliding. In *The Gods Themselves* Asimov takes both of the two paths I have suggested are open to him, and they are incompatible in one novel. He cannot present simultaneously his bleak evaluation of the crisis situation in which we find ourselves and his buoyantly optimistic story line. We all know that he does not believe that someone is going to discover a pocket-frannistan and save us all. That Asimov can write "Against Stupidity" and "The Gods Themselves" I take as a hopeful sign. That he chose to cap them off with "Contend in Vain?" I take as an indication that he is not yet certain whether he is looking to his future or to his past. (One might add to this such of his most recent stories as "Feminine Intuition," "The Computer That Went on Strike," and "Mirror Image.")

"Waterclap" integrates two projects that must fascinate Asimov both as a science writer and as a science fiction writer: the exploration of outer space and the exploration of our own oceans. He could have written an essay asserting in nonfictional terms a possible relationship between the two, but instead he wrote a story demonstrating in fictional terms that space-ocean exploration is not either-or but both-and. A fanatical believer in space exploration comes to Ocean-Deep to sabotage the installation so that funds for it will be cut off and channeled into space exploration instead. At the crucial moment he does not destroy Ocean-Deep because he becomes convinced that "the purpose of Ocean-Deep is to devise the ultimate vessels and mechanisms that will explore and colonize Jupiter" (*World's Best Science Fiction: 1971*, pp. 123–24). The speaker goes on to describe "Project Big World" in the most optimistic science fictional and Asimovian terms:

> Look about you and see the beginnings of a Jovian environment—the closest approach to it we can achieve on Earth. It is only a faint image—but it is a beginning. Destroy this . . . and you destroy any hope for Jupiter. On the other hand, let us live and we will, together, penetrate and settle the brightest jewel of the solar system. And long before we can reach the limits of Jupiter we'll be ready for the stars, for the Earth-type planets circling them—and the Jupiter-type planets, too. [P. 124]

"We'll be ready for the stars": the ultimate symbol in science fiction for human success and freedom. The happy ending here is an affirmation of the necessity for people to work together to solve their problems, despite sometimes conflicting aims and motivations. In contrast the happy ending of *The Gods Themselves* was a parallel universe pulled out of a hat. And while, at the end of *The Gods Themselves*, everyone lived happily ever after, the ending of "Waterclap" is not really an ending: the Galactic Empire is not yet come, and there is much to do.

In my mind, the nature of Asimov's future in science fiction depends on his willingness to resolve the disparity between his fiction and his nonfiction, between *The Caves of Steel* and his interview in *Boston*. That he can resolve them is clearly demonstrated in "Against Stupidity" and "Waterclap." But these two items represent only a small part of his most recent fiction, and nostalgic excursions with Susan Calvin, Lije Baley, R. Daneel Olivaw, the positronic robots, and perhaps even the Foundations have taken a disproportionate amount of his science fiction time and energies.

Personally, I hope Asimov can shake off his past successes and move in the direction indicated by "Against Stupidity" and "Waterclap." I would welcome Asimov's return as a full-time science fiction writer, taking fiction seriously as a medium in which to say the most important things he has to say. Then he could announce to us all—in the words of Estwald at the end of "The Gods Themselves"—"I am permanently with you now, and there is much to do—"

Bibliography

This is a listing of items used and mentioned in this study. For a more complete bibliography of science fiction criticism see Thomas Clareson, ed., *Science Fiction Criticism: An Annotated Checklist* (Kent State University Press, 1972). For full bibliographies on Isaac Asimov see Marjorie Miller, *Isaac Asimov: A Checklist* (Kent State University Press, 1972) and Matthew Tepper, *Asimov Science Fiction Bibliography* (Chinese Ducked Press, 1970). (All but two of Asimov's novels and collections are published in hard cover by Doubleday & Company, Inc., and these editions form the copy texts for the quoted citations, with two exceptions: *The Caves of Steel* and *The Naked Sun* citations are from *The Rest of the Robots*, and the Lucky Starr juveniles are from the paperback editions.)

PRIMARY WORKS

Asimov's Novels and Collections

Asimov's Mysteries. 1968.
Before the Golden Age. 1974.
The Caves of Steel. 1954. (In *The Rest of the Robots.*)
The Currents of Space. 1952.
David Starr: Space Ranger. 1952. Signet, 1971.
The Death Dealers. Avon, 1958.
The Early Asimov. 1972.
Earth Is Room Enough. 1957.
The End of Eternity. 1955.
Fantastic Voyage. 1966.
Foundation. 1951.
Foundation and Empire. 1952.
The Gods Themselves. 1972.

I, Robot. 1950.
Lucky Starr and the Big Sun of Mercury. 1956. Signet, 1972.
Lucky Starr and the Moons of Jupiter. 1957. Signet, 1972.
Lucky Starr and the Oceans of Venus. 1954. Signet, 1972.
Lucky Starr and the Pirates of the Asteroids. 1953. Signet, 1972.
Lucky Starr and the Rings of Saturn. 1958. Signet, 1972.
The Martian Way and Other Stories. 1955.
The Naked Sun. 1957. (In *The Rest of the Robots.*)
Nightfall and Other Stories. 1969.
Nine Tomorrows. 1959.
Opus 100. Houghton-Mifflin, 1969.
Pebble in the Sky. 1950.
The Rest of the Robots. 1964.
Second Foundation. 1953.
The Stars Like Dust. 1951.

Asimov's Uncollected Fiction

"Belief." *Astounding Science Fiction* 52 (October 1953).
"Button, Button." *Startling Stories* 28 (January 1953).
"The Computer That Went on Strike." *Saturday Evening Post,* Spring 1972.
"Darwinian Poolroom." *Galaxy Science Fiction* 1 (October 1950).
"Dreamworld." In *The Best from Fantasy and Science Fiction,* 5th series. Anthony Boucher, ed. Doubleday, 1954.
"Each an Explorer." In *The Year's Greatest Science Fiction and Fantasy, 2nd Annual Volume.* Judith Merrill, ed. Dell, 1957.
"Exile to Hell." *Analog Science Fact–Science Fiction* 81 (May 1968).
"Feminine Intuition." In *Twenty Years of the Magazine of Fantasy and Science Fiction.* Edward L. Ferman and Robert P. Mills, eds. Putnam's, 1970.
"The Greatest Asset." *Analog Science Fiction–Science Fact* 88 (January 1972).
"Ideas Die Hard." *Galaxy Science Fiction* 14 (October 1957).
"Mirror Image." *Analog Science Fact–Science Fiction* 89 (May 1972).
"The Monkey's Fingers." *Startling Stories* 29 (February 1953).
"Rain, Rain, Go Away." *Fantastic Universe* 11 (September 1959).

"Take a Match." In *New Dimensions II*. Robert Silverberg, ed. Doubleday, 1972.

"Waterclap." In *The World's Best Science Fiction: 1971*. Donald A. Wollheim and Terry Carr, eds. Ace, 1971.

Fiction by Others

Asimov, Isaac, ed. *The Hugo Winners*. Vol. I. Doubleday, 1962.

——, ed. *The Hugo Winners*, Vol. II. Doubleday, 1971.

——, ed. *Where Do We Go From Here?* Doubleday, 1971.

Bova, Ben, ed. *Science Fiction Hall of Fame*. Vol. II. Doubleday, 1973.

Bradbury, Ray. *The Martian Chronicles*. Bantam, 1951.

Clarke, Arthur C. "The Sentinel." In *Mirror of Infinity*. Robert Silverberg, ed. Harper & Row, 1970.

Clement, Hal. *Mission of Gravity*. *Astounding Science Fiction* 51 (April, May, June, July, 1953).

Conklin, Groff, ed. *The Best of Science Fiction*. Crown, 1946.

De Camp, L. Sprague. *Lest Darkness Fall*. Galaxy Novel 24, 1949.

Hamilton, Edmond. "The City at World's End." *Startling Stories* 21 (July 1950).

——. "The Star Kings." *Amazing Stories* 21 (September 1947).

Heinlein, Robert A. *The Man Who Sold the Moon*. Signet, 1951.

——. "Requiem." In *Famous Science Fiction Stories: Adventures in Time and Space*. Raymond J. Healy and J. Francis McComas, eds. Modern Library (G-31), 1957.

——. "The Roads Must Roll." In *Science Fiction Hall of Fame*. Vol. I. Doubleday, 1970. Also in *Famous Science Fiction Stories: Adventures in Time and Space*. Raymond J. Healy and J. Francis McComas, eds. Modern Library (G-31), 1957.

Herbert, Frank. *Dune*. Chilton, 1965.

Kummer, Frederick Arnold, Jr. "The Treasure of Asteroid X." *Amazing Stories* 13 (January 1939).

Marguiles, Leo, and Friend, Oscar J., eds. *My Best Science Fiction Story*. Merlin Press, 1949.

Silverberg, Robert. *Dying Inside*. Ballantine, 1972.

——, ed. *Science Fiction Hall of Fame*. Vol. I. Doubleday, 1970.

Van Vogt, A. E. "Black Destroyer." In *Famous Science Fiction*

Stories: Adventures in Time and Space. Raymond J. Healy and J. Francis McComas, eds. Modern Library (G-31), 1957.

Verne, Jules. *Twenty Thousand Leagues Under the Sea.* Bantam, 1962.

Wells, H. G. *The Time Machine; The War of the Worlds.* Fawcett, 1968.

SECONDARY WORKS

Books

Aldiss, Brian. *Billion Year Spree: The True History of Science Fiction.* Doubleday, 1973.

Asimov, Isaac. *Is Anyone There?* Doubleday, 1967.

Blish, James. *The Issue at Hand.* Advent, 1964.

Clareson, Thomas, ed. *Science Fiction Criticism: An Annotated Checklist.* Kent State University Press, 1972.

Goble, Neil. *Asimov Analyzed.* Mirage, 1972.

Knight, Damon. *In Search of Wonder.* 2d ed. Advent, 1967.

Meredith, Robert C., and Fitzgerald, John D. *The Professional Story Writer and His Art.* Apollo, 1967.

Miller, Marjorie. *Isaac Asimov: A Checklist.* Kent State University Press, 1972.

Tepper, Matthew B. *Asimov Science Fiction Bibliography.* Chinese Ducked Press, 1970.

Wellek, René, and Warren, Austin. *Theory of Literature.* 2d ed. Harcourt, Brace, 1956.

Wollheim, Donald A. *The Universe Makers: Science Fiction Today.* Harper & Row, 1971.

Articles

Asimov, Isaac. "Scientific Inquiry: A *Boston* Interview with Isaac Asimov." *Boston* 61 (December 1969).

——. "Social Science Fiction." In *Modern Science Fiction.* Reginald Bretnor, ed. Coward-McCann, 1953.

De Camp, L. Sprague. "The Sea-King's Armored Division." *Astounding Science Fiction* 28 (September, October, 1941).

Geis, Richard E. *The Alien Critic.* August 1973.

Moskowitz, Sam. "Isaac Asimov." In *Seekers of Tomorrow: Masters of Modern Science Fiction.* World, 1966.

Wilhelm, Kate. "Something Happens." In *Clarion.* Robin Scott Wilson, ed. Signet, 1971.

Index

Action vs. summation, xviii–xix, xxiv

"Ad Astra," 4

Aldiss, Brian, vii, 104–6

Alien Critic, The, 147

"All the Troubles in the World," 216

Amazing Stories, xxv, 4, 7, 229

Analog, 19, 240

". . . And Now You Don't," xxv

"Anniversary," 228, 229–31

"Asimovian," 255–58

Asimov's career in science fiction, xxiv–xxvii

Asimov Science Fiction Bibliography, The, vii

Asimov's Mysteries (1968), xxvii, 51, 78, 192, 196, 215, 221–33, 240

Astonishing Stories, 4

Astounding Science Fiction, xxv, 3, 4, 13, 15, 19, 35, 36, 41, 50, 61, 63, 111, 112, 192, 196, 207, 234, 235, 241

"Author! Author!," 183, 185–88, 189, 221, 245

Balkis-type character, 124–26, 133–35, 139, 162–63, 238–39, 243

"Barton's Island," xxv

Before the Golden Age (1974), xxvii, 3, 20

"Belief," 241–42

Belisarius, 84–86 *passim*

Best of Science Fiction, The, 190

"Billiard Ball, The," 228, 233

Billion Year Spree, vii, 104

"Black Destroyer," 235

"Black Friar of the Flame," 15–16, 19

"Blind Alley," 189–90, 191, 195

Blish, James, 101

Boardman, John, 147

Bonestell, Chesley, 158

Boston, 261, 271

Bradbury, Ray, 228

Bradbury, Walter I., 113, 151

"Breeds There a Man . . . ?," 213, 217, 233, 235–36

Bretnor, Reginald, 27, 245

"Bridle and Saddle," 62

Browning, Robert, 112 n

"Button, Button," 240, 241

"Callistan Menace, The," 4–7, 10, 11, 13, 19, 143, 259

Campbell, John W., Jr., xxv, 3, 4, 7, 11–19 *passim*, 26, 35, 36, 37, 50, 51, 61, 62, 65, 78, 107, 111–14 *passim*, 188, 196, 207, 234, 241–42, 255

"Catch That Rabbit," 36, 39, 40, 43

Caves of Steel, The (1954), 35, 51, 115, 132, 152, 154, 155, 159–71, 172, 174, 176–79, *passim*, 188, 221, 227–28, 238, 262, 269, 271

"C-Chute," 233, 237, 239

Central character, xviii, xx, xxii, 90–91, 106, 232, 236, 256

Character, xviii, xx–xxi, xxiv

Characterization, xx–xxi

Chaucer, x, 129

Chekhov, 5

Christie, Agatha, 222, 224

City at World's End, The, 119

Clarke, Arthur C., 227

Clement, Hal, xxii

Complication, xviii, 106

"Computer That Went on Strike, The," 262, 270

Conflict, xviii, 106, 235, 237

Conklin, Groff, 190

"Cosmic Corkscrew, The," 3–4, 19, 192

Critical stories, 244–52

Currents of Space, The (1952), viii, 115, 116, 137–41, 145, 164, 211, 225, 257

"Darwinian Poolroom," 234, 240–41

David Starr: Space Ranger (1952), 152, 156

"Dead Hand," 83

"Dead Past, The," 208–13, 214–18 *passim*

Death Dealers, The (1958), 114

"Death Sentence," 188–89, 190, 206

De Camp, L. Sprague, 85, 192

Decline and Fall of the Roman Empire, 85

"Deep, The," 202

Delany, Samuel R., 57

Destination Moon, 198

Deus ex machina, 50, 71, 73, 79, 87, 120, 166, 235, 243

Dianetics, 112

Dimension X, 26, 64

Disch, Thomas, 57

Donne, John, 29

"Dreaming Is a Private Thing," 213, 249–51

"Dreamworld," 240

"Dust of Death, The," 221, 224–25

Dying Inside, xvi

"Dying Night, The," 215, 221, 223–24, 225, 228

"Each an Explorer," 241, 242–44

Early Asimov, The (1972), xxvii, 3, 4, 13–19 *passim*, 111, 117, 183–97

Earth Is Room Enough (1957), xxvi, 20, 196, 208–15, 233, 240, 246, 248–49

Elgin, Suzette Haden, 159

Ellison, Harlan, 57, 148

Emerson, Ralph Waldo, 20, 21, 112

"Encyclopedists, The," 62, 63, 64, 67, 68–74, 75–78 *passim*, 120

End of Eternity, The (1955), 115, 141–50, 191, 192, 194, 195, 220, 231

"Escape!," 35, 36–37, 45

"Evidence," 37, 45–47

"Evitable Conflict, The," 35, 37, 45, 47–49

"Exile to Hell," 240, 241

Exposition, 39–40, 64, 68, 75, 144, 256–57, 265

Fantastic Story Quarterly, 111

Fantastic Universe, 240

Fantastic Voyage (1966), 114, 196

Fantasy and Science Fiction (*F+SF*), 111, 221, 225, 240, 258, 260

"Feeling of Power, The," 213, 215–16

"Feminine Intuition," 259, 262, 270

"First Law," 36, 50–51

"Foundation," 62

Foundation (1951), 61, 63–82

Foundation and Empire (1952), 61, 82–92

Foundation Series, xxi–xxvii *passim*, 12–20 *passim*, 25, 35, 61–108, 112–15 *passim*, 120, 132–43 *passim*, 152, 154, 163, 164, 183, 184, 189–97 *passim*, 206, 228, 259, 260, 263, 266, 268

"Franchise," 214

Frankenstein complex, 38, 171, 213, 218

Freeman, R. Austin, 221–22

French, Paul, 151

"Fun They Had, The," 214

"Galactic Crusade," 15

Galaxy Science Fiction, 111, 159, 196, 217, 234, 240

"Galley Slave," 52–53

Geis, Richard E., 147

"General, The," 16, 82–86, 90, 92

"Gentle Vultures, The," 216

Gilbert and Sullivan, 62, 245–46

"Gimmicks Three," 213

Gnome Press, 63

Gods Themselves, The (1972), xxvi, xxvii, 18, 114, 145, 148, 184, 188, 220, 259, 263–70

Gold, Horace L., 159, 234, 240

"Greatest Asset, The," 262

Greenberg, Martin, 63, 64, 67

"Green Patches," 233, 234–35, 236, 242

"Grow Old With Me," 112–14, 125, 234

Gunn, James, 125

"Half-Breed," 13, 19, 66

"Half-Breeds on Venus," 13, 19

Hamilton, Edmond, 119

Heinlein, Robert A., xxv, xxvii, 66, 165

"Hell-Fire," 214

Herbert, Frank, xxii, 20, 207

Holmes, Sherlock, and Dr. Watson, xx, 153

"Holmes-Ginsbook Device, The," 240, 241

"Homo Sol," xxv, 13, 15, 16–18, 19, 50, 78, 92, 185, 189, 190, 216

"Hostess," 233, 237–39, 240

Hugo Winners, The (1962), xxvi

I, Robot (1950), xxvi, 35, 36–49, 54, 162, 189, 196

"Ideas Die Hard," 241

If, 240

"Imaginary, The," 13, 19

"I'm in Marsport Without Hilda," xix, 215, 220, 228–29

"Immortal Bard, The," 213, 214, 240, 249, 251–52, 260

"In a Good Cause," 239–40

Initial situation, xviii, 24–25, 106, 235, 237

In Search of Wonder, 85, 144, 168, 197

Isaac Asimov: A Checklist, vii

Is Anyone There?, 245

Issue at Hand, The, 101

"It's Such a Beautiful Day," 240

"Jokester," 213, 217, 236, 245

Jonson, Ben, ix

"Key, The," 221, 225–27, 228, 257

"Kid Stuff," 213, 246, 248

Kimoy, Ernest, 26–27

Knight, Damon, 85, 144, 168, 197, 201

Kummer, Frederick Arnold, 7, 10

Lafferty, R. A., 57

"Lastborn," 196, 217

"Last Question, The," 20, 35, 53–54, 215

"Last Trump, The," 213

"Legal Rites," 185

"Lennie," 52

Lest Darkness Fall, 85

"Let's Get Together," 51

"Liar!," xxv, 13, 19, 36, 37, 43–45, 119

"Little Lost Robot," 36, 54

"Little Man on the Subway, The," 185

"Living Space," 214–15

"Loint of Paw, A," 240

Lovecraft, H. P., 57

Lucky Starr and the Big Sun of Mercury (1956), 152–58 *passim*

Lucky Starr and the Moons of Jupiter (1957), 153–59 *passim*

Lucky Starr and the Oceans of Venus (1954), 158

Lucky Starr and the Pirates of the Asteroids (1953), 154

Lucky Starr and the Rings of Saturn (1958), 152, 154, 168

"Lucky Starr" juveniles, xxvi, 114, 115, 151–59, 162, 163, 184, 191

"Man Who Sold the Moon, The," 66

Marguiles and Friend, 49, 50

"Marooned Off Vesta," xxv, 4, 7–10, 11, 12, 19, 21, 25, 72, 119, 143, 153, 164, 184, 192, 204, 218, 222, 228, 229–31, 259

Martian Chronicles, The, 228

"Martian Way, The," xxvi, 197–202, 203, 207, 213, 215

Martian Way and Other Stories, The (1955), 20, 196, 197–208, 233

Maugham, Somerset, 121

"Mayors, The," 62, 68, 69, 73, 74–78

"Merchant Princes, The," 63, 79–82, 87, 89

Meredith and Fitzgerald, viii

Merritt, A., 57

Merwin, Sam, Jr., 112–13, 234

"Message, The," 214

Miller, Marjorie, vii, ix

Milton, John, 28, 95

"Mirror Image," 259–60, 270

"Misbegotten Missionary," 234

Mission of Gravity, xxii

"Monkey's Fingers, The," 246–48

"Mother Earth," 191, 194–95, 206

"Mule, The," 88–92, 103, 104, 113, 132

My Best Science Fiction Story, 50

Naked Sun, The (1957), xxvi, 35, 51, 114, 115, 132, 148, 152, 155, 162, 171–79, 196, 228

Narrative point of view, xviii, xix–xx, xxiv, 43, 199–201, 231, 237–38, 256

Narrative techniques, xviii–xxiv, 256

"Nature," 20

New Dimensions II, 266

"Nightfall," xxi, xxiv, xxv, 14, 18, 19–29, 45, 50, 62, 78, 108, 112, 114, 183, 185, 192, 196, 203, 206, 220, 225, 233, 234, 235, 260

Nightfall and Other Stories (1969), xxvi, xxvii, 20, 21, 56, 170, 196, 213, 233–40, 245

Nine Tomorrows (1959), xxiv, xxvi, 20, 196, 213, 215–20, 233

Niven, Larry, xxii, 18, 159

"No Connection," 189, 190–91

"Not Final!," 183–85, 189, 191

"Obituary," 228, 231–33

Opus 100 (1969), xxvii, 35, 62, 105, 151, 244, 258

Palmer, Ray, 4

Pebble in the Sky (1950), xxv, xxvi, 15, 82, 111–31, 132–43 *passim,* 149, 152, 161, 163, 171, 174, 183, 191, 196, 234, 243

"Pilgrimage," 15

Plot, xviii, xx–xxiv *passim,* 106–7, 197, 235, 237, 256–57

"Plutonium-186," 263–68 *passim*

Poe, Edgar Allan, 223

Poetics (Aristotle), 85

Pohl, Frederick, xxv, 4, 13, 19, 36, 113–14, 185

"Profession," 215

Professional Story Writer and His Art, The, viii

"Psychohistorians, The," 63–68, 69, 76

Psychohistory, 65–66, 81

"Rain, Rain, Go Away," 240, 241

"Reason," xxv, 13, 16, 19, 36, 39, 40, 41–42, 43, 50, 55

"Red Queen's Race, The," 191–94, 195, 221

"Requiem," 66

"Resolution," xviii, 235

Rest of the Robots, The (1964), 35, 49–53, 54, 213

"Ring Around the Sun," 13, 19

"Risk," 54, 55

"Roads Must Roll, The," 165

"Robbie," 14, 36, 37, 38–39, 42, 49

"Robot AL-76 Goes Astray," 36, 49–50, 189

Robot Stories, the, xxv, xxvii, 13, 16, 19, 20, 35, 36, 37, 45, 51, 52, 55, 108, 114, 119, 153, 155, 159, 162, 183, 184, 189, 192, 196, 215, 216, 259, 263

Romance of the Rose, The, 267

"Runaround," 36, 37, 39, 40–41, 42, 55, 62, 155

"Sally," 240

"Satisfaction Guaranteed," 49, 51–52, 213

Science fantasy, xv

Science fiction, description of, xv–xvii

Science Fiction Hall of Fame, 197

Science Fiction Writers of America (SFWA), 19, 197

"Sea-King's Armored Division, The," 192

"Search by the Foundation," 90, 95–100, 107, 111, 132, 164

"Search by the Mule," 92–97, 103–4, 132, 164

Second Foundation (1953), 61, 82, 85, 92–100

"Secret Sense, The," 14–15, 19

Sense of wonder, the, xxiv, 158, 202

"Sentinel, The," 227

Setting, xviii, xxi–xxii, xxiv

Shakespeare, ix, 106, 247–48, 251–52, 260

Silverberg, Robert, xvi, 263, 265, 266

"Singing Bell, The," 221, 222–23, 224, 225, 228

Six Characters in Search of an Author, 188

Smith, Clark Ashton, 57

"Social Science Fiction," 27, 85, 245

Solution, xviii, 106, 235

"Someday," 213, 215, 216, 245

"Spell My Name with an S," 217, 236

Sputnik, xxvi, 179, 260

Star Kings, The, 119

Stars Like Dust, The (1951), 115, 131–37, 138, 139, 141, 145, 164

Startling Stories, xxvi, 112–13, 234, 240, 246

"Stowaway," 4

"Strange Playfellow," 14, 36

Style, 10–11, 21–22, 48–49, 54–57, 101–2, 139, 255, 258

"Sucker Bait," 203–8, 213, 215, 242

"Super Neutron," 13, 19

Super Science Stories, 36

Symbolism, 48

"Take a Match," 259, 262, 266

"Talking Stone, The," 221, 223, 224

Tamerlane, 85, 86

Tepper, M. B., vii, ix

"That Thou Art Mindful of Him," 260

Theme, xviii, xxii–xxiv, 107–8

Theory of Literature, viii

Three Laws (or Rules) of Robotics, the, 37, 39, 40, 41, 42, 46, 51, 55, 62, 66, 112, 155, 162, 172, 178

Thrilling Wonder Stories, 4

Time Machine, The, 263

"Time Pussy," 192

"Traders, The," 63, 79, 87

"Treasure of Asteroid X, The," 7–8

"Trends," xxv, 4, 11–13, 15, 235

Triangle (1961), 115, 123, 130, 132, 139, 141, 142, 143, 152, 162, 163

TV Guide, 244

Twain, Mark, xvi

2001: A Space Odyssey, 158, 227

"Ugly Little Boy, The," 20, 196, 215, 217–20, 232

Uncollected Stories, 240–44

Universe Makers, The, vii, 108

"Up-to-Date Sorcerer, The," 245–46

Van Vogt, A. E., 207, 235

Verne, Jules, 157

"Victory Unintentional," 36, 50, 184

Vincent, Harl, xxv

War of the Worlds, The, 190

"Waterclap," 263, 270, 271

"Watery Place, The," 214

"Weapon Too Dreadful to Use, The," 14, 15

Wellek and Warren, viii

Wells, H. G., xvi, xxi, 190, 263

When Worlds Collide, 198

Where Do We Go from Here?, 156

Wilhelm, Kate, 10

Wolfe, Thomas, 112

Wollheim, Donald A., vii, 108

Wonder Story Annual, 111

"Youth," 202, 203, 240, 241

Zelazny, Roger, 57, 159